ON·TAP

THE ODYSSEY OF BEER AND BREWING IN VICTORIAN LONDON·MIDDLESEX

"*Wholesome beer, that has a little life in it, is all that is wanted in general.*"

William Cobbett, *Cottage Economy*, 1831

ON·TAP

THE ODYSSEY OF BEER AND BREWING IN VICTORIAN LONDON·MIDDLESEX

Glen C. Phillips

CHESHIRE CAT PRESS

P.O. Box 2611   Sarnia   Ontario   N7T 7V8

CHESHIRE CAT PRESS
P.O. Box 2611
Sarnia, Ontario
N7T 7V8
905-576-1506 (c/o William P. Moran, Bookseller)

Printed in Canada by
Capital Printing
London, Ontario

Canadian Cataloguing in Publication Data
Phillips, Glen Christopher, 1967–
    On tap: the odyssey of beer & brewing in Victorian London-Middlesex

Includes bibliographical references and index.
ISBN 9-921818-21-1

1. Brewing industry — Ontario — Middlesex — History — 19th century.   2. Brewing industry — Ontario — London — History — 19th century.   3. Beer industry — Ontario — Middlesex — History — 19th century.   4. Beer industry — Ontario — London — History — 19th century. I. Title.

HD9397.C23M52 2000   338.4'766342'0971325   C00-931213-7

Multiple copies of this book may be purchased for special promotional programs and corporate gifts by contacting the publisher at the above address or telephone number.

CONTENTS

Preface & Acknowledgements

In 1988, the idea for this book first popped into my head. At the time, I was doing the research for my first book, *The Ontario Soda Water Manufacturers and Brewers Gazetteer and Business Directory*, a reference list of historic pop works and breweries which operated in Ontario from 1851 to 1930. That book project introduced me to London-Middlesex's rich brewing heritage. I had long since known about Carling and Labatt of London and Bixel of Strathroy, but I was intrigued to learn of the Tupholmes in Delaware, John Allaster in London East and dozens of other brewers in the county. It struck me that the collective story of these early beer-makers would make an excellent subject for another book.

Well, to make a very long story short, after ten years of off-and-on research and two more years of intensively mining the historical record, writing, wrestling with the computer and editing, editing and more editing — with the writing, wrestling and editing being accomplished in the midst of a move from London, Ontario to Dublin, Ireland — I can finally say that my twelve-year-old dream is, at last, a reality. All that I now require is a nice pint of stout and a long rest!

In the great hunt for historical facts and period images, I have greatly relied upon the expertise of librarians, archivists and museum curators. In particular, I would like to thank Nellie Swart of the Labatt Archives, John Lutman, Theresa Regnier and Deb Caley of the J.J. Talman Regional Collection at the University of Western Ontario, Mike Baker of the London Regional Art and Historical Museums, Arthur McClelland of the London Room at the London Public Library and Shirley Lovell of the Ingersoll Museum. I would also like to acknowledge the assistance I received at the D.B. Weldon Library, the Middlesex Registry Office, the Brantford Public Library, the Brant County Museum, the Metropolitan Toronto Reference Library, the Archives of Ontario, the United Church Archives, the National Library of Canada, the National Archives of Canada, the Cleveland Public Library, the Wheeling Public Library, the Oglebay Museum in Wheeling, the National Library of Ireland and the National Archives of Ireland.

Many others also helped in the preparation of this work. Loren Newman, publisher of *The Canadian Brewerianist*, Canada's fabulous printed forum for collectors of brewery memorabilia, and Glen Austin, a dynamic and knowledgeable brewer, formerly of Labatt London and now with the Latrobe Brewing Company, each read various chapter drafts. Their advice greatly enhanced the quality and accuracy of the manuscript. I would also like to tip my hat to David Dillon of the Geology Department at the University of Western Ontario. David took time out from his very busy schedule to give me a concise, illustrated overview of London-Middlesex's geology. Monika Pomper, members of her family and her friends teamed together and translated some old German brewing documents into English for me. Their efforts helped immeasurably. And Professor Ben Forster and my fellow classmates in the graduate course in Canadian Business History at UWO offered valuable suggestions for a paper I wrote on local brewing history.

Private collectors also answered my calls for help. Carl Miller and Thaddeus Podratsky provided me with crucial details about the American angles to this story. Steve Peters kindly allowed me access to his considerable research files on historic breweries in St. Thomas-Elgin and London-Middlesex. Meanwhile, Dave Craig and Frank Mrazik generously sent me photocopies of old bottle labels and other historical documents in their collections. Just as generous were Arthur Bixel, Jim Butler, Don Cosens, Jim Maitland, Keith McCallum, Paul Miller and John Saddy, who loaned me the use of various brewery artifacts for photographic reproduction. Their treasures have greatly added to the visual appearance of this book. I would further like to applaud Alan Noon, Roland Schubert and John Tamblyn for their photography. Moreover, I would be remiss if I did not mention the folks at Capital Printing and Capital Imaging in London for doing a bang-up job at setting up and printing this book.

Finally, I would like to thank Don and Marilyn Fulton of Little Rapids, Ontario. They helped in countless ways and supported me through thick and thin. More particularly, Don and Marilyn raised a fine person in their eldest daughter, Crystal. I should know, since I married her. Crystal's patience has been a tremendous strength, especially given that she tolerates an often cranky writer in her husband. Crystal's scholarly talents, her fearless editorial skills and her remarkable ability to empathize with a fellow writer are truly amazing. Above all, her love sustains me. This book is for Crystal.

Glen C. Phillips,
Dublin, Ireland, March 2000

Patrons

The author and publisher would like to acknowledge the following for their interest in brewing heritage and for their support of this publication.

Ask Alice Books, London

Attic Books, London

Glen Austin

Dan Brock

Butler Plumbing & Heating, Strathroy

Colour by Schubert Custom Photofinishing, London

Dave Craig

Don & Marilyn Fulton

Gatherick Press, London

Gordon Holder

Jim Maitland

Mayer Heritage Consultants Inc., London

William P. Moran, Bookseller, Oshawa

C.G. Paton

Steve Peters

Siskinds, The Law Firm, London

Ken Tupholme

Sandra Wilton

INTRODUCTION

Painted onto the east facing wall of Strathroy's Derby Inn there lives an imaginative tribute to the county's brewing heritage. In this mural, one can spy representations of beer barrels marked with such mysterious words as Bixel and the Western Steam Brewery. To most passersby, these names have little meaning and yet these brewers once put Strathroy on the map, so to speak. Further tributes to local beer history can be found in London, where one will find Carling Street, Carling Heights, Carling Arena, Labatt Park, the Labatt Pioneer Brewery at Fanshawe Pioneer Village and, of course, the modern Labatt brewery just off Richmond Street south of Horton. Indeed, these symbols serve as interesting reminders of the important place beer has assumed in local historical development. Moreover, of the big three names on the Canadian beer scene today — Carling, Labatt and Molson — Carling and Labatt originated in London. Interestingly, no other city in Canada can boast of such historical connections. And thereby hangs a tale.

The following pages explore why nineteenth-century London-Middlesex, a region removed from Ontario's population nexus and an area largely unblessed with natural transportation advantages, such as navigable waterways, became one of Victorian Canada's most important brewing centres. At its very heart, this book argues that, contrary to what many historians of Canada's economic past have suggested, beer was a very transportable product — profitably so, in fact — and that this characteristic was fundamental to the building of brewing empires in the nineteenth century. Naturally, such issues as taste quality, railway access, capital strength, marketing skills and overall entrepreneurship also played very significant roles in shaping the Victorian brewing landscape, but everything was ultimately predicated upon the fact that beer could be shipped near and far.

Now, while questions of transportability may seem somewhat mundane in our day and age of multi-lane expressways, jet flights and even space travel, one must remember that issues of transportation and transportation development figure prominently in all branches of history, whether local, national, international, ancient, medieval, modern, economic, social, political or military.

Interestingly, historians have not only failed to acknowledge beer's transportability, but have also missed how that reality influenced the domestic industry. These failures have spawned some fairly misleading historical depictions of Ontario's brewing history. For instance, in a report about the value of the 1871 census to industrial history, Elizabeth and Gerald Bloomfield unsatisfactorily conclude that beer's "perishable and bulky nature" forced the concentration of the brewing industry in large urban centres. Similarly, Ian Drummond once remarked in the *Canadian Historical Review*: "It is obvious that many industries, especially those whose inputs or outputs were heavy in relation to their values, or whose markets were local, enjoyed a large margin of 'natural protection.' Among such industries were. . . distilling and brewing."

However, we shall see that nineteenth-century beer, while certainly bulky, was hardly as fragile as the Bloomfields suggest. Indeed, brewers in the British Isles shipped their brews across the Atlantic by boat in order to reach thirsty Canadians. Moreover, as if to counter a major plank in Drummond's overall assertion, we shall discover that, owing to beer's transportability, a notable degree of market integration marked Ontario's brewing industry throughout the 1800s and that this commercial situation had tremendous bearing upon brewing developments in London-Middlesex.

In addition, it appears that the above statements about the localized nature of the brewing industry are overdrawn. True, many Victorian brewers were locally oriented, but, as the course of affairs in London-Middlesex indicates, healthy local markets in bigger urban centres simply allowed some brewers, such as Carling and Labatt, access to the capital required to compete on a larger geographic stage. In this regard, brewing became concentrated in large urban centres because brewers in those places used local market advantages to build regional/national enterprises that could fight for sales in outside communities. Yet again, we return to the transportability of beer.

At any rate, our story begins with a somewhat fanciful chapter, which is followed by two generalized overview chapters that lend important context to local brewing developments. The rest of the book largely follows a chronological path and highlights the early years of brewing in the county, how the railway age changed local dynamics, the battle between German lager and its heavier Anglo-Irish counterparts, the influence of the temperance movement and the rise of sophisticated marketing practices. Since no place ever existed in isolation, this work necessarily draws upon wider events to explain local developments.

Admittedly, this history is a case study and covers a specific period of time. However, there is considerable interpretive value in the approach herein taken. First of all, given the prominence of the Carling and Labatt names in today's brewing circles, documenting the nineteenth-century origins of these two brewers is, in and of itself, an important historical exercise. In addition, the case study technique permits a detailed examination of the past, which, in turn, can be used to test the historical situation elsewhere. It would be wonderful to shine a bright, deeply penetrating light into every single geographic corner of Canada's entire brewing history, but, for all too obvious reasons, such a project is simply impossible. Nevertheless, it is strongly believed that the pattern of brewing progress in Victorian London-Middlesex will prove helpful in the study of Canada's wider brewing heritage.

The scope of this book is limited to the nineteenth century because that century witnessed the beginning of brewing in London-Middlesex and saw the foundations of the modern industry laid down. On this score, the nineteenth century is an era not so removed from our own. As unbelievable as it may first sound, our society is still largely fashioned upon the great technological, social and commercial changes of the Victorian age. Indeed, we are merely a reflection of our predecessors, as our descendants will be of us. It is important to know the Victorians if we want to know ourselves.

Before plunging into our vat of beer history, a little historical "shop-talk" will benefit readers. Above all, your author takes the view that centuries properly begin with "01" and end with "00." This is because there was no year zero. Thus, in these pages at least, the nineteenth century ended on December 31, 1900. As to geography, this book focuses upon the brewing history which unfolded upon the soil enclosed by the modern boundaries of Middlesex County (at one time, Middlesex included what is now Elgin County). Moreover, the term "London-Middlesex" has been used either for variety or to imply the city and county in one fell swoop. For those unfamiliar with Ontario's constitutional history, Upper Canada was the name for the province from 1791 until 1841 and Canada West from 1841 until 1867.

Finally, when and where appropriate, the term "Carling" implies the firm of William & John Carling, Carling & Company or the Carling Brewing & Malting Company, Limited. Also, the old spelling of "license" has been used instead of its modern counterpart. In addition, please keep in mind that many of the dollar figures herein mentioned, while appearing quite small to our modern eyes, were actually fairly substantial in a relative sense. And unless otherwise noted, all volumes are in imperial measure.

BLACKFRIARS BRIDGE WITH THE CARLING BREWERY IN THE BACKGROUND, CIRCA 1876

CHAPTER ONE

Two Fantastic
Trips back in Time

IMAGINE FOR A moment that you have just invented the world's first time-travel machine. Now, having a passion for beer and brewing history — You're reading this book, after all! — your heart is set upon visiting some of Middlesex County's historic breweries. The only problem is that you can only make two trips before the rigours of time travel will permanently wreck your mental and physical health. So, with this restriction in mind, you decide to visit the location of the present Labatt brewery once in 1828, when John Balkwill started brewing at the site, and then again in 1900, when John Labatt was in the midst of building up his empire. With great anticipation, you calibrate your time machine and off you go through that mystical wormhole which links the present to the past.

In a cloudy thud, you tumble onto the corner of Dundas Street near Wellington. It's a chilly October 8, 1828 and you're on the edge of the infant village of London, Upper Canada. The only thing you recognize is the vague outline of a somewhat Gothic courthouse poking into the western sky. Although the building is not quite finished, it's the tallest structure around and serves as an excellent landmark. As you walk along Dundas towards your beacon, you can't help but chuckle at how primitive the place looks. Most buildings are made of logs or rough-hewn planks and are one or one-and-a-half storeys short. Most peculiarly, houses are shuffled in amongst crude shacks that serve as stores. Even more strange to your twenty-first-century eyes are the tree stumps which chequer the street. While these wooden protrusions are supposed to be cut close enough to the ground so that wagon axles can pass over them, the impatient cursing of two frustrated teamsters tells you otherwise. The soft mud which serves as road pavement in these parts has artificially increased the height of the stumps. Stymied by a snapped rear axle, the teamsters have been rudely reminded of this fact. Still, this ill-defined core of a young London seems to be full of more people than the modern downtown. Within a block of the courthouse, you know to turn south, as this street, recently named Talbot, will lead you to your destination. Not long after you cross York Street, you notice two things. One, there is no busy railway line to stop you. Two, the air is filled with that sweet smell so unique to a boiling brew kettle. The fragrance coaxes your thirst.

Within a few short minutes, you're at the brewery. The building standing before your eyes would be absolutely dwarfed by the modern Labatt plant. It's made of logs, the bark peelings from which litter its outside perimeter. As the imperfectly joined and sealed timbers indicate, this brewery was hastily put together. While running your hand along a wall to test the rough wood, a thick Devonshire accent interrupts your inspection. "Balkwill's the name. John Balkwill. What's it that you need?" Turning around, you are met by the stocky silhouette of the brewery's owner. You apologize for manhandling his building. Since the concept of manhandling something made of logs and plaster strikes him as funny, your apologetic gesture is happily accepted. Balkwill then explains that his brewery was indeed erected in a hurry so that he could get his beer quickly to market. "The demands of the ledgers, you know," he explains. You ask for a tour of the place and he obligingly agrees.

Once inside, you discover a beehive of activity carried out by an army of three labouring amidst a rather grainy and hoppy atmosphere. The army consists of a man superintending the boiling copper kettle, another filling barrels and a lad of no more than fifteen years rolling full barrels outside to an awaiting cart. While surveying the interior, you notice that gravity and human muscle serve as the brewery's only sources of motive power. Save the kettle, everything else is made of wood, even the mixing tools. Moreover, the only technical instrument you spy is a crude saccharometer kept on a shelf near the mash tun. Another notable rarity in this historic brewery is the glass bottle, a ubiquitous sight in a modern brewery. Upon asking Mr. Balkwill about this, he responds, "Ah yes, glass bottles are scarce out here. Even pottery ones are hard to find. Occasionally, we might stumble across some used bottles and make do with them, but we deal mostly in barrelled ale and porter."

Next, the brewer invites you into his office to enjoy a sample or two. He sends the lad, who bears the name Robert, to fetch some porter. In the meantime, you scan the office and are surprised at its plainness. Balkwill has a simple pine desk, upon which are piled some ledgers, a crude inkwell and a small heap of handwritten invoices. The invoices are particularly interesting in that no two of them are the same size and that the cotton-rag paper upon which Balkwill has scribbled various

BEER QUOTE —
He that buys land buys many stones,
He that buys flesh buys many bones,
He that buys eggs buys many shells,
But he that buys good ale buys nothing else.
          John Ray, *English Proverbs*

names and figures closely resembles the paper you made by hand in high school art class. The man superintending the brew kettle calls out and your host summarily excuses himself. At this moment, nosey curiosity gets the better of you and you thumb through the stack of invoices. As you expected, all of Balkwill's customers are in the village and next-door in Westminster and London Townships. This is truly a local brewery. Before you get a chance to check out Balkwill's selling prices, Robert returns with two mugs of porter. Closely on his heels is an apologetic John Balkwill. "Sorry 'bout that — my man on the copper reckoned the brew had run its course, but wanted my opinion before drawing it through the hop-jack."

With a friendly grin on his face, Balkwill hoists his mug of dark, chocolate brown liquid and you join him in the traditional toast of "Cheers!" Before the porter has a chance to hit the back of your tongue, you notice that it's almost room temperature and carries few bubbles. You wouldn't call it flat, but you certainly wouldn't say it's anywhere near the fizzy article of the new millennium. It's somewhere in between. As for taste, it definitely has one! Balkwill's porter is quite bitter at first, but boasts a sweet, malty finish. As the beer slides down your throat, you give it an A+. After all, you are a proponent of strong tasting brews that challenge the palate. To your amazement, while you were revelling in your first sip, the brewer had nearly consumed his entire mugful. He, too, notices this and jokingly wonders aloud, "So, my tablemate does not fancy porter, eh?" You politely protest by explaining that you just wanted to take your time. Privately, you were simply savouring the rare moment that no one else from the future has ever enjoyed. If Balkwill only knew your secret!

The next round consists of five mugs of reddish-amber ale. The first and second mugs are taken by you and your host, the third by Joseph, the kettle superintendent, the fourth by Richard, the barrel-filler, and the fifth by Robert. Initially, you are shocked that a fifteen-year-old has been offered a drink, but then you realize that it was a nineteenth-century custom for all brewery employees to enjoy a beer or two at the end of a hard day's work. Besides, no law of the time kept Robert from having his pint anyway. The ale is much more restrained than the porter, but ends with a slightly more bitter and dry finish. As ales go, you consider it quite robust and hardy. After another round of Balkwill's ale and more good chatter, you decided that it's time to take your leave. As you walk away from the brewery, you just can't believe what an extraordinary experience the day has been. This serves to whet your appetite for the voyage to Labatt's brewery in 1900. With the click of a button, you're gone. Whoosh!

This time around you land on Richmond Street just south of the Thames River.

BEER LORE — The saying, "Mind your P's and Q's," stems from an accounting method adopted by English tavernkeepers during the 1700s. To keep track of bar tabs, they would record customers' orders upon a slate headed with the letters P and Q. The P was for pints and the Q was for quarts. When squaring up, drinkers literally had to mind their P's and Q's, lest a disorganized or unscrupulous tavern owner overcharge them.

You dust yourself off, turn northwards and cross the nearby bridge. The seventy-two year contrast is startling. Where John Balkwill's crude log brewhouse once stood there now towers the massive complex that is John Labatt's brewery. From out of the cluster of four multi-storey brick buildings, a large smoke stack, that ultimate symbol of Victorian industrial progress, crowns London's skyline. Dozens and dozens of workers buzz about the place.

Most interestingly, you spot two teams of burly labourers racing each other to load up several drays. Each team appears to be charged with about a gross of full barrels. Unbelievably, the strongest combatants can heave these one- and two-hundred-pound vessels around like they were filled with feathers. As these Herculean strongmen hoist the barrels from the ground, others receive them and then speedily arrange them atop the wagons. Still other contestants roll the barrels out to the lifters. Within minutes, the teams are down to their last few kegs. A crowd has gathered around to watch and the cheering becomes louder and louder. By this time, you are close enough to see the muscular determination in each strained expression. The feathers now become beer. Amidst the grunts and groans, you discover how the teams were divvied up. The grey hairs poking out from beneath caps, the occasional bald spot, facial wrinkles and the portly mid-sections give the one side away as the older labourers. Meanwhile, members of the younger team are blessed with full heads of bright hair, smoothly chiselled faces and the classic proportions of youthful physiques. Despite the handicaps of age, the older crew wins the day by two barrels. "Experience over youth!" yells out the victorious captain. "We'll see about that tomorrow!" retorts one of the defeated. Everyone then has a good laugh. However, it dawns on you that both teams have won the contest — a gruelling, back-breaking chore has been made far lighter through some spirited competition.

At battle's end, you approach a rather cheerful looking man in a suit. The suit identifies him as someone in authority. His reply to your request for a tour is marked by a melodious Irish accent somewhat tempered by living in Canada. "I would be delighted. By the way, the name's Dennis Mason. I'm Mr. Labatt's head brewer. Shall we start with one of the maltings?" You agree and the brewer leads you north through the rear of the brewery yard to the six-storey malting tower on the south side of Simcoe Street between Talbot and Richmond. For the life of you, you can't imagine where Balkwill's brewery once stood. The maze of buildings rising from this block of land has made orientation with the vagueness of 1828 an impossible task. One comparison is easy to make, however. Four or five, or maybe even six or seven of Balkwill's little log breweries would easily fit inside this malting building alone!

BEER LORE — During the reign of King Charles II of England, the following law was passed: "No common brewer is to sell, deliver, or carry out any beer or ale to his customers in any city, town-corporate, or market-town, before notice [is] given to the officer, but between three in the morning and nine in the evening, from 25th March to 29th September, and between five in the morning and seven in the evening, from 29th September to 25th March, on forfeiture of 20 shillings per barrel." Now, aren't you glad that The Beer Store keeps convenient opening hours?

Mason notices your amazement and beams, "Impressive, isn't it?"

Inside, bigness is everywhere. The oak and iron pillars are broad and sturdy. The malting floors are wide and expansive. And the kiln is absolutely huge. Even the grainy aroma is big. You learn from one of Labatt's several maltsters that the floor is being scrubbed in anticipation of another malting. With a grin on his face, he jokingly declares that malting is the most crucial step in beer-making and that kettle work is a mere afterthought. Mason, taking up the jovial challenge and ready to defend the honour of his trade, responds that malting always leads to bigger and better things. As you leave the malt building, Mason quietly confides that malting is actually a very serious business. After all, Labatt's maltsters are responsible for barley investments worth tens of thousands of dollars. He casually notes that their talents command healthy recompense. With a proud voice, the brewmaster further notes that brewing skills also bring good pay. "Speaking of brewing, it's off to the brewery next," he announces.

Mason takes you out the front of the malthouse and westerly along Simcoe Street. Soon, you and your guide turn left and stroll another hundred feet or so to the brewhouse. Nearly every worker in the yard greets Dennis Mason with the titles "Mister" and "Sir," but one senior employee affectionately calls him "Denny." The first thing you notice about the brewery is that it's literally draped in vents. Mason casually notes that the brewhouse needs to be kept cool during the warmer months or else the whole brewing process becomes difficult to manage. As with the malthouse, everything about the brewery is large. The kettle is large, the vats are large and the machinery is large. All over the place, canvas belts whirr round and round and drive all sorts of mechanized appliances. These belts, along with countless gears, cogs and fly wheels, have replaced the cumbersome hand-tools used during Balkwill's time. Precision instruments can be spied everywhere and steam powers the entire mechanical works, although human hands are still required for many jobs.

Mason then gives you a tour of the cellars. Made of brick and stone with vaulted ceilings, these huge underground caverns burst with row upon row of casks filled with ripening malt liquor. The air is chilly and thick with a beery smell. Also inspecting the cellars is a man in his early sixties. Impeccably groomed muttonchops and a bushy moustache lend his face a dignified Victorian appearance. As you try to place him, Dennis Mason gives his identity away. "Good afternoon, Mr. Labatt." After replying in kind, the brewery owner politely introduces himself. His genial and pleasant manner seems to fly in the face of nineteenth-century stiffness. He quickly sets you at ease. Labatt invites you to his

BEER QUOTE —
Give me a bumper; fill it up;
See how it sparkles in the cup;
O, how shall I regale!
Can any taste this drink divine,
And then compare rum, brandy, wine
Or aught with Nappy Ale?
Unknown

office for a taste of his flagship brand, India Pale Ale. Delighted, you naturally take him up on his generous offer.

The first thing you observe about John Labatt's office is that it reflects the zest the man has for his business. Hanging prominently on the walls are brightly lithographed promotional items. One of the lithographs is trimmed in a gilded frame. You instantly recognize it as the famous poster which shows two refined gentlemen about to sample some of Labatt's finest. In your time, it's a very collectable artifact and a specimen in pristine condition can fetch hundreds of dollars. Pictorial advertising calenders also adorn the office walls. Scattered across his oak desk are trade journals, technical publications and brewing books. A finely cut set of crystal inkwells centres everything. Standing atop the fireplace mantle is a framed collection of medals that Labatt's beers have won at international taste competitions. Your host rightfully glows when he talks of these awards.

While retrieving a quart bottle from a table in the corner, he enquires, "How 'bout that I.P.A. now?" It pours smoothly and gently fizzes in the glass. You glance up at the framed poster and can't help but laugh at the resemblance between you and Labatt and the two printed gentlemen. Labatt also notices the parallel and joins your mirth. The ale has a slightly nutty bouquet and its flavour is sharp with a hint of sweetness. Its tiny bubbles tickle the palate. In a word, it's terrific. No wonder Labatt has claimed so many medals for it. Over the I.P.A., you and the brewer chat about his business. He proudly notes that his beer is shipped by rail across the breadth of Canada to agencies in Saint John, Quebec City, Montreal, Ottawa, Toronto, Winnipeg, Regina, Calgary, Edmonton and Vancouver. John Balkwill's sales area absolutely pales by comparison. John Labatt also tells you that his brewery is one of the largest in the country, but that he has strong competitors in Carling at the other end of Talbot Street, Sleeman of Guelph, O'Keefe, Dominion and Copland of Toronto and Molson and Dow of Montreal. In addition, he concedes that temperance crusaders have plagued him ever since he got into brewing at London back in the 1860s. Still, he is quite happy about the way things have turned out for him and he smiles contentedly.

You join the brewer in another glass, but decline a third because it's getting late in the afternoon. You say your good-byes and make your way out of the brewery. Before starting your time machine, you take one last look at Labatt's in 1900 and marvel at the remarkable changes you've witnessed since 1828. You wonder how it all happened during those seventy-two years. The questions leap into your head. Unable to make another personal visit to the past, you'll just have to read the rest of this book in order to quench your curiosity.

CHAPTER TWO

Beer & Brewing in the 19th Century

NOT SURPRISINGLY, LARGER forces of tradition and innovation shaped the brewing landscape in Victorian London-Middlesex. In this respect, county breweries were hardly unique, since they exhibited features common throughout the wider world of brewing. Chronicling these similarities lends us crucial perspective and sets the stage for our story.

BEER AS CULTURAL BAGGAGE

Beer travelled a long distance over a long time before it arrived in Canada. According to scholarly estimates, the world's first beer was brewed in ancient Mesopotamia sometime between 6,000 and 4,000 B.C. This makes beer older than wine. The brewing art was next adopted in Egypt around four or five thousand years ago. Having learned from the Egyptians how to brew beer, the ancient Romans spread the beverage throughout their vast empire. By the Middle Ages, malt liquor had become an entrenched part of northern Europe's dietary and social culture. Not surprisingly, the Europeans who colonized what is now Canada carried their beer-drinking habits with them. The French, although usually preferring fortified wines, came with a mild taste for beer. After the fall of New France, the English, Welsh, Scottish and Irish, along with their American kinsmen, arrived in British North America with a pronounced appreciation of heavy ale, porter and stout. To this mix, Alsatian, Belgian and German immigrants added lighter ale, lager and bock. Naturally enough, settlers' demands for beer gave rise to the Canadian brewing industry.

THE EARLY YEARS OF BREWING IN CANADA

Along with such basic pursuits as flour milling and lumbering, brewing stands as one of the earliest industries in Canada's history. Perhaps the first notable brewery on Canadian soil was the one conducted by the Jesuits at Quebec City during the 1630s. Another early brewery was the *Brasserie du Roi* (King's Brewery) that Jean Talon, New France's dynamic Intendant, had in operation in the same place from 1671 to 1675. However, the brewing industry did not have much luck in Canada until the British, Irish and their Loyalist American cousins began pouring into the colony a century or so later. By the end of the 1700s, these migrants, steeped in a beer-drinking culture, had given brewers the required market demand for industry permanence in St. John's, Halifax, Quebec City and Montreal. Precisely when and where the first commercial brewer operated in Ontario remains a prisoner of time. The late historian William Canniff suggested that it was Loyalist Henry Finkle who, sometime during the 1780s, began to make beer to supply his tavern in Ernestown Township. However, this claim is not supported with verifiable evidence. On the other hand, the archival record points to the Kingston brewery of Joseph Forsyth & Company, established prior to the fall of 1793, as the province's first.

Nonetheless, early Ontario brewers fired their kettles in or near major settlements, such as Kingston, York (Toronto) and Niagara. In these growing centres, brewers found their customers. On this score, beer writer Ian Bowering has keenly emphasized the positive influence that the British military had upon the infancy of brewing in the province. Knowing that garrisoned regulars were given a daily ration of five or six pints of small beer before 1800 or thereafter were paid a stipend of "beer money," brewers established themselves in places with a fixed military presence. By 1842, the industry consisted of ninety-six breweries spread across the whole province. Twenty years later, the provincial number of breweries crested at 155. At century's end, dominance by large regional and national breweries was clearly evident. By the revenue year ending June 30, 1901, the number of breweries in Ontario had fallen sharply to sixty-two. At the time, four centres — London, Kitchener-Waterloo-Guelph (the heart of German Canada), Hamilton and Toronto — accounted for forty percent of the entire country's beer output.

Most brewers in Victorian Canada were male and of Irish, English, Scottish and German origins. A few were also of Belgian and Alsatian heritage. Great brewing family names from the Victorian era, such as O'Keefe, Cosgrave, Copland, Sleeman, Davies, Kuntz, Huether, Molson, Dow, Boswell, Oland, Keith, McDonagh, Shea and, of course, Carling and Labatt, lasted well into the twentieth century. Incidentally, the typical brewery owner supported the Conservatives. This was not necessarily because of Sir John A. Macdonald's crafty politicking, his protective economic policies or even his legendary fondness for stiff drink. In a nutshell, the Conservative Party was good for business because it opposed the concept of all-out prohibition.

BEER LORE — As their surviving written records indicate, ancient Mesopotamians could count upon their brewers for dark beer, white beer, reddish beer, beer for ceremonial sacrifices, beer for divine repasts and a beer "from the Netherworld." Yikes!

WATER

Nineteenth-century beer was made with four basic ingredients: water, barley (generally), hops and yeast. As is the case today, a clean supply of water was of the utmost importance. Despite Canada's abundance of lakes, rivers and streams, surface waters were not well suited for brewing owing to the degree of organic matter they naturally held and because of contaminants from animal waste and industrial effluent. Necessarily, brewers sought underground sources. Now, imagine a giant pan and resting on top of that pan is a thick filter pad. Essentially, this is the geologic structure which underpins most of Middlesex County. The pan is formed by layers of bedrock, limestone, shale and glacial till and the filter consists of sand and gravel. Through the filter percolates rain water which is cleansed of its organic substances and yet infused with the carbonates and sulphates that enhance the brewing process. Since this water cannot pass through the pan, it eventually collects into pools and underground streams or rises to the surface in springs. Middlesex County's breweries were located over these subterranean water bodies.

BARLEY

Victorian brewers obtained fermentable sugar from barley, corn, oats, wheat, rye, rice and even peas if they were desperate enough. Brewers preferred barley because it was best suited to traditional malting techniques. Still, owing to early agricultural shortcomings, brewers were often forced to settle for second best on the grain market. As Edward Allen Talbot accurately observed in 1825: "Barley averages about twenty bushels per acre; but it is little cultivated in Upper Canada." Ever the pragmatic bunch, brewers did something ingeniously simple to correct this objectionable state of affairs — they actively encouraged barley culture by offering farmers ready cash for the grain. It should come as little surprise that such an inducement worked its intended magic in an economy where coin could be all too scarce. In Middlesex, the brewers' call found an eager reply. Around 1830, for example, local farmers paid scant attention to the crop. But by 1851, they had transformed Middlesex into the province's tenth most productive barley county. As the century moved forward, Middlesex farmers grew more and more barley to feed local brew kettles. In return, brewers filled the farmers' pockets with more and more money.

Incidentally, just as brewers paid cash for their barley, they generally sold their beer for cash. Significantly, cash sales provided them with crucial pools of capital from which they not only purchased raw materials, but also financed plant

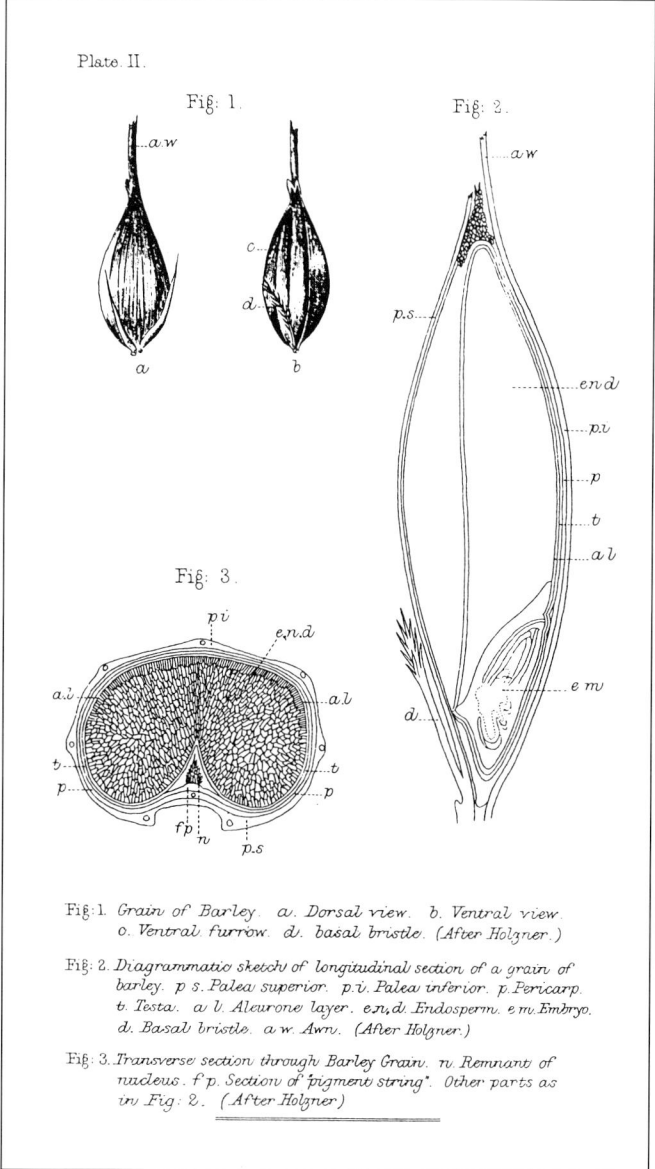

Fig: 1. *Grain of Barley. a. Dorsal view. b. Ventral view. c. Ventral furrow. d. basal bristle. (After Holgner.)*

Fig: 2. *Diagrammatic sketch of longitudinal section of a grain of barley. p.s. Palea superior. p.i. Palea inferior. p. Pericarp. t. Testa. a.l. Aleurone layer. en.d. Endosperm. e.m. Embryo. d. Basal bristle. a.w. Awn. (After Holgner.)*

Fig: 3. *Transverse section through Barley Grain. n. Remnant of nucleus. f.p. Section of "pigment string". Other parts as in Fig: 2. (After Holgner)*

DIAGRAM OF A BARLEY KERNEL FROM *A TEXT-BOOK OF THE SCIENCE OF BREWING*, 1891
Victorian brewers preferred barley as their source of fermentable sugar, and through their mass purchases of this grain, they played a very important role in the agricultural economy.

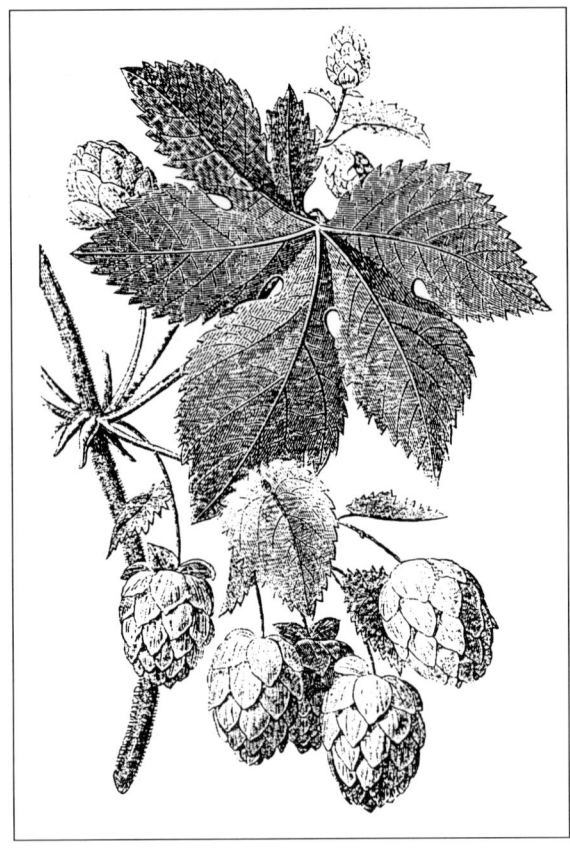

ENGRAVED PRINT OF A HOP PLANT, CIRCA 1850
To impart beer with its characteristic bitter flavour and sharp aroma, brewers drew upon the resins found in the strobile (cone) of the female hop plant. The same resins also helped to preserve beer by preventing bacteria growth.

construction and expansion. Of course, the realities of pioneer existence occasionally saw brewers resort to bartering for their grain.

HOPS

Resins from the strobile of the female hop plant (*humulus lupulus*) give beer its bitter flavour. Released during the actual brewing phase of beer-making, the resins also serve as natural preservatives. Since early brewers paid good cash to acquire hops, farmers eagerly took to raising this vine-like cousin of the nettle. Indeed, Middlesex County — particularly its northeastern corner — was one of Canada's most important hop-growing regions until the late 1870s. The strong connection between local hop-growing and local brewing activity is impossible to dispute. As the *London Free Press* noted on November 16, 1865: "About 5,000 pounds of hops came into this city yesterday, and sold at an average of 23 cents per pound." Where these hops were destined was so obvious that the paper did not bother with comment. Agricultural census returns outline the pattern of hop production in the county:

1851 – 20,968 lbs. (first in the country)
1861 – 31,216 lbs. (third in the country)
1871 – 174,529 lbs. (first in the country)
1881 – 2,494 lbs. (almost last in the country)
1891 – 2,067 lbs. (almost last in the country)
1901 – 713 lbs. (virtually last in the country)

Low prices tied to increased supply, competition from hop districts in Brant and Prince Edward Counties, the remarkable growth of the international hop trade and attacks by parasites during the late 1870s account for the near collapse of the industry in Middlesex evident from 1881 onwards.

GRAIN & HOP DEALERS

Early in the century, brewers bought their grain and hops directly from area farmers. However, the appetites of rapidly expanding breweries soon outstripped local farming capabilities. Consequently, industrial breweries, such as Carling and Labatt of London and Bixel of Strathroy, increasingly relied upon large-scale grain and hop dealers from across Canada and in the United States, Britain and Bavaria.

Buying in these worldwide arenas was speculative and not without its headaches. A supply-contract that Carling had with W.R. Snelgrove, a hop broker from Brighton, Ontario, is an excellent case in point. On September 29, 1881, Snelgrove agreed by "a writing under his hand" to sell the brewer three tons of golden cluster hops at a rate of sixteen and a half cents per pound. The hops were contracted for future delivery at the brewery. The hop market was then quite volatile and subject to great price fluctuations caused by the effects of bumper harvests and crop failures. On October 10, Snelgrove telegraphed Carling and gave notice that he would not deliver the hops. Over the previous ten days, the world price of hops had shot up by a whopping fifty percent owing to the near failure of the crop in England. In all likelihood, Snelgrove preferred to find (or had found) a customer willing to pay the new market price of twenty-four cents per pound. Carling then had no choice but to buy at the inflated rate. Understandably, the brewer bought from a party other than Snelgrove. Thenceforth, Carling only dealt with the delinquent merchant through the courts and successfully sued him for $510 in damages plus legal costs.

YEAST

Yeast is the fermenting agent used to make beer. A unicellular organism, it feeds upon grain sugar and, with the help of oxygen, converts it into ethyl alcohol and carbon dioxide (beer bubbles). Early brewers in Canada obtained their primary yeast cultures either by emigrating with their own specimens, buying samples from other brewers or collecting and cultivating natural strains. The last method was highly unpredictable and came with the risk of unwanted yeast species and/or bacterial intrusions spoiling fermentation. At any rate, yeast from one brew was saved for use in the next. This practice often nurtured unique strains, as yeast gradually evolved in the closed environment of the brewery. Brewers sold excess yeast to bakers, other brewers, distillers, vinegar-makers and householders.

BARLEY MALTING

Before the brewing process begins, barley must be turned into malt. At its essence, malting is the process whereby grain starches are converted into fermentable

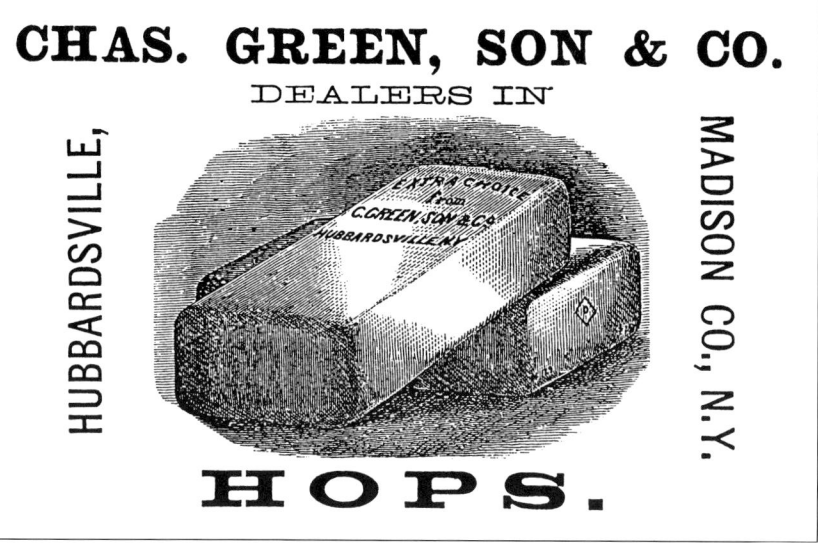

GRAIN MERCHANT AD, 1899 (UPPER) AND HOP DEALER AD, 1872 (LOWER)
Voracious demand for barley and hops carried brewers into national and international commodities markets.

A Typical Malthouse Interior, 1882 (upper) and Maltsters at Labatt's Brewery, circa 1900 (lower) *Malting demanded skill and simple back-breaking effort. The broad wooden spades were used to turn the malt over in order to expose it to the air. Courtesy, Labatt Archives*

sugars. Well into the nineteenth century, malting was as much an art as it was a science. The maltster began his task by spreading barley kernels across the large stone, brick or metal floor of the malthouse. Next, the barley was steeped in water until it was ready to germinate, at which point the water was drawn off and the mass of barley was left on the floor where it was purposely exposed to oxygen. Depending upon temperature and humidity fluctuations, germination could take anywhere from two to fourteen days. During this process, the maltster's artful skill and experience came into play. The trick was to halt germination when naturally occurring enzymes had converted most of the barley's starch into simpler sugars, but had not yet begun to consume those same sugars for further growth. For the early maltster, this step was chiefly one of visual inspection, touch, taste and smell. To arrest the enzymatic action, the malt was either floor- or kiln-dried. Brewers sold their leftover malt to nearby distilleries or even to local competitors.

THE BREWING PROCESS

Beer brewing followed the same basic pattern throughout the nineteenth century. Of course, some variance marked the industry. For instance, pioneer brewers, often lacking one instrument or another, improvised out of necessity and large-scale brewers modified techniques to suit the demands of efficiency and economies of scale. Nevertheless, the process was by batch and always began with malt and water. To maximize the solubility of its sugars, malt was ground into a flour, and to take advantage of gravity's motive power — gravity was free, after all — water was pumped into a large reservoir near the top of the brewery.

The next step, mashing, called for the ground malt to be mixed with water heated to between 160° and 190° Fahrenheit (cooler temperatures are used today) in a mash tun (vat) fixed at a level below the water reservoir. The water's temperature helped to solubilize and draw out the sugar from the malt. The mash was heated and mixed until it reached its greatest possible sweetness (measured by the tongue or by a special tool called a saccharometer). Now

WHISKY DISTILLERIES

In basic terms, whisky is simply distilled beer. More particularly, whisky distillation is the process whereby distiller's beer — or wash, to use the proper distillery jargon — is purified by vapourizing it with heat and then allowing it to condense. Since alcohol boils out of wash faster than water, the resulting distillate contains a much higher alcohol level than the original fermented liquid. Keeping this in mind, distilleries in Victorian London-Middlesex were also breweries in that they manufactured high wines (grain spirits of around fifteen to thirty percent alcohol by volume) and whiskies from beer brewed out of mashes of rye, corn, wheat and barley. Of course, distilleries were only breweries insofar as the initial stage of distilling required them to be. Ultimately, however, they were not really breweries in the truest sense of the word.

Every township in Middlesex was home to at least one distillery at one time or another. The county's first distillery was probably the one established by Ebenezer Allen in Delaware sometime during the late 1790s. Half a century later, the number of local distilleries stood at a dozen. The fact that distilling was an ideal adjunct to grain milling helps explain why distilleries were spread over a wider local area than breweries. However, county distilleries were fairly small. In the mid-1850s, for instance, the typical one produced an average of only 5,800 gallons of proof spirits per year. In other words, the industry was of little local consequence.

Competition from the province's largest distilleries in Windsor, Waterloo, Toronto, Belleville and Kingston (each producing well over 100,000 gallons annually) played a strong part in forcing the closure of the modest producers in London-Middlesex. New excise rules that required freshly distilled liquor to be warehoused for several months before its sale was permitted — a capital intensive proposition — also spelled the doom of the local distilling industry. The county's last four distilleries all ceased production in 1863. Much to the chagrin of those charged with collecting Her Majesty's inland revenue, the only local whisky distilling to occur thereafter was of an illicit nature.

called wort, the solution was then drained into an underback (*lauter tun* in German breweries). While flowing into the underback, the wort passed through a perforated false-bottom in the mash tun. This straining measure removed most of the grain particles from the wort. Trapped barley husks also helped to filter the wort. In a technique called sparging, hot water was sprayed onto the heap of leftover solid matter. The purpose of sparging was to wash any remaining sugars into the underback. In the underback, finer particles settled out of the wort. Depending on the batch's intended volume, the entire mashing process could take anywhere from a few hours to a day or two. Spent grain was eaten by the brewery's dray horses or sold to farmers for use as animal feed.

Actual brewing took place in a wood-fired or steam-heated copper kettle into which the wort from the underback was pumped. Hops, either whole or chopped, joined the wort in the kettle. Boiled anywhere from a few to several hours, the spiced wort now took on the flavour characteristics of beer. Heat from the kettle also rid the mixture of micro-organisms, paving the way for effective yeast growth during fermentation. While the wort boiled, the atmosphere throughout the

BEER LORE — In 1617, the vice-chancellor of Oxford University had one John Shurle appointed as the school's official ale tester. Shurle's annual pay was one gallon of strong ale and two gallons of strong wort.

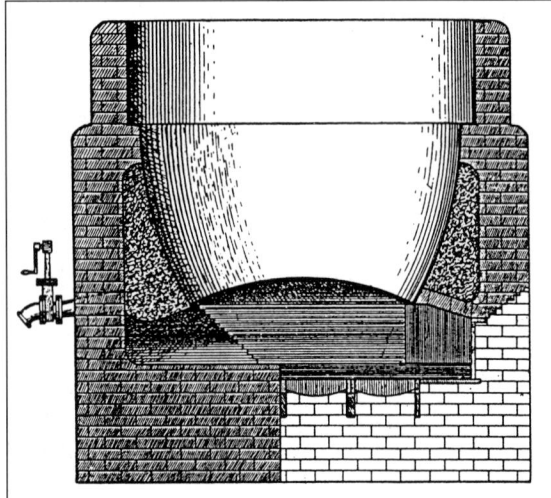

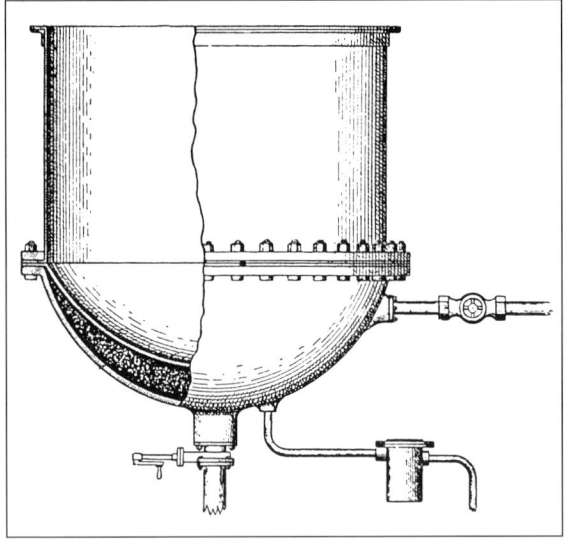

A WOOD-FIRED KETTLE (UPPER) AND A STEAM-HEATED KETTLE (LOWER), BOTH CIRCA 1885
With few exceptions, nineteenth-century brew kettles were made of copper. Wood-fired kettles were usually anchored in brick and mortar housings, although some models were freestanding. Steam pipes, connected to a central boiler, fed steam-heated kettles.

neighbourhood of the brewery assumed a distinctly sweet and grainy bouquet (residents in today's London are well acquainted with this). Once brewed, the wort was passed through a filter known as a hop-jack or hop-back. Made of straw, horse hair or tightly woven fabrics, such as felt, the hop-jack strained the hops out of the boiled wort. Brewers recycled hops recovered in this manner for use in subsequent brews.

Before the wort found its way into fermenting tuns, its temperature had to be reduced instantly to about 65° Fahrenheit. If cooled too slowly, the wort would become contaminated with bacteria and acidify to the point where fermentation would be difficult and the taste of the final product would be compromised. Early brewers accomplished this by limiting brewing activities to the fall, winter and early spring (summer was generally too hot) and by cleverly using simple devices, such as shallow, open-faced pans designed to maximize the exposure of hot wort to cool air. Often, pipes filled with cold spring or river water were snaked through the pans to enhance the cooling effect. Alternatively, some brewers trickled hot wort over chilled metal plates. The cooled wort was next drained into fermenting tuns. At this stage, yeast was introduced to work its magic upon the grain sugar. Ale, porter and stout fermentation took place at temperatures between 65° and 72° Fahrenheit and lasted from around four to six days. Lager fermentation required much cooler temperatures and lasted from one to three or four weeks. Fermented wort was then called beer.

New beer was drawn off into casks for aging in cellars or underground caverns. This could take anywhere from about ten days for regular beers to two years for old stock ales. However, given the pressing need to satisfy customer demand, most beer was aged for less than six months. During the aging process, a small amount of yeast was added to each cask of beer in order to continue fermentation and keep the beer fresh by consuming any remaining oxygen. Secondary fermentation also freed up precious space in fermenting tuns for subsequent batches of wort.

Fining or clarifying beer generally occurred just after secondary fermentation. Substances, such as isinglass (a gelatinous material obtained from fish, especially sturgeon), chalk, ground oyster shells, charcoal or spent hops were mixed into the beer. As these compounds settled, they attracted and absorbed the extremely fine particles that otherwise would have made the beer muddy. Usually, but not always, beer clarified in this manner was racked either before a secondary aging period or before final packaging in kegs and bottles. Racking simply involved using a siphon to separate the bright beer from the sediment drawn out by the fining agent.

SCIENCE & TECHNOLOGY
The great march of science and technology wielded a profound impact upon Victorian breweries and affected each and every step in the brewing process. While

documenting every change is beyond these pages, it is important to outline the three most significant trends — advances in brewing chemistry, improvements to cooling technology and the introduction of steam power — that allowed breweries to become larger and more efficient and to produce clearer and more consistent brews.

ADVANCES IN BREWING CHEMISTRY

Growing understanding of brewing chemistry (zymurgy) marked the entire century. In 1800, the typical brewer truly knew very little about the chemical and biochemical processes by which he turned grain into beer. His trade was one of artful tradition and he brewed with the blind faith that things would work because they had done so before. Owing to his imperfect knowledge, mistakes were common and spoiled brews the result. However, with the same blind faith, he would simply start over.

BREWHOUSE COOLING PANS FROM CHEMISTRY, THEORETICAL, PRACTICAL, AND ANALYTICAL, 1882 *Boiled wort had to be cooled quickly before it was introduced to the fermenting tuns. Passing hot wort through pans containing metal tubes filled with cold river or spring water usually did the trick. This cooling method was quite popular with brewers in Victorian London-Middlesex.*

Over the century, the brewer gradually became more of a scientist and less of an artisan. Indeed, on the eve of the twentieth century, some brewers had earned university degrees in biology or chemistry and many had trained at professional brewing academies, although apprenticing still remained the most popular means of learning the trade. Behind the industry-wide move to science was a legion of laboratory researchers, including the eminent Louis Pasteur, who investigated everything from the chemical composition of barley and hops to the biochemistry of fermentation (Pasteur's chief contribution). Their discoveries, once disseminated through scientific and industrial literature, provided brewers with an immense pool of accurate and tested knowledge. By the 1890s, the typical brewer was thoroughly acquainted with the chemistry of malting, mashing, kettle-brewing and fermentation and he better understood the importance of hygiene in the prevention of bacterial spoilage. Armed with myriad statistical tables, specific gravity charts, gauges and other instruments, as well as new-found scientific know-how, the late Victorian brewer brewed with greater precision and control. Overall, the frequency of mistakes shrank, efficiency improved, product quality became better and more consistent and, most importantly, the potential for profit increased.

BEER LORE — Driving a wagon or carriage while under the influence of intoxicating liquor, including beer, was a punishable offence in Victorian Canada only if one drove the vehicle furiously or recklessly.

IMPROVEMENTS TO COOLING TECHNOLOGY

Improvements to cooling technology freed the nineteenth-century brewer from a seasonal prison wherein summer heat confined the brewing season to the fall,

LABATT'S NEW BREWERY (LEFT OF HOUSE AT RIGHT), LOOKING NORTH FROM NEAR THE FOOT OF TALBOT STREET, WINTER, CIRCA 1876
Improved cooling, refrigeration and heating techniques allowed Victorian brewers the freedom to brew year round. Thanks to such triumphs over Canada's harsh seasonal realities, breweries of the era evolved into large-scale industrial enterprises. Courtesy, J.J. Talman Regional Collection

winter and early spring. The most notable advancements in this regard were ammonia-based refrigerators and artificial ice-making machines. During the second half of the 1800s, various kinds of these mechanical devices were developed across the brewing world. Significantly, they afforded the brewer the luxury of crucial temperature regulation over the hot summer months.

On the face of things, Canadian brewers appear to have been behind the times in adopting the latest cooling technology. However, it should be noted that these appliances were expensive and not entirely reliable. More importantly, the annual wintertime harvest of natural ice — surprise, surprise! — blessed Canadian brewers with a relatively inexpensive option. In 1864, for instance, eight tons of delivered ice only cost twenty dollars. Nonetheless, refrigeration machines started to make their presence felt in Canada towards the end of the century, when large breweries began to deplete private ice sources and outstrip local and regional ice dealers' supply abilities. Around 1900, for example, Carling installed an artificial ice plant.

Besides ice, early brewers, as we have already seen, also relied upon spring and river water as a refrigerant. Of course, subterranean storage facilities were naturally cooled by the ground to between 60° and 65° Fahrenheit and straw could be used as insulation. Other cooling techniques were related to architectural innovations. Over the century, architects learned to design breweries with an eye to improving internal air flow. For instance, cupolas, wall vents, doors and windows were better placed to exhaust hot air. Moreover, architects increasingly recognized the value of strategic ice storage within the brewery. When Londoners Robinson & Tracy drew up plans for Robert Arkell's new brewery, they ensured that ice could be warehoused so that it refrigerated the necessary parts of the building. Better heating technologies also permitted brewing during the coldest of winter days.

THE INTRODUCTION OF STEAM POWER

During the first half of the 1800s, most Canadian breweries relied upon gravity, human sinew and horse muscle as sources of power. However, the introduction of steam technology — the very foundation of Victorian manufacturing progress — revolutionized the brewing industry over the third quarter of the century. For instance, steam-driven pumps moved liquids much more rapidly than clumsy hand-pumps ever could. Indeed, steam pumps allowed colossal volumes of hot water, wort and beer to travel throughout the brewery with comparative ease. Even more importantly, steam engines, blessed with relatively immense strength, freed breweries from the inefficiencies of all too exhaustible human and animal energy. Time-saving steam-powered machinery, such as automatic malt mills, gear-driven malt turners, mechanical mash mixers and belt-controlled barrel washers, replaced hand tools. Significantly, since steam pumps and steam engines largely superseded gravity as a motive force, brewing appliances no longer had to be arranged in a vertical manner. As a result, breweries of the second half of the century could be built according to much bigger horizontal plans

Steam was also directly applied to the brewing process. For two reasons, the steam-heated kettle was an improvement over the traditional wood-fired copper. One, steam kettles distributed heat evenly to the wort. Two, they gave the brewer precise control

BREWERY AD FROM THE LONDON FREE PRESS OF JANUARY 27, 1871
As steam revolutionized how breweries were designed, powered and operated, many brewery owners were sure to incorporate the great watchword of the age — steam — into their breweries' names. In Victorian Canada, a steam brewery was one that possessed the latest technology — a steam-heated kettle. (computer enhanced)

BEER LORE — The Picts of ancient Scotland brewed a beer flavoured with the heather flower. Now, that's just bonnie!

THE NEW CARLING BREWERY, TALBOT AND ANN
STREETS, CIRCA 1876
*The steam engine saw brewery architecture move away
from the centuries-old tower plan. The new Carling
brewery, built in the mid-1870s, was a typical horizontal
brewery of its time. Courtesy, J.J. Talman Regional
Collection*

over boiling temperatures. Another steam application shaped the brewing industry in a remarkably different way. Trains, essentially steam boilers on iron wheels, facilitated the shipping of beer across Canada and it was only during the railway age that breweries blossomed into regional and national concerns. While steam technology presented decided advantages, its adoption was an expensive option that entailed significant capital outlay, hefty repair charges and constant fuel bills. Nevertheless, steam power ultimately translated into improved efficiency and enhanced production capacity. Moreover, its associated costs were outweighed by increased profit potential. Naturally, those brewers who could afford such promising technology readily acquired it.

OTHER TECHNOLOGIES

A host of other technologies also found their way into Victorian breweries. For instance, pneumatic malting drums boosted the speed and accuracy of malting. Better filtration techniques greatly reduced the need for clarifying agents. And the telegraph, the telephone, the typewriter and even the multi-ringed office binder improved communication and overall business administration. Ironically, in this bold age of steam, some technological leaps still relied upon human power. Perhaps the most notable example of this was the hand-operated mechanical bottling machine. Although much slower than the automatic bottling lines of the early 1900s, these machines were vastly superior to the old method of hand-corking.

THE BREWERY WORKFORCE

The typical Victorian brewery employed both skilled and semi-skilled workers who, on average, laboured from ten to twelve hours per weekday and from four to eight hours on Saturdays. Interestingly, maltsters were on call seven days a week and usually lived within shouting distance of the brewery in case they were instantly needed to terminate a malting that had dared to finish ahead of schedule. Skilled workers possessed specialized talents that were only acquired by apprenticeship or, less commonly, through formal training in schools. Their ranks included maltsters, brewmasters, brewers, coopers, engineers and accountants. Naturally, maltsters, brewmasters and brewers applied their valuable knowledge and experience to the brewing process. (The technical difference between a brewmaster and a brewer was that the former had attained the highest level of qualification, while the latter was one or two steps behind in professional standing.) Coopers made and repaired barrels, engineers (stationary engineers in modern terms) operated and maintained steam engines, heavy machinery and other mechanical appliances, and accountants brought financial wizardry into the brewery office. Semi-skilled workers performed jobs that required relatively little training. They included bottle washers, bottlers, labellers, packers, cellar and warehouse clerks, teamsters, janitors, night-watchmen and general labourers. This last group did odd jobs around the brewery, such as shovelling grain, turning malt, kegging, loading wagons and otherwise lending a hand when and where needed.

Most brewery employees were males aged sixteen years or older. Workforce maleness was deemed necessary to carry out the heavy tasks associated with brewery jobs. However, it was not unknown to see women employed as bottle

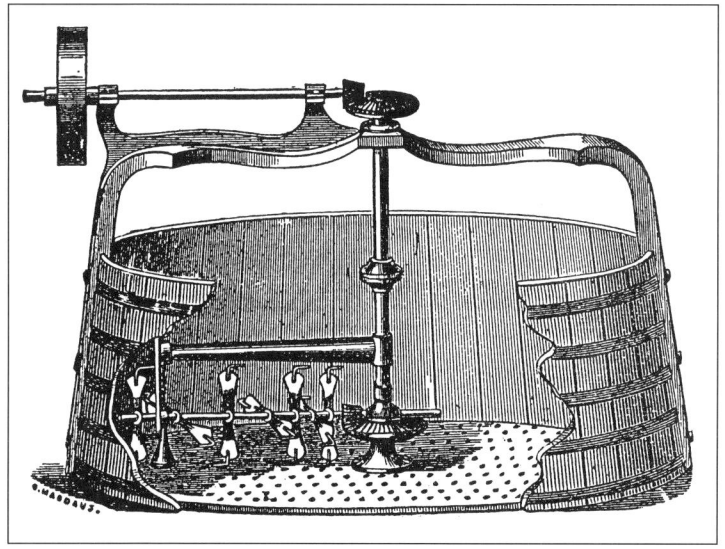

THEODORE KRAUSCH'S PATENTED PROPELLER MASHING MACHINE FROM *THE AMERICAN BREWERS' GAZETTE* OF DECEMBER 15, 1872
Over the last third of the 1800s, mechanical mash mixers, similar to the one pictured above, were installed in breweries across Canada. Cranked by steam-powered drive belts and gears, these appliances were far more efficient than hand-operated tools and saved the brewer time, energy and labour costs.

BOY WANTED. – APPLY AT KENT BREW-
ERY.　　　　　　　　　　　　　　G14v

20 GOOD ACTIVE BOYS WANTED TO WORK in bottling department.　Apply Carling
Brewing & Malting Co.　　　　　　D26v

BOYS WANTED – FOR BOTTLING DE-
PARTMENT.　Apply　at　Labatt's
Brewery, Simcoe street.　　　　　　E9v

Help Wanted Ads from the London Free Press Issues for (top to bottom) July 14, 1886, April 26, 1887 and May 9, 1893
Brewers often employed boys between the ages of twelve and sixteen to work as bottlers over the summer months. (all computer enhanced)

BEER QUOTE — "They who drink beer will think beer."

Washington Irving, *The Sketch Book*, "Stratford"

washers, bottlers, labellers, case packers and secretarial staff. Still, the sexism of the era kept females from occupying skilled positions. Interestingly, children of both genders and as young as ten, but usually twelve or older, were to be found in Victorian breweries. They were charged with washing, filling, labelling and packing bottles and with such chores as skimming drowned rodents off vats and fishing the same creatures, whether dead or alive, out of barrels. Under the tutelage of more senior workers, teenage boys served their malting, brewing and coopering apprenticeships. Of the many who worked in local breweries, three Carling employees particularly stand out because of their surnames. The first, William Sleeman, a "beer carrier" (teamster) during the mid-1850s, was probably a member of Guelph's famous brewing family. The second and third, John Barrel, a labourer during the mid-1850s, and Ed Barrel, a teamster during the 1880s, bore a family name that was a natural for brewery work.

Animals constituted the "forgotten employees" at any Victorian brewery. Most obviously, strong draft horses served as the motive power for wagons and carts. Before steam engines, horses also powered malt mills and pumps. Equine workers were usually joined by cats and dogs who laboured to keep the resident rat and mouse population in check — after all, these pesky little rodents loved to feast upon malthouse grain. Dogs also doubled as roving nighttime security systems.

Of course, the brewery owner headed the workforce. In the vast majority of cases, this person was a fully trained brewmaster, who oversaw every phase of production and looked after the promotional end of the business. In this sense, the proprietor was the Victorian equivalent of the modern plant manager, corporate affairs branch, human resources department and marketing division all rolled into one.

BREWERY WAGES
Interestingly, census returns for 1871 reveal that Ontario brewery employees were better paid than most other factory workers in the province. Out of the sixty-two most significant industries evaluated in the census that year, brewery wages stood seventeenth highest. More specifically, brewery workers then earned an average of $326 in annual wages. Meanwhile, labourers in the cheesemaking, saw milling and cigar manufacturing industries respectively earned $122, $193 and $223 per year. Skilled tradesmen claimed the lion's share of wages within the brewing industry. Brewery owners had no choice but to reward these employees with handsome pay packets, as the talents of experienced maltsters, brewmasters, brewers, coopers, engineers and accountants fetched premium rates in a tight labour market.

BARRELS, CASKS & KEGS

Most beer in nineteenth-century Canada was traded in wooden vessels known as barrels or casks (the words were interchangeable, although barrel was most frequently used). The term keg usually denoted a container smaller than a standard barrel. Made of strong and durable oak, casks were ideally suited for bulk shipment of beer near and wide. The following are the names and corresponding sizes for common Victorian beer barrels, which came in either imperial measure or wine measure:

Butt or Pipe	108 gallons
Puncheon	72 gallons
Hogshead	54 gallons
Standard Barrel	36 gallons (or 31 gallons)
Kilderkin	18 gallons
Firkin	9 gallons
Pin	4½ gallons

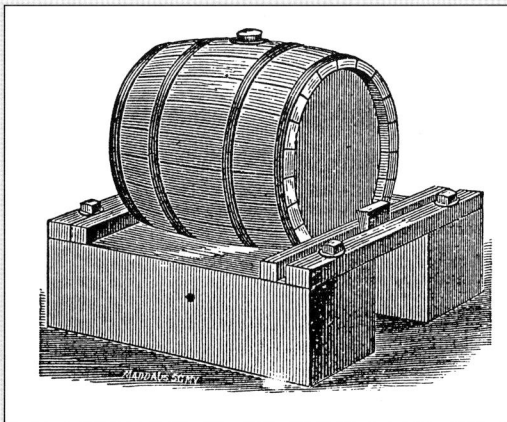

A TYPICAL VICTORIAN BEER BARREL

By the end of the 1800s, hogsheads, standard barrels, kilderkins and firkins were the Canadian brewer's sizes of choice.

COOPERS POSING OUTSIDE JOHN LABATT'S COOPERAGE, CIRCA 1880
Courtesy, Labatt Archives

Brewery coopers manufactured, repaired and cleaned barrels. They worked with draw-knives, crummy-knives, round-shaves, saws, brace-and-bits, bick-irons, swifts, hammers and mauls to transform staves, hoops and headings into the finished product. Under normal conditions, a properly made barrel would last for several years. Keeping these containers free of grime was crucial for turning out good product. To "neutralize and dissipate all putrescence" in dirty casks, coopers used everything from hand-scrubbing to jets of steam to sulphuric acid or chloride of lime. Another cleansing technique called for coating the inside of a barrel with pitch and setting fire to the pitch. The heat acted as a sterilizing agent. Of course, the flame was extinguished before it charred the interior.

BOTTLES

After barrels, bottles were the next most frequently used container for packaging beer in the 1800s (jugs came third, pails and buckets last). Bottles came in two basic sizes — the pint and the quart — and were made of hand-blown glass or pottery. Glass bottles could be embossed with a brewer's name, location and product type, while pottery bottles could have the same identifiers stamped across their shoulders. However, the vast majority of the century's beer bottles were unmarked, except by labels. Like today, brewers charged returnable deposit fees on their bottles.

A TYPICAL LATE VICTORIAN BEER BOTTLE *Courtesy, Jim Maitland*

Owing to a combination of their relatively high cost and breakability, glass beer bottles were not as prominent during the first half of the 1800s as they were during the second half. Advancements in glassmaking technology, which lowered the price of bottles and enhanced their strength, allowed brewers to rely upon bottling more and more as the century marched onwards. By 1900, roughly one-third of all Canadian-made beer came in bottles.

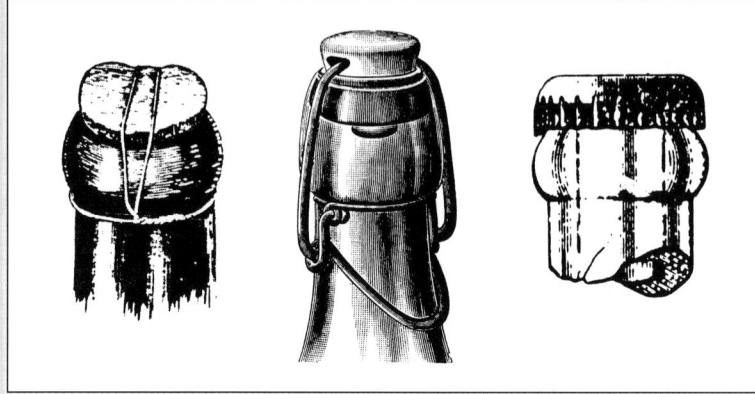

LEFT TO RIGHT — A CORK CLOSURE, THE LIGHTNING STOPPER AND THE CROWN CAP

Improvements to bottle closures also marked the course of the 1800s. The most basic stopper was the cork. Prone to popping out of pressurized bottles or simply drying out and letting beer go flat, corks often had to be secured with wire ties or tinfoil wraps. In 1875, Charles de Quillfeldt developed his lightning stopper. Essentially a rubber-lined porcelain plug fastened by a wire bail, this closure was more reliable than the cork. Even more reliable was William Painter's crown cap of 1892. Best suited to semi- and fully automatic bottling machinery, the crown cap soon became the standard in the brewing industry. Indeed, a modified version of Painter's closure — the "twist-off" cap — is still with us. Of course, the daunting expense of converting bottle inventories and bottling lines to these new closures postponed the demise of the humble cork until the early 1910s.

Retaining skilled workers was crucial to turning out good product and maximizing business efficiency, and the best means to keep skilled workers was to compensate them well. Semi-skilled labourers, while not earning nearly the princely sums of their skilled colleagues, still made a decent living. At the bottom of the brewery pay scale were women, children and apprentices, although boys who received formal training in the brewing trades obtained lasting benefits that far outweighed their modest wages.

WORKPLACE HAZARDS

One drawback to relatively high pay levels was that breweries could be dangerous places for the unwary, inattentive, careless or just plain unlucky. Wet floors, slippery ladders, steam valves, hot pipes, boiling kettles, whirling engine belts, falling heavy objects and shattering glass bottles all harboured ill-will. A less obvious hazard was carbon dioxide. This gas could suffocate anyone who dared to lean over a batch of fermenting wort. Moreover, pressure exerted by carbon dioxide in beer could burst bottles and cause metal hoops to fly off barrels with sinister speed. Hoops unfastened in this manner could cut right through a human body.

Although horrible accidents were quite infrequent, they did unfortunately occur. The *London Free Press* of July 11, 1887 recounted one such event:

> John Bullen, who is employed in the Carling brewing and malting establishment as a labeller, met with a very painful accident on Thursday last. He was engaged in putting a label on a bottle when the bottle burst, lacerating his hand in a frightful manner, and severing several arteries. The blood flowed profusely from the wound, and was not stopped until the assistance of Drs. Moore and Gardiner had been secured. The arm was opened near the elbow, and the main artery sewed up.

Thankfully, Bullen recovered and continued working for Carling into the twentieth century. Fatal accidents were rarest of all and only two of them were ever recorded in Victorian Middlesex. In early 1863, George Barber, an engineer at Labatt's, lost his life after falling into a boiling kettle. Revealing the brotherly spirit which typified London's brewing community, employees at both Labatt's and Carling's contributed to a fund in aid of Barber's widow and child. Eighteen years later, one Thorneycraft was crushed to death in the belting and machinery at the Carling brewery. Despite such gruesome occurrences, official records show that breweries were far safer workplaces than flour mills, lumber mills, foundries and other factories.

WORKFORCE EXPANSION & SPECIALIZATION

Workforce expansion and specialization marked the evolution of the brewing industry. During the first half of the 1800s, the typical brewery workforce rarely numbered more than five or six people. As scientific and technological progress allowed breweries to grow physically, the demand for labour paradoxically increased. While steam power replaced manual labour in many areas of the brewery, it simultaneously boosted the need for human muscle in other parts,

DENNIS MASON, CIRCA 1910
In the late 1860s, while in his early twenties, Irish immigrant Dennis Mason (also spelled Denis) began his career at Labatt's as a general labourer. Within a few years, he had worked his way up the ladder to brewer. In the mid-1880s, Mason was promoted to head brewer, a position he held into the twentieth century. Michael Walsh was Mason's counterpart at Carling's. Courtesy, Labatt Archives

LABELS FOR JOSEPH HAMILTON'S LONDON PORTER AND LONDON AMBER ALE, 1889
While dark ale, porter and stout dominated most of Victorian Canada's beer world, brewers hardly ignored changes in public taste. Joseph Hamilton supplied steadfast traditionalists with his London Porter and accommodated those who wanted something a bit lighter with his Amber Ale.

especially in the malthouse, kegging room, aging cellar, bottling department and shipping bay. Of course, greater output also required more teamsters to carry beer out of the brewery. Barrel-makers were the only ones who suffered appreciably at the hands of steam technology. As the century progressed, machine-made barrels gradually made coopers less and less essential, although they were still needed in smaller numbers to repair barrels. By 1900, larger breweries employed a hundred or so workers and half again during the busy summer bottling season.

Until mid-century, brewery employees, despite whatever particular training and status they may have had, were expected to perform jobs throughout the entire brewery. They were so expected due to economics of small-scale production. After all, a maltster, once finished with malting, could keg beer, rather than collect pay for being idle. A similar logic also saw the brewery owner labour alongside his workers. However, as breweries moulted into factories, economics of large-scale production dictated workforce specialization. For example, fast-paced year-round production kept maltsters in the malthouse and brewers in the brewhouse. Furthermore, specialization saw workers organized into administrative hierarchies. Bottlers answered to a foreman, brewers to the head brewmaster, junior engineers to a chief engineer and so on and so forth. Of course, under this pyramid structure, everyone was responsible to the brewery owner or his designate. Workforce specialization also affected the brewery proprietor, who moved away from daily brewing chores and almost exclusively into what we now call corporate planning and management.

STYLES OF BEER

Beer in Victorian Canada fell into the ale, porter, stout and lager families. Ale, porter and stout were (and still are) closely related in that their yeasts worked on top of the wort in the fermenting tun. Ale, brewed with moderate quantities of hops, ranged in colour from light amber to bright red to dark brown. Porter and stout, made from roasted malt and very generous amounts of hops, were consequently much darker and generally thicker than ale. Indeed, stout, essentially the boldest, darkest and thickest style of porter, appeared in the mug as midnight black and flowed with the consistency of cream. Interestingly, the heavy qualities of porter and stout could cover up minor mistakes in their brewing. Forgiving in this manner, they were well-suited for manufacture in the primitive breweries of the pioneer era. Ales, porters and stouts ranged in taste from sweet to bitter and were brewed according to English, Irish and Scottish traditions. Given the predominance of British and Irish brewers and the generally British and Irish character of the population, it is not surprising that these beverages ranked as the most popular beer styles during the 1800s.

Lager takes its name from the German word *lagern*, which means "to store." It is a fitting appellation given that the beer's Bavarian creators aged it by storing it over the winter in deep underground caverns. What truly distinguishes lager from British and Irish beers is that it is produced with a yeast that works at relatively cold temperatures and at the bottom of the fermenting tun. This particular brewing process results in a smooth and mellow malt liquor. Moreover, as lighter-coloured beverages, lagers have been traditionally brewed with paler malts and fewer hops than their Anglo-Saxon and Hibernian counterparts. As a Germanic beer, lager naturally dominated in regions settled by those of German ancestry, such as Waterloo County and parts of Wellington, Perth, Huron, Bruce and Grey Counties. Indeed, George Rebscher, who added a lager brewhouse to his tavern business at Berlin (now Kitchener) in 1837, was the first North American lager brewer (he beat John Wagner of Philadelphia by several years). Besides lager, German settlers also brought their dark bock beers and wheat-based weiss beers.

Other nineteenth-century beers included those spiced with spruce shoots, maple syrup, treacle, raspberries, cherries, etcetera. However, these flavoured beers were generally produced in the pioneer's home brewery and not commercially. Still, maple beer stands as the most Canadian of beers ever made. Small beer was ale made from the second and third spargings of mash. The resulting wort was low in sugar and thus bore a beer with a small alcohol level — hence the name "small beer." The perfect substitute for dirty drinking water, it was consumed by families, including children, as part of the daily diet and routinely by labourers on work breaks. By mid-century, small beer had passed out of favour, chiefly owing to improved access to clean water.

THE TREND TO LIGHTER-BODIED BEERS

Heavy ales, porters and stouts dominated the Canadian beer landscape during the first two-thirds of the 1800s. However, starting in the 1860s, these dark brews began to lose significant ground to pale and amber ales. By the 1880s, these latter two beverages reigned supreme. Besides surpassing the once eminent position of dark beer, pale and amber ales also waged a subtle and sneaky campaign of dilution against their heavier cousins. Chiefly fought in taverns and saloons during the 1870s and 1880s, this battle saw light ale mixed into porter and stout to create half and half or 'arf and 'arf as it was affectionately known. By century's end, pale and amber ales constituted not quite one-half of the Canadian beer market, while heavy ales, porters and stouts made up nearly one-third. While the struggle unfolded between dark and light brews in the British and Irish vein, lager further lightened the character of Canada's beer world over the last half of the 1800s. Indeed, by 1900, about twenty-five percent of all beer annually consumed in the country was lager.

LABEL FOR CARLING BREWING & MALTING CO.'S HALF AND HALF, CIRCA 1885
The growing popularity of half and half — porter mixed (or diluted) with ale — stands as a strong symbol of the Victorian consumer trend towards lighter-bodied beers.

BEER LORE — In 1188, King Henry II levied the first English tax on beer. Known as the Saladin tithe, it was intended to offset the cost of financing Crusades to the Holy Land.

ALCOHOL CONTENT

Stories of pioneer beer containing twenty to thirty-five percent alcohol are absolute hogwash, since brewer's yeast dies when wort attains an alcohol content of around fourteen percent. Grain-based beverages with higher alcohol volumes are distilled high wines and whiskies which, by definition, are not beers. At any rate, it is difficult to discover the alcohol level in most nineteenth-century beer because brewers were not then legally compelled to disclose such information. However, analysts' reports submitted to the federal government reveal that late Victorian beer generally clocked in at four to eight percent alcohol by volume (strikingly similar to the range of today's beer). In 1886, for example, tests showed that Carling's lager and draft beer were respectively 4.93% and 6.57% alcohol by volume. Meanwhile, John Hamilton's draft beer was 4.89% and John Labatt's was 6.16%. Immediately prior to the turn of the century, the following percentages by volume were recorded for brands produced at Middlesex County's two largest breweries:

Carling's Amber Ale – 8.63%

Carling's Export India Pale Ale – 6.63% to 8.72%

Carling's Pale Bitter Ale – 4.25% to 4.64%

Carling's XXX Porter – 6.24% to 7.09%

Labatt's India Pale Ale – 3.9% to 5.86%

Labatt's XXX Stout – 6.65% to 6.86%

EARLY TASTE TESTS

Sadly, we will never be treated to the delightful privilege of sampling historic Canadian brews. As one might suspect, early opinion varied widely on the quality of domestic beer. At one extreme, that whiny volcano of complaints about pioneer life, Catharine Parr Traill, flowing with proverbial British beer snobbery (even then!), lamented that the Canadian article was not "like the sweet, well-flavoured, home-brewed beer of the English farm-houses." Conversely, Hugh Murray, an intrepid Scotsman who travelled across British North America in the late 1830s, discovered in the Canadas "ale and beer of excellent quality." While it is impossible to discover whose opinion lies closer to the truth, the consuming public, as we shall see, certainly enjoyed the beers brewed in London-Middlesex. Of course, arguments about the quality of Canada's beer have raged on ever since, especially whenever Canadians and Americans sit down together and share some brew.

BEER LORE — In Tudor England, civic officials known as ale conners were charged with testing the purity of locally brewed beer. Perhaps the most notable ale conner was William Shakespeare's father.

CHAPTER THREE

Beer & Drink Culture
in the 19th Century

NATURALLY, BEER DRINKING in the nineteenth century was part of a wider drink culture. To understand the social context in which beer was consumed, it is helpful to look at this drink culture. After all, the whos, whats, whens, wheres and whys are key parts of our story. Of all these dimensions, the barroom loomed largest, since it was the most prominent place of public drinking and was of fundamental importance to brewers' financial health.

THE OVERALL DRINK CULTURE

Besides malt liquors, our ancestors consumed all manner of beverage alcohol: wine, brandy, port, sherry, cognac, fermented cider, mead (made from honey), whisky, gin, rum, vodka (then fairly rare), schnapps, cordials, liqueurs, bitters, mixed drinks and so on and so forth. Men drank, women drank and children drank. Interestingly, statutory age restrictions were phenomena of the late 1800s and early 1900s, although, regardless of legal developments, nineteenth-century social conventions frowned upon minors being served liquor in licensed places and childhood intoxication received sharp approbation. Still, youngsters often joined their elders in a glass of beer or wine at the dinner table.

At the risk of sounding facetious, Victorians drank because they had inherited the cultural practice from their forebears. More specifically, the historical record reveals that they imbibed for reasons of hospitality, celebration, social union, health (alcohol in beverage form and as a medicinal solvent), refreshment, nutrition, physical warmth (a mistaken concept), boredom, frustration and, unfortunately, addiction. Interestingly, these impulses match those which precipitate drinking in our age. Also, they drank practically everywhere and anytime, including at home, work, taverns, saloons, stores, dances, building-bees, elections, hospitals, prisons and church (for sacramental purposes and occasionally because of tedious

THE BRYCE & MILLS STORE, HAMILTON ROAD AT ADELAIDE STREET, CIRCA 1875
In the nineteenth century, beer could be bought at the neighbourhood corner store. Bryce & Mills, general dealers and licensed liquor merchants, proudly carried John Labatt's ale and porter. Courtesy, J.J. Talman Regional Collection

---

BEER LORE — The Oland family of Moosehead Beer fame once ran a brewery in Woodstock, Ontario.

sermonizers or, from the perspective of some clergy, because of dull congregations).

THE RETAIL LIQUOR TRADE

Although many nineteenth-century drinkers privately manufactured their own liquid pleasures — either legally in the case of beer, wine, cider and mead or illicitly in the case of distilled spirits — most acquired strong drink on the retail market. During the 1800s, legitimate retailers of beverage alcohol included brewers, distillers, commercial winemakers, tavern- and hotelkeepers, saloon operators and licensed merchants. In particular, licensed storekeepers played a significant role in the distribution of beer since they were "The Beer Stores" of their day.

HOTELS, TAVERNS & SALOONS

The most prominent public drinking in the nineteenth century occurred in hotels, taverns and saloons. Under the law, hotels and taverns were the same in that each provided meals and lodgings to the travelling public and stabling for horses. The popular distinction between the two was one of size. Taverns were smaller and generally located in outlying areas, while hotels were larger and situated in urban centres. Still, Victorian Canadians often used the terms interchangeably (as will we). Nevertheless, hotels played an important economic role in an era when slower and less efficient means of travel necessitated overnight stopovers, even for short journeys of ten to fifteen miles by horse. The saloon — a word which now conjures up visions of drunken sprees and tough-guy brawls in the Wild West — was simply a restaurant that was licensed to serve alcoholic beverages.

Tavernkeepers in Middlesex (and elsewhere) prided themselves upon their abilities to accommodate the public with genial service and friendly old-country atmosphere. For instance, shortly before Confederation, Vincent Ockley pledged that "good, hearty 'British cheer' will always abound" in his hotel. Meanwhile David Haystead promised that "Those who call with D.H. will find the host a thorough Englishman, who will treat his guests in a thoroughly English Fashion." Still other hotelkeepers simply stamped their outgoing personalties onto their establishments. In July of 1859, for instance, a commercial reporter observed that thirty-five-year-old hotelman Robert Arkell, "rather a roistering, jolly, noisy fellow," kept "a ditto house." Of course, aside from offering the usual comforts of bed, board and stabling, the county's tavernkeepers typically met the public with liquid greetings. As James F. Dundas, proprietor of London's freshly renovated Central Inn, proclaimed in 1864: "Those who desire a foaming tankard of Ale, good Wines and Whiskey, [and] a superior glass of Brandy… will hereafter know where to call."

LONDON'S MARKET SQUARE WITH THE MARKET SALOON VISIBLE AT THE FAR LEFT, CIRCA 1865
Full of ambience and good cheer, saloons were popular points of call with the imbibing public. When this photograph was originally taken, about two dozen saloons were clustered in and around London's market square. Courtesy, J.J. Talman Regional Collection

THE BARROOM

Restrained imitations of British and Irish pubs, barrooms in Victorian London-Middlesex, whether they belonged to saloons, countryside taverns or large urban hotels, shared certain features, most of which are still with us in more modern forms. Naturally, central to the barroom was the bar, which could range from rough-hewn pine planks to elaborately carved masterpieces of oak, maple and black walnut. Atop, under and behind the bar were stored bottles and decanters of wine,

BEER LORE — The word beer comes from *bibere*, which is Latin for drink.

LOBO'S JUNCTION HOTEL (ABOVE LEFT), 1878, STRATHROY'S ALBION HOTEL (ABOVE RIGHT), 1878 AND LONDON'S TECUMSEH HOUSE HOTEL (LEFT), 1889 *Aside from providing the travelling public with beer, bed and board, nineteenth-century hotels, whether they were located in town or country, also functioned as community centres. Folks gathered in their barrooms to catch up on local gossip, exchange business and political news and trade tall tales. Where and when other facilities were lacking, hotels also served as meeting halls for social organizations, school boards, municipal councils and even court sessions. Incidentally, the Tecumseh House was reputed to be the largest hotel west of Toronto and the Junction Hotel building still stands at the northeast corner of Egremont Drive and Nairn Road.*

liquor, beer and soft drinks, as well as the glasses, tumblers and mugs necessary to serve thirsty customers. In order to free up counter-space, barrels of ale, porter, stout and lager were often kept in the cellar immediately beneath the bar's beer pump and taps. Lined up along the bar were stools and within the barroom itself were scattered tables and chairs. Heat came from wood-stoves and light from candles, oil lanterns and gas lamps. A kitchen was invariably adjacent to or near the barroom.

THE MORKIN HOUSE BAR, LONDON, 1905
Although taken in the early 1900s, this image nonetheless reflects the look of a late Victorian barroom. If you jump into the photo, you will discover a Labatt poster above the doorway to the right. Can you spot the two brewery ads etched into the mirror? Courtesy, J.J. Talman Regional Collection

AD FOR JAMES SMITH'S ALBION SALOON, RICHMOND STREET, LONDON FROM THE *LONDON FREE PRESS* OF JULY 3, 1869
Besides being an Englishman to his very core (Albion is an ancient word for England, after all), Jimmy Smith was also a clever marketer. While one might speculate about the popularity of the tripe, frogs' legs were clearly a big hit. Note that the saloonkeeper called for 12,000 of the amphibians. By the way, a talking parrot greeted and otherwise entertained Smith's customers.

Besides drinks, patrons could nibble upon a variety of finger foods, including oysters, sardines, frogs' legs, sausages, pigs' feet, cheese, crackers, biscuits, pastries, pretzels, nuts, fruits, vegetables, raisins, chocolates, candies and other confections. Meals included potato dishes, pork, beef, beef tongue, fish, fowl and lobster, as well as soups, salads and sandwiches. Some food was free, especially salty snacks which promoted thirst and thereby boosted bar sales. After dining, customers could relax with a cigar or a plug of chewing tobacco, items which no well-appointed bar was lacking. Most taverns and saloons also stocked newspapers, popular magazines, hunting and sports journals and books for the reading pleasure of their customers.

The law placed limits on when one could legally raise a full glass of cheer — usually from 11 a.m. or noon until 9 or 10 p.m. on weekdays, until 11 p.m. or midnight on Saturdays and never on the Sabbath, except when legitimate travellers and boarders took their meals. Of course, as court records clearly indicate, some tavern- and saloonkeepers obliged the parched after hours and on Sundays. In addition, barrooms in the county's larger taverns and hotels were, by social custom, generally a male preserve, save for serving staff. Females were expected to frequent their own private "dining parlours." In small taverns, the sexes were more likely to mingle owing to lack of space for separate quarters divided according to gender.

BARROOM AMBIENCE

The diversions and the decorations found in barrooms of the era were designed to appeal to men and their sense of masculinity. Quite obviously, games (whether legal or not), such as bagatelle, skittles, Mississippi, cards, billiards, drinking contests, cockfights and even friendly wrestling matches, allowed male patrons to express their competitive instincts and gambling prowess. Winners were hailed as better men, while losers went home with bruised egos and, of course, lighter pockets. Even the lowly spittoon (or cuspidor in more genteel circles) found a role to play in this masculine culture. After all, any man worth his salt could launch a missile of spent chaw right into one of these tin, copper or red-ware pots. The fact that barroom floor boards were invariably stained with second-hand tobacco juice surely demonstrates that men of the time were not always worth their salt. Manly decor complemented the manly pursuits practised in the barroom. For example, glass cases filled with stuffed birds and other creatures, mounted staghead, displays of taxidermic fish and lithographed hunting scenes appealed to the Victorian male's belief that it was his rightful destiny to dominant nature. Moreover, aquatints of sporting events and hand-coloured prints of rather buxom women with large eyes and pouting lips struck chords with men on different psychological and physical levels.

Other barroom entertainments ranged from the playfully amusing to the grotesquely bizarre. At London's American House hotel in early 1857, the clairvoyant Madame De Mark, "the best living Divine of the Past, Present and Future," healed metaphysical ills and imparted her sage advice about friendships, marriage, trip-planning, business matters, law and medical treatment. Around the same time, Rhody M'Guire, "Professor of Boxing," received "Pupils for instruction in the Art of Self-Defence" nearby at Dulmage's Hotel. On a darker level, Victorian freak-show promoters engaged licensed establishments as makeshift exhibition halls. A few days before Confederation, Tennessean Susan Grisham was put on display at London's City Arms Hotel. From the ankles up, there was nothing remarkable about the woman. However, each of her feet resembled "an immense turnip," and together they weighed an estimated fifty to sixty pounds. Throngs turned out to gawk at poor Susan's feet.

Ultimately, however, barroom ambience was cleverly cultivated to draw and keep customers. After all, hotel and saloon proprietors were in business to make profits, and the longer patrons stayed, the longer they ate and drank, and the longer they spent their money. Simply put, inviting atmosphere and good beer were perfectly suited to boosting the bottom lines of bar owners and brewers alike.

ROWDYISM

We would be kidding ourselves if we thought that barroom customers always governed themselves in a proper fashion. Overindulgence occasionally got the better of some bar patrons. Emboldened by alcohol and influenced by the macho social customs of their day (and possibly by their own psychological demons), such individuals often behaved in unruly and obnoxious fashions, vandalized property, provoked fights and otherwise disturbed the peace. Perhaps, the most notorious locals in this regard were the transplanted Irish of Biddulph Township, including

FRANCIS EVANS CORNISH, LONDON'S MAYOR FROM 1861 TO 1864, CIRCA 1860
Without a doubt, F.E. Cornish was Victorian London-Middlesex's single most notorious imbiber. Aside from his drunken carousing, Cornish thought nothing of using free beer to buy votes. He later headed west and became Winnipeg's first mayor. Courtesy, J.J. Talman Regional Collection

SETTING THE STANDARDS

Given that those born in the British Isles made up most of the consuming public in nineteenth-century Canada, it should not be surprising that the qualities of British and Irish beers set the standards by which Canadian beers were measured. After all, British and Irish immigrants arrived in the New World with great bonds of affection — a fierce loyalty, some might say — for the brews of the Mother Country. They wanted Canadian ales to taste like those from Burton-on-Trent or Canadian porters to remind them of those from old London or Canadian stouts to match the creamy texture and flavour of those from Dublin. In short, they wanted a sip of home to delight their palates.

Comparisons were endless. Consequently, popular expectations were only satisfied if Canadian ales and porters were deemed to resemble those produced by the great English breweries of, say, Bass, Allsopp or Messrs. Barclay & Perkins. Of course, the merits of Canadian stout had to pass the test against the most famous of all stouts — Guinness.

Comparisons with the standard-setters occasionally found their way into print. As the *London Prototype* determined of Carling's ale and porter in early 1861: "We question very much if either of the articles can be excelled by the old 'Bass' himself." Some years later, the *Strathroy Dispatch* heralded the beer from Delaware's Tupholme brewery as "a nectar" that "promises to emulate the fame of Guinness." Quite purposely, Canadian brewers and their sales agents often advertised that domestic brews compared favourably with old country beer.

No. of Licensed Establishments, 1870-1900		Hotels/Taverns	Shops
1870	London	80	31
	Middlesex*	163	31
1880	London	45	29
	Middlesex*	134	18
1890	London	56	13
	Middlesex*	93	6
1900	London	35	8
	Middlesex*	68	4

* Does not include London.

the legendary Donnelly clan, who fought many a battle in area taverns. Surprisingly (or perhaps not), some of the rowdiest imbibers came from what were supposed to be the most respectable of circles. Francis Evans Cornish, mayor of London from 1861 to 1864, is probably the most famous rambunctious drinker in the county's history. His alcoholic exploits are the stuff of legend. In a drunken impulse to defend his wife's honour, he once thrashed the local army garrison's second-in-command. A minor diplomatic stir, the incident nearly caused the British military to leave London. And in his capacity as police magistrate, then a mayoral prerogative, Cornish sometimes found himself in the peculiar position of having to lecture himself about the evils of liquor and then fine himself for public drunkenness.

It should be stressed, however, that those in the county's licensed trade hardly tolerated the disruptive behaviour of rowdies. For instance, London saloonkeeper Martin Haystead, who could be a bit of bruiser himself, was widely known for his ability to eject unruly customers by his own hand. And hotelkeeper Edward Morkin, another Londoner, had few qualms about criminally charging drunken troublemakers, even if one of their ranks happened to include his own son. Financial imperatives motivated this self-policing. For two important reasons, a drinking establishment with a reputation for violence did not remain in business for long. One, responsible clientele found somewhere else to drink. Two, license commissioners had the legal power to revoke liquor permits held by less than vigilant license-holders. In short, besides flowing beer taps, orderliness also helped to stuff the cash drawer.

DRINK & SOCIAL UNION

Commonly held beliefs that nineteenth-century taverns and saloons were nothing but wellsprings of social disharmony and drunken violence must be tempered with the knowledge that, for reasons of self-interest, journalists and temperance pamphleteers tended to exaggerate the problems associated with the barroom. To the mainstream press, reports about bar brawls and bacchanalian excess made good copy and, just like today, news about such scandal and outrage helped to sell newspapers. After all, who would have wanted to read endless columns about the responsible drinking habits of their neighbours? And for plainly obvious reasons, dry crusaders had a definite stake in emphasizing the evils of the liquor trade. As we shall see, their campaign agenda called for the utter obliteration of the barroom from society.

Interestingly, Victorian Canadians used drink to make and cement friendships. For instance, alcoholic beverages brought people together at barn-raisings, wood-chopping bees, harvests and dances. In taverns and saloons, treating others to a round was (and still is) a prevalent gesture of sociability. Spontaneous sing-a-longs over drinks at the bar furthered the coming together of people. However, perhaps the most profound form of social union achieved through drink sprang from the English custom of toasting. As a French visitor observed of Upper Canadians in 1795: "The ingenuity of the English in devising toasts, which are to be honoured with bumpers, is well known. To decline such a toast would be deemed uncivil."

Clearly not wishing to be deemed uncivil, Middlesex residents followed suit. Across the county's hotel- and saloonkeeping landscape, toasts abounded during public dinners and private banquets for local cultural clubs, political party associations, agricultural societies, fraternal organizations, sports teams, labour unions, factory workers, store employees and hosts of other groups. When they raised their cups in fellowship, these drinkers invariably confirmed their affinity for one another under the Union Jack and they led off with pledged affections for Queen Victoria, Prince Albert, the British army and navy, the Canadian militia and "our adopted country." To keep the mirth flowing, the next round of toasts usually became even more creative and acknowledged such people and things as the Duke

London District,

TO WIT :

In General Quarter Sessions of the Peace, held at London, this Sixteenth day of April, **1832** ;

IT IS ORDERED,

That as Inns and Houses of Public Entertainment are established and authorised for the convenience and accommodation of Travellers, and not for the encouragement of Tippling and Drinking :---

No Inn-keeper shall suffer or allow any person whatever, to be Tippling, or unnecessarily Drinking, in or about the Inn or Premises.

No Inn-keeper shall allow or suffer profane language or obscene conversation in his House.

No Inn-keeper shall allow or suffer any Gaming at Dice, Cards, or otherwise, in his House, or in any place adjoining thereto.

That every Inn-keeper shall keep good and sufficient Sheds, Stable, and Barn, for the safe keeping of Horses, Carriages, and Wagons; and shall have some person at all times in attendance to take charge of the same.

That every Inn-keeper shall provide and keep at least Four good Beds, for the use of Travellers, besides those required for the use of his Family.

J. B. Askin,

Clerk of the Peace, London District.

The Patriot Office, London.

BROADSIDE ANNOUNCING THE LONDON DISTRICT TAVERN REGULATIONS FOR 1832
Throughout the 1800s, a raft of municipal and provincial laws, rules and regulations governed the operation of licensed houses. Courtesy, Ontario Archives

of Wellington, the memory of Nelson, whatever day was being celebrated, the weather, various elected politicians, "mine host," agricultural prosperity, etcetera.

Of course, locally made beer often filled clinking glasses. For example, cheer from the breweries of Carling and Labatt "added considerably to the humor" of the dinner organized for participants in Westminster Township's plowing match for 1867. And at the third annual banquet of the Strathroy Gun Club, held at the Prangley House hotel on December 10, 1896, ale from the same breweries assumed a prominent spot on the evening's menu.

CHAPTER FOUR

The Birth of a Local
Industry, 1827 to 1852

UNFORTUNATELY, LARGE VOIDS in local archival heritage make it difficult to
document in any great detail the progress of the county's brewing industry until the
1840s. Still, what can be unearthed fits a pattern of economic life typical of
anywhere and anytime in Canada's frontier past. The first settlers largely made do
on their own. They grew their own food, made their own clothes and brewed their
own beer. As the population grew and became more urban, so did demand for
commercially made products. This process encouraged the establishment of local
breweries and saw the forces of market internationalization and integration play
greater and greater roles in the county's beer landscape. Quickly rising to the top of
the area's municipal hierarchy, London soon supported Middlesex's most significant
concentration of brewing activity. Finally, as minor players came and went, two of
Canada's eventual brewing giants — Carling and Labatt — got their start and began
their fairly rapid climb to dominance in the southwestern region of the province.

The First Beer in London-Middlesex
Exactly who introduced the first brew into the county is one of history's secrets,
although that person was likely an itinerant who visited the area sometime before
the end of eighteenth century. Perhaps, a French fur trader who ventured up La
Tranche (now the Thames River) from Lake St. Clair sometime during the 1740s
or 1750s was the first. Then again, maybe a member of John Graves Simcoe's party
brought along a bottle or two of British ale while on the Lieutenant-Governor's
official trek into western Upper Canada in early 1793. Indeed, it may have been
Simcoe himself, since he was quite fond of beer. Still again, surveyors, first active in
the county during the late 1790s and early 1800s may have carried the first beer
into the area. If the French, those in Simcoe's entourage or early surveyors did not
hoist the county's inaugural mug of beer, then such honours surely belong to

HOME BREWING IN ENGLAND, 1736
Taken from Bailey's Dictionarium Domesticum, *this woodcut depicts a housewife busy with her brewing chores. Brewing remained a domestic responsibility of many English housewives well into the nineteenth century. Indeed, many of London-Middlesex's earliest homebrewers were immigrant women, who had carried the practice across the Atlantic.*

BEER QUOTE — "What two ideas are more inseparable than beer and Britannia? What event is more awfully important to an English colony than the erection of its first brewhouse?"

Sydney Smith, *Lady Holland, Memoir*

Middlesex's first settlers who began to arrive in Delaware, Lobo, London, North Dorchester, West Nissouri and Westminster Townships during the first two decades of the 1800s. These hardy pioneers not only arrived with a taste for beer, but also knew how to manufacture the beverage. Of course, all of this is historical conjecture based upon cultural assumptions about the earliest Europeans to have set foot in London-Middlesex. Our answer remains a prisoner of time and there it will likely stay.

JOHN DIMOND'S FIRST BREWERY

While many early settlers brewed beer for personal consumption, the historical record does not reveal with absolute certainty when, where or by whom Middlesex's first commercial brewery was established. In all likelihood, an early tavernkeeper, confronted with the absence of other supply alternatives, opened the first one.

The earliest extant reference to a local brewery comes from the *Gore Gazette* of November 22, 1827. Commenting upon the building boom triggered in London by the village's designation as the new seat of the London District, the newspaper simply acknowledged that a brewery, among other sundry buildings, was in the course of construction. Understandably, the report's author focused attention upon the most important news emanating from the village — the erection of the budding capital's Gothic courthouse — and neglected to mention who owned the brewery. However, according to Goodspeed's *History of the County of Middlesex*, published in 1889, John Dimond conducted the first brewery in London on the north side of North Street (now ironically Carling Street). Dimond's enterprise probably stood near the site of the city's present courthouse and was likely the brewery to which the *Gore Gazette* referred. Without question producing the heavy English ales, porters and stouts of his day, Dimond only ran this brewery until sometime in 1828, when he sold out or rented to William and George Snell, immigrants from Devonshire, England.

JOHN BALKWILL

That same year, another Devonman, John Balkwill, built a small log brewery on the banks of the Thames River just a few blocks south of the village's core. Little did Balkwill realize that he had laid the foundations of what is now Canada's largest brewing company — Labatt. In 1832, William and George Snell combined their beer business with Balkwill's at the latter's brewery. The connection between the Snells and Balkwill was more than just commercial — the two families were related by marriage. Interestingly, and revealing how tightly the fabric of pioneer society could be woven, Balkwill was also connected to the Carlings through marriage.

Sometime during the mid-1830s, George Snell severed his connection with Balkwill's brewery. William Snell continued his involvement with the business until sometime between 1838 and 1842, when he established his own brewery in Yarmouth Township. In 1839, it appears that John Balkwill brought Christopher C. Coombs into partnership under the name Balkwill & Coombs. Balkwill assumed sole management of the brewery the next year.

JOHN STEPHEN

The only other pre-1840 brewery reference is John Stephen's advertisement in the *London Sun* of January 26, 1832. In the ad, Stephen, who brewed somewhere in Westminster Township (possibly adjacent to the rising village of London), announced that he had "Strong Beer" for sale and that he would reward area farmers with cash for their barley. Given the seasonal nature of Stephen's advertisement, we can conclude that he had fired his kettle as early as the harvest of 1831. Aside from what can be gleaned from this newspaper insert, nothing else can be found out about John Stephen's brewery. At any rate, his is the earliest brewery that can be pinpointed in Middlesex outside London's boundaries.

ST. THOMAS CONNECTIONS

While early facts are few and far between, we can still trace in some detail two wider developments that had strong bearing upon the local brewing scene. One, in the nearby village of St. Thomas, some personal ties, which later had a profound impact upon London's brewing progress, were being cemented together during the 1830s. Two, around the same time, the overall beer market in Upper Canada was becoming increasingly more internationalized and integrated.

The connections made in St. Thomas present a fascinating interweaving of personalities. In 1833, William Peacey and English brewmaster George W. Smith established a brewery on New Street in the village. Linked to this brewery, if not in a proprietary capacity, then as a relative of Peacey, was another Englishman, Samuel Eccles. As if to complete a triad of sorts, Smith married Eccles' sister, Mary, on December 2, 1833. One of the three official witnesses to this union was Henry Arkell whose family included a young son called Robert. To add yet another name to this mix, shortly after the Eccles-Smith wedding, Irishman John Kinder Labatt settled in Westminster Township near present-day Glanworth and not far from St. Thomas.

Upon the untimely death of his new bride, George W. Smith left St. Thomas and eventually operated breweries in Pittsburgh, Pennsylvania as early as 1835 and in Wheeling, Virginia (now West Virginia) as early as 1847. As Smith sought his fortune in the United States, Samuel Eccles assumed control of Peacey's brewery

STRONG BEER.

FOR sale at John Stephen's Westminster
  Cash paid for Barley
Westminster, 29th, Sept., 1831   10tf

BREWERY AD FROM THE *LONDON SUN* OF JANUARY 26, 1832 AND PRIZE LIST, ST. THOMAS BRANCH, LONDON DISTRICT AGRICULTURAL SOCIETY FROM THE *LONDON HERALD* OF APRIL 15, 1843
Stephen's ad is the earliest surviving example of brewery advertising from nineteenth-century Middlesex. Samuel Eccles and John Kinder Labatt were good friends long before they bought the London Brewery. In 1843, Eccles sat as branch president of the society, while Labatt occupied one of its vice-presidencies. Note the misspelling of Labatt's surname. (computer enhanced)

The Premiums awarded were as follow, for the	
Best 3 yrs. old Bull,	John Pierce,
2d best, do. do.	Major Nevills,
Best 2 yrs. old, do.	Garratt Smith,
Best yearling, do.	J. K. La Batt,
2d best, do. do.	J. K. La Batt,
Best Bull Calf,	Captain Drake,
Best Milch Cow,	Henry Payne,
2d best, do.	Anson Paul,
Best 2 yrs. old Heifer,	Samuel Eccles,
2d best, do. do.	John Partridge,
Best yearling Heifer,	Samuel Eccles,
2d best, do. do.	Lesslie Pierce,
Best Heifer Calf,	Samuel Smith,
2d best, do. do.	Samuel Eccles,
Best yoke of Oxen,	Lesslie Pierce,
2d best, do. do.	J. K. La Batt,
Best yk. 4 yrs.old steers,	Joshua Robier,
2d best, do. do.	Joshua Robier,
Best do. 3 yrs. old, do.	Geo. Thompson,
Best pair yearling steers	Samuel Eccles,
2d best, do. do.	Lesslie Pierce,
Best fat Cow,	Henry Payne,
2d Best do. do.	Joshua Robier,

THE LABATT SAGA

Often shaped by great forces of history, the Labatt family story is a fascinating tale. The earliest traceable Labatt ancestor is André Labat (also La Bat or de Labat), who was born in Guyenne, France sometime during the mid-1600s. A devout Huguenot, André lived amongst fellow Protestants in one of Catholic France's most Protestant regions. This was to have some dire consequences.

The 1680s and 1690s were fraught with terrible religious strife between Protestants and Catholics throughout Western Europe. In 1685, Louis XIV, the staunchly Catholic French monarch, revoked the Edict of Nantes, a royal decree that afforded French Protestants religious freedom. This ushered in an era of violent persecution against the Huguenots. The Labat family was hardly spared. For instance, a Labat was killed at Clairac in the mid-1680s, a victim of the hordes who did the bidding of Marillac, the "Scourge of Saintonge and Poitou." Outnumbered and fearful of losing life and limb, thousands of Huguenots fled France for the safety of Protestant England, Flanders and the Netherlands. The André Labat family settled in either Flanders or the Netherlands.

Meanwhile, anti-Catholic bigotry found fertile ground in Protestant Europe. In England, King James II's Catholic sympathies inflamed Protestant passions. During the Glorious Revolution, James fled to France. In James' place, the arch-Protestant Dutch royals, William and Mary, were installed as joint sovereigns. James later secured French military support in his bid to restore himself to the English throne. In 1689, James mounted his attack against England from Irish soil. William met James in Ireland.

What does all of this have to do with André Labat? In a word, everything. To bolster his army, William recruited displaced French Protestants in Flanders and the Netherlands. André Labat answered the call and eventually became a captain in La Mellonière's regiment. Incidentally, Labat may have served a prior term in William's army beginning in 1686. An able soldier, Labat was aboard the *Mountjoy* when it "broke the boom" at the narrows of Culmore during the relief of Derry (1689). He also saw action during the famed Battles of the Boyne (1690) and Aughrim (1691).

In return for his loyal service, Labat was rewarded with a military pension and a lease to a parcel of land in Portarlington, Queen's County (now County Laois), Ireland. In the village, the Labats joined dozens of other disbanded Huguenot soldiers and their families. All of them were planted under the aegis of Henri de Massue de Ruvigny, one of King "Billy's" generals and later Lord Galway. To seed Catholic Ireland with even more Protestants, de Ruvigny had been granted 58,000 acres of land in Queen's County, most of which comprised the forfeited estates of Sir Patrick Trant, one of the many unlucky Irish supporters of James II.

If anything, Portarlington's Huguenot society was a transplanted French one. Indeed, French remained the written and spoken language of the village's Huguenot Church until 1817! And although they originally hailed from some of France's renowned wine regions, these settlers brought with them a great love of beer, especially for a type of home-brewed small beer that they drank at the breakfast table. This cultural practice also survived well into the nineteenth century. The Labats later moved several miles north of Portarlington into King's County (now County Offaly).

Owing to a murky Irish historical record, the Labatt genealogy suffers for want of detail until the 1800s. Still, the direct line to John Kinder Labatt can be pieced together. André, the patriarch, died in 1736. One of his sons, Andrew (anglicized form of André) and his wife, Christina Peppard, had a boy whom they also named Andrew. In turn, this Andrew and his wife, Rose Harte (Hart), had yet another Andrew. He married a woman named Bell (her given name is not known) and they had at least two sons.

Generally using anglicized surnames, these sons were Samuel Bell Labatt and Valentine Knightly Chetwood Labatt (also spelled Knightley Chetwode). Samuel moved to Dublin and became a prominent medical doctor during the mid-1800s. At the same time, several other Labatts, undoubtedly members of the same clan, but whose connection to Samuel cannot be determined, also practised medicine in the Irish capital.

Named in honour of Valentine Knightly Chetwood, a member

of the Irish landed gentry and High Sheriff of Queen's County from 1758 to 1759, Valentine Labatt and his wife, Jane, lived in Mountmellick, Queen's County and had a family of seven that included a son born in 1803. This son was christened John Kinder. The children of this marriage did not know their father for long, however. On December 12, 1813, Valentine died. His father, Andrew, who was to outlive him by fifteen years, had his body interred at the Killaderry graveyard in Daingean, King's County. In 1822, Valentine's widow married Benjamin Gatchell.

The Mountmellick in which John Kinder Labatt grew up was exceptional in the southern Irish scheme of things both ethnically and economically. Not far from the original Huguenot settlement of Portarlington, the town had a fair number of residents with French surnames. It also contained an even larger contingent of Quakers. These and other Protestants dominated town affairs and gave the place a notable arch-Protestant flavour. However, what truly distinguished Mountmellick was that it was one of the few southern communities to be anchored by an industrial economy.

Weaving counted as the most important manufacturing pursuit and all manner of woollen cloth, fabric and lace radiated from the place. Mountmellick also boasted a flour mill, a tannery, two soap factories, several potteries, a large distillery and three breweries. James Calcutt owned and operated one of these breweries, which he founded in 1806 at the unlikely age of fourteen! A branch of Ireland's Grand Canal afforded local manufacturers access to distant markets in Dublin and Britain's thriving cities. On the strength of the local economy, the town's population more than doubled from about 2,000 in the late 1810s to over 4,500 by 1831.

The hum of Mountmellick was not lost on a young John Kinder Labatt. The busy town taught the boy crucial lessons about the virtues of hard work, the value of transportation to local success and the direct relationship between manufacturing activity and prosperity at a time when the industrial revolution was quickly reshaping the Western World. Labatt's childhood experiences would serve him well in his later years.

Sectarian strife worked against Mountmellick's fortunes during the late 1820s and early 1830s, when underground groups of Catholics, billing themselves as Blackfeet, Whitefeet and White Boys, waged clandestine and often brutal attacks against Protestant power-holders and those Catholics who either aided their Protestant neighbours or refused to obey partisan directives. The basic ideology fuelling these secret brotherhoods was an extreme disaffection with British rule in Ireland. It was, after all, an era when laws largely kept Irish Catholics from voting, owning property and generally running their own affairs in their own country.

Some of the worst outrages occurred in the Mountmellick area and local newspapers bulge with stories about roaming gangs, threats, assaults, gunfire, arson and murder. Many Protestants fled for safety. For instance, James Calcutt, who had grown tired of having his teamsters beaten, his brewery wagons ransacked and his beer stolen, moved to Cobourg, Upper Canada in 1832. As legend has it, his chief tormenter, one James Demsey, arrived in Cobourg sometime later aboard a steamboat. Before Demsey could disembark, a giant wave reached out of Lake Ontario and dragged him beneath the surface. A few days later, his lifeless body washed up onto the beach at the foot of Calcutt's waterfront brewery.

Sectarian violence may have also seen John Kinder Labatt move to England. In August 1833, he married Eliza Kell at Twickenham in the original Middlesex. Later that year, they emigrated to Upper Canada and settled on lot 18, concession 8, Westminster Township. In 1843, Labatt bought an adjacent 200-acre farm from Colonel Thomas Talbot for £50. The Labatts' arrival, like that of Yorkshireman Thomas Carling some fifteen years earlier, would prove to be of tremendous consequence to Canadian brewing history. John Kinder and Eliza had the following children (birth year bracketed): Robert Pritchard (1835), Ephraim (1837), John (1838), Charlotte (1840), George Thomas (1843), Eliza (1844), Maria (1847), Jane (1849), Frances Louisa (1851), Emma (1853), Ismena (1855), Louisa (1858), Charles Knightley Chetwode (1859) and Mary Caroline (1861). All but Maria, Emma, Louisa and Charles Knightley Chetwode lived to adulthood.

ADS FEATURING BRITISH BEERS FROM THE *LONDON GAZETTE* OF OCTOBER 28, 1837 (UPPER) AND THE *LONDON TIMES* OF JUNE 6, 1845 (LOWER)
As these retail advertisements symbolize, the beer world in early Victorian London-Middlesex had a notable international flavour. (computer enhanced)

after the latter's death in 1842. While running this brewery, Eccles and the farmer from Westminster, John Kinder Labatt, became acquainted with each other through their membership in the St. Thomas branch of the London District Agricultural Society and through their business dealings with each other (Labatt was a barley farmer, after all). In partnership, they bought the London Brewery in 1847. About a decade later, Labatt arranged a brewing apprenticeship for his son, John, under George W. Smith of Wheeling. As for Robert Arkell, he moved to London upon reaching his majority. At first, he involved himself with the hotel trade. Later, he moved into the malting industry and then into brewing at the village of Kensington, a London suburb.

THE INTERNATIONAL FLAVOUR OF THE MARKET
Throughout the first half of the nineteenth century, brewers in London-Middlesex (and the rest of the province, for that matter) found that their markets were becoming more and more internationalized and integrated. Internationalization stemmed from Upper Canada's position at the western end of Britain's North Atlantic trading empire. Although timber and wheat from the colonies and immigrants and manufactured wares from the British Isles dominated this cross-ocean economy, ales and porters from the "mother countries" occupied their fair share of space in the holds of merchant vessels bound for British North America.

Of course, one might conclude that, because of their high bulk-to-value ratio and supposedly perishable nature, malt liquors were hardly suited to transport over such great distances. However, one must not ignore the fact that barrelled liquids made ideal ballast for ships returning from the British Isles to the colonies. In addition, British beer at the time was actually far from fragile. The chemical nature of generously malted and hopped English porters and stouts rendered those beverages fairly resistant to bacterial spoilage. Moreover, all beer, including slightly less self-preserving ales, found ideal storage conditions in ships' holds which were naturally cooled by the frigid waters of the North Atlantic. As early as the first decade of the nineteenth century, British beer had become a notable feature in the newspaper advertisements of Lower Canadian importers. By the 1830s, foreign beers had found their way into Middlesex. For instance, London merchants routinely stocked Hibbert's Porter and Leith Ale. Of course, such retailers sought to quench the thirst of customers who longed for a taste of 'ome.

EARLY MARKET INTEGRATION
Fairly early in the nineteenth century, Canadian brewers, following in the footsteps of their British counterparts, also recognized that their beers made friends near and

afar. In hopes of boosting their incomes, they organized sales agencies in distant communities. By doing so, they initiated a sharp turn towards domestic market integration and essentially set the course for the rise of large regional and national breweries and the gradual decline of small local breweries. Shining examples of this process are found in the entrepreneurship of four brewers from outside Middlesex, who maintained agencies in the county's largest municipality, London, during the 1830s and 1840s. Three of them, Weir & Black, the Luke Brothers and Samuel Eccles, were based in St. Thomas and the other, Joseph & Henry Slagg, operated in Chatham. Hardly intimidated by Upper Canada's mud-paved roads, the Slaggs shipped their ale by wagon some sixty miles overland to their London agent, former brewer John Dimond. Outside brewers likely did not ignore the rest of Middlesex; however, limitations in the surviving historical record make it impossible to pinpoint exactly when and where they shipped their beer.

THE LURE OF LONDON

Although imported and domestic beers were transported across Upper Canada, we must not ignore the importance of the localized trade in beer. After all, most beer consumed during the first three-quarters of the 1800s was produced and quaffed locally. One should keep in mind that primary success in any consumer products industry in nineteenth-century Canada depended upon a healthy home market. Indeed, the robust nature of London's home market fated the place to become the county's brewing hub.

In London, brewers found a vibrant consumer dynamism. Above all, the town was blessed (or cursed if one happened to be a teetotaller) with demographics close to the hearts of ale and porter brewers in the British tradition. Census returns for 1851 reveal that ninety-eight percent of the town's residents were from or could trace their direct ancestry to the great beer-drinking nations of England, Scotland and Ireland. Moreover, the majority of Londoners belonged to those religious denominations not prone to temperance fervour at the time. Two other demographic factors further distinguished the place from the rest of Middlesex. One, London's rapid growth greatly benefitted local brewers. From 1840 to 1850, the town's population trebled from 1,716 to 5,124 residents. By 1855, the year of cityhood, the local populace had leapt to 10,000. Two, London became a garrison town not long after the 1837 Rebellion. Home to eight regiments between 1838 and 1853, it was awash in a sea of thirsty British troops. The combination of bored soldiers, their pay packets and their desire for beersome pursuits greatly enhanced the local brewing economy.

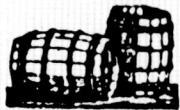

ECCLES' Superior Ale!

In Barrels, half Barrels, and thirds, always on sale at JOHN SCOTT'S, Exchange Hotel, Dundas St., London.

SAMUEL ECCLES in returning thanks to his customers in London and its vicinity; for the liberal support they have given him, since he has carried on the Brewing business at St. Thomas, begs to apprise them that he has appointed Mr Scott, Exchange Hotel, his sole agent in London, for the sale of his Ale, which in consequence of the depreciation in the price of Barley, will be supplies at £1 5 0 c'y. per Barrel.

S. E. hopes that at the above reduced price, and by making a uniform good article, he will receive a continuation of that support, which *has hitherto* been given him.
St. Thomas, Sept. 27, 1844.   8–1y

BREWERY AGENCY NOTICES FROM THE *LONDON TIMES* OF MAY 30, 1845 (ABOVE) AND THE *LONDON GAZETTE* OF APRIL 23, 1842 (BELOW)
London's dynamic beer market was simply too tempting for outside brewers to resist. Eccles found it so good that he eventually left St. Thomas to brew in London.

CHATHAM ALE.
J. & H. SLAGG, Brewers of the Ale well known as McCrae's, are now delivering a supply to their Agent,   JOHN DIMOND.
London, Nov. 8, 1841.   2

THE MILITARY BARRACKS AT LONDON
(NOW VICTORIA PARK), CIRCA 1842
The British Army stationed several regiments in London from 1838 until 1853 and then again beginning in the 1860s. To brewers' eyes, these barracks represented hundreds of beer-thirsty soldiers paid in cash. Courtesy, J.J. Talman Regional Collection

LONDON'S HOTEL & SALOON TRADE

London's mushrooming population, its status as a district and then a county seat, its role as a regional market town and its position as a thriving commercial centre fostered a vibrant local hotel- and saloonkeeping culture. Largely centred around the courthouse and market square, as well as dotting the town's main fairways, hotels and saloons appealed to resident and out-of-town beer drinkers alike. Not unexpectedly, the size of London's inn- and saloonkeeping landscape expanded with local population growth. In 1843, the town contained twenty-three licensed hotels and saloons. Eight years later, according to *The Canada Directory*, the number had jumped slightly to twenty-six. Having nicely weathered the temporary withdrawal of the garrison in 1853, London's licensed victualling community stood at fifty hoteliers and twenty saloon owners in 1856. The number of liquor merchants in London also grew quite swiftly. In 1845, the town had about a half dozen liquor dealers. Eleven years later, the newly incorporated city issued twenty-two shopkeepers' licenses.

BREWING IN LONDON DURING THE 1840S & EARLY 1850S

Understandably, commercially ambitious Victorians sought predictable and financially secure environments in which to establish themselves. As a thriving wellspring of opportunity, mid-nineteenth-century London fit this model quite nicely and attracted business interests like a magnet. The town's dynamic licensed liquor trade, pronounced military presence and rising population were strong drawing cards for the several brewers who arrived on the local scene during the 1840s. Significantly, two of these new arrivals, along with their descendants, were to give London its lasting fame as one of Canada's major brewing centres.

CARLING ARRIVES

In the spring of 1818, twenty-one-year-old Thomas Carling, an ambitious son of Yorkshire, England, embarked upon a cross-Atlantic voyage that would change the course of Canadian brewing history. Despite one month at sea and several arduous weeks making his way inland from Quebec City, the stalwart immigrant quickly set himself to his chosen task on the Upper Canadian frontier. Settling on lot 14, concession 8, London Township (near Arva), he worked hard to clear a farm and soon reaped the rewards of his labour. In 1824, for reasons that remain unclear, he traded farms with John Smith. This move put the Carlings on lot 26, concession 6, London Township (near Hyde Park). As local folklore has it, the beer he brewed privately for family and friends commanded a popular following. Undoubtedly recognizing that his beer would also find favour with the British troops garrisoned in nearby London, Carling retired from farming in 1843 and built a wooden brewery on the northeast corner of Waterloo and Pall Mall Streets (now Siskinds, The Law Firm). Possessing a sharp eye for business, Thomas Carling had strategically located his brewery within sight of the town's regimental barracks.

It is interesting to note that 1840 has mistakenly become enshrined as Carling's establishment date. While this is hardly the fault of modern corporate marketers, it is a bit off the mark nonetheless. According to the census returns for 1842, Thomas Carling was still farming in London Township. Moreover, Carling's obituary, nineteenth-century business directories and the late Dr. Clarence T. Campbell, a local historian and Carling family friend, all give 1843 as the year when the Yorkshireman began brewing in London. It seems that the error stems from loose interpretations of Goodspeed's *History of the County of Middlesex* which notes that

THOMAS CARLING, CIRCA 1860
One of London Township's pioneer settlers, Thomas Carling brought his talent for brewing to London in 1843. The beer-making business that he established not far from the town's military barracks grew into one of Canada's largest. Courtesy, London Public Library

BEER QUOTE — "No soldier can fight unless he is properly fed on beef and beer."
　　Duke of Marlborough, Commander of the British forces during the War of Spanish Succession

JOHN CARLING, CIRCA 1860
Although originally apprenticed as a leather tanner, John Carling, along with his brother William, jumped at the chance to purchase their father's brewery in 1849. John brought to the business a flair for promotion and financial management, while William added his considerable talent as a brewer. A likeness of William has yet to surface from the past. Courtesy, National Archives of Canada

the brewery was "established by Thos. Carling about the year 1840." The 1840 date first appeared in early twentieth-century Carling advertisements and has been taken at face value ever since.

Although later described by his granddaughter as "a very primitive little brewery, with a white horse walking around and around in a circle, turning the mill that ground the malt," Thomas Carling's endeavour met with considerable fortune in the beer-thirsty town. To accommodate business growth, in August 1844, he acquired three lots adjacent to the original brewery lot. A few years later, Carling boasted a manufacturing capacity of 150 barrels per week — a level which dwarfed that of his local competition.

WILLIAM & JOHN CARLING

In the spring of 1849, Thomas sold the brewery to two of his sons, William and John (his other son, Isaac, had since established a leather tannery in Exeter, Canada West). Partnering themselves as W. & J. Carling, the younger Carlings enjoyed the same brisk ale and porter sales that their father had. Indeed, a healthy cash flow easily allowed them to meet their obligations to the London Building Society on the mortgage they had obtained to buy out their father.

With keen commercial instincts — undoubtedly inherited from their father — the brothers embarked upon an ambitious phase of expansion in the fall of 1852. Real estate was key to this project and the Carlings purchased neighbouring parcels of land over the ensuing year. When all was said and done, the brewery grounds had been enlarged to a total of three and one-fifth acres. The next part of the brothers' plan called for massive physical additions to their plant. For the necessary capital, William and John secured a loan of £1,000 from The Trust and Loan Company of Upper Canada. Cash in hand, the brothers then built onto their brewery during the fall of 1853. The project was wise for two reasons. One, improving manufacturing efficiency has always been fundamental to industrial success. Two, new challenges and opportunities were rapidly approaching London railway spike by railway spike. Clearly, the partners saw future dividends in being prepared.

LABATT ARRIVES

John Kinder Labatt came to London as junior partner to brewmaster Samuel Eccles, when the two acquired the London Brewery at Simcoe and Talbot Streets from John Balkwill in 1847. That they, like Thomas Carling, had given up economic pursuits elsewhere truly speaks to London's drawing power. After all, Eccles had left behind a well-established brewery in St. Thomas to relocate in London, while Labatt had pulled up stakes from his prosperous farm in Westminster Township to join Eccles.

However, the partners may not have had a chance to buy into the London Brewery in the first place if financial circumstances had been better for John Balkwill. Balkwill's problems stemmed from a spiral of indebtedness and a devastating fire.

JOHN BALKWILL'S HARDSHIP

In 1841 and 1843, a cash-strapped Balkwill borrowed a combined total of £1,300 from Christopher C. Coombs and Thomas Cronyn. Why he required the money is unclear, but as was the Victorian business custom, the brewer mortgaged his land as security for these loans. The property involved embraced lots 14 and 15 — the brewery lots — on the south side of Simcoe Street. In the summer of 1844, he was released from the £300 mortgage held by Cronyn and one of the two mortgages held by Coombs. However, Balkwill's need for funds was still acute and he borrowed £650 from George Jervis Goodhue. To secure Goodhue's loan, Balkwill mortgaged lots 11, 12 and 13 on the south side of Simcoe Street, remortgaged brewery lot 14 and took out a second mortgage on brewery lot 15 (Coombs still held a mortgage on this parcel of land). Gravely, Balkwill waded into 1845 burdened by a substantial debt load.

While Balkwill pledged his land as loan security, he rented out the brewery. His first tenants were his brother, William, and Thomas W. Shepherd. Styled as the firm of Shepherd & Balkwill, they ran what they billed as the London Brewery during the summer and early fall of 1844. In November, William Balkwill returned to the hotel business, leaving Shepherd to conduct the brewery on his own account. What prompted these leasing arrangements has been lost to time, but it seems logical that John Balkwill was involved with some pursuit outside of brewing and viewed his brewery as a greatly needed source of extra income during a financially pressing time.

THE GREAT FIRE OF 1845

Fires could be unmerciful in early Victorian Canada, a country studded with jumbles of bone-dry wooden buildings that formed the villages and towns of the era. Sunday, April 13, 1845 stands as one of the blackest dates in London's history. Shortly before noon that day, flames broke out at the Robinson House hotel on the southeast corner of Dundas and Ridout Streets. Fanned by a steady wind from the north-northwest, the fire quickly swept across London's core. An anonymous letter-writer to the *Toronto Herald* later described the awful scene he observed in the town's southern extreme at about half-past two that afternoon:

> The house where the family of Col. Clench lives was burning when I came away, and the Hon. Mr. Goodhue's house is [sic] already burned.

DETAIL FROM A MAP OF LONDON, 1878
This detail shows the lots on which John Balkwill's brewery stood. At the time the map was drawn, the concern was under John Labatt's proprietorship.

SAMUEL ECCLES, 1878
Born in North Leach, Colchester, England on January 5, 1802, Samuel Eccles was a fully trained brewmaster. He bought the London Brewery from John Balkwill and took John Kinder Labatt into partnership to operate the business. Upon selling his share in the brewery to Labatt, Eccles retired to a life of farming in Yarmouth Township. He died at the grand old age of ninety-one on December 8, 1893. Courtesy, J.J. Talman Regional Collection

Mr. Balkwell's [sic] brewery, which is still further south of Col. Clench's house was in imminent danger when I returned. They were making great exertions to save it, but I fear it will go. . . To the southeast of Balkwell's brewery the fire has extended some distance, and although the houses in that quarter are very scattered, yet nothing can impede the progress of the devouring element.

The concerns of our witness proved frightfully valid. In the wake of the conflagration, John Balkwill's brewery was but one of the 110 dwellings, shops and industrial buildings that had been reduced to heaps of ash and scorched rubble. It is not known whether Balkwill carried any insurance or how much, but it is painfully obvious that the Great Fire of 1845 further compromised his already precarious financial state of affairs. After all, the giant blaze left him with little, apart from what few things were saved before the fire reached the brewery and what fewer things, if any, could be salvaged after the fire had subsided. Most seriously, he no longer had a brewhouse to rent out or operate personally. In short, 1845 was a virtual write-off for Balkwill.

Once bitten and twice shy, Balkwill rebuilt in stone the next year. For capital, he again turned to Goodhue and granted as security to his lender a series of second mortgages on lots 11 through 14 and a third mortgage on lot 15. Needless to say, this put the new brewery in unhealthy circumstances. Still, the uneasy situation was partially smoothed by Shepherd's return as brewery tenant. Now at least, Balkwill had a steady source of revenue and, unlike his lessee, he did not have to spend time and energy fighting to reclaim local market share recently lost to Thomas Carling, John Dimond and James Grant, all of whose breweries escaped the Great Fire of 1845.

SAMUEL ECCLES BUYS THE LONDON BREWERY
A weighty debt load ultimately got the better of Balkwill. In early February 1847, he sold the London Brewery and the two brewery lots on Simcoe Street to Samuel Eccles. To finance the purchase, Eccles borrowed £828 from Goodhue. While the exact selling price is unknown, the money enabled Balkwill to settle his debts with Coombs and Goodhue. Balkwill retained ownership of lots 11, 12, 13 and the eastern part of 14. A few months after buying out Balkwill, Eccles took John Kinder Labatt into partnership. Perhaps using buy-in money from Labatt, Eccles dramatically reduced his mortgage obligations to Goodhue by some £350.

Labatt's entry into the brewing industry was rooted in his friendship with Eccles. In 1846, Labatt went to England to administer some of his investments in that country. While there, he reassessed his current vocation and determined that, despite his success in harvesting the land, a change was in order. As he wrote to his wife: "I fancy I should like brewing better than anything else, but that is impossible." At this point, it should be noted that the farmer had long since enjoyed brewing up private batches of beer for his family and neighbours. Undoubtedly recalling the industrial success of Mountmellick, Ireland, Labatt also wrote to Eccles and asked the St. Thomas brewer "to be on the lookout for something for me." Eccles obviously kept his friend's request firmly in mind. After selling his farm, borrowing £500 from his aunt Maria and probably liquidating his English assets, Labatt joined Eccles at the London Brewery in the fall of 1847. The new firm was styled Eccles & Labatt.

LONDON BREWERY RECEIPT, MARCH 8, 1848
As this document reveals, Eccles & Labatt, proprietors of the London Brewery, enjoyed the patronage of such eminent persons as Colonel Thomas Talbot and Colonel Richard Airey. Note that John Kinder Labatt signed on behalf of Samuel Eccles, the firm's senior partner. Courtesy, J.J. Talman Regional Collection

Although the exact terms of their partnership have yet to surface, land records reveal that Labatt's investment in the business was fairly substantial and for the long term. According to an indenture dated October 28, 1847, Labatt bought from Eccles the western part of brewery lot 14 and the eastern part of brewery lot 15 on the south side of Simcoe Street for £650. That Eccles relinquished ownership of the land on which the brewery stood suggests that Labatt was slated to own the entire business at some future date. Lending further credence to this theory is that, throughout the life of the partnership, Labatt acquired land adjacent to the brewery (notably the eastern part of brewery lot 14 and lots 13 and 14 on the north side of Grey Street). It is also interesting to note that the partners' business relationship fell along the lines of mentor and protégé. An experienced brewmaster, Eccles passed his commercial knowledge on to the neophyte Labatt. Not content with modest success, the aggressive immigrants diligently cultivated a large and profitable trade. Fortune in London smiled upon them. As a field agent with the credit-reporting house of R.G. Dun & Company noted in 1850: "They brew the best beer in this part of the Country & have an extensive bus[iness]." And indeed they had.

ECCLES SELLS THE LONDON BREWERY TO LABATT

When Eccles retired to a life of farming in Yarmouth Township in 1855, he sold his half share in the brewery to his partner for £5,368, an amount that truly reflected the firm's achievements. Eccles hardly expected his friend to buy the brewery up front, however. Rather, the two settled upon an eight-year instalment schedule.

BEER LORE — The letters X, XX, XXX once used to describe beer were indicators of specific gravity — the more Xs, the heavier the beverage.

JOHN KINDER LABATT, CIRCA 1865
Of French ancestry, John Kinder Labatt was born at Mountmellick, Queen's County, Ireland in 1803. He came to Upper Canada to farm, but later joined forces with Samuel Eccles to run the London Brewery. From Eccles, Labatt learned the ins and outs of commercial brewing. At the time this photograph was originally taken, Labatt was a well-to-do man of capital. Courtesy, Labatt Archives

Secured by a mortgage on the brewery land, Labatt was to remit the following payments on the first day of June in each of the follow years: £440 in 1856, £428 in 1857, £416 in 1858, £704 in 1859, £674 in 1860, £844 in 1861, £802 in 1862 and £1060 in 1863. The rationale behind the irregular instalment amounts is not clear, but why Eccles crossed out the interest provision on the pre-printed mortgage form is perfectly understandable as a warm gesture of friendship. Eminently positioned in a profitable business, Labatt had no problems meeting the payments. He carried the brewery to even loftier heights over the next decade. Incidentally, Labatt may have had William Barker and one A. Lefroy as partners from sometime in 1856 until August 1857.

JOHN DIMOND'S SECOND BREWERY

Besides Thomas Carling and Eccles & Labatt, two other parties established breweries in London during the 1840s. In John Dimond's case, he re-established himself in late 1841. Lured back into the trade by rising local demand for beer, he formed a partnership with Joseph Slagg, one half of the Chatham brewing firm for whom he had served as agent. According to the census for 1842, the partners styled themselves as Slagg & Dimond, a name incorporating a rather unusual contrast in terms. Their brewery stood on property owned by Dimond on lots 1 and 2 on the north side of North Street in the Mount-Goodhue survey. On March 2, 1843, they dissolved their firm by mutual consent. Dimond carried on and, anxious to capture a chunk of the lucrative hotel trade in the busy town, he advertised that he could accommodate customers with full, half and quarter barrels of his Superior Ale. In 1850, adopting a practice then not unknown in Canadian brewing circles, he expanded into whisky distilling. Three years later, perhaps unable or unwilling to face stiff competition from the Carlings and Eccles & Labatt, Dimond retired from brewing for a new life in East Williams Township. Ever the entrepreneur, he established flour and saw mills, a tannery, a real estate business and a general store in the township. Clustered around Dimond's ambitions sprang the village of Nairn. One cannot help but wonder if he ever stocked any of his former competitors' beer at his general store.

JAMES GRANT

Sometime between the spring of 1841 and the spring of 1844, James Grant, a native of Strathspey, Scotland, established a brewery on the northwest corner of King and Clarence Streets (the site of the demolished Smuggler's Alley Mall). Seeing greater opportunities in the construction trade, Grant left the beer business and subsequently leased out his brewery. One of his early tenants was Richard Rich who

GOVERNMENT & TAXATION

The primary relationship between government and brewers during the 1800s can be summed up in one word — taxation. From the start, brewery owners were required to pay municipal taxes based upon the assessed values of their breweries. Surprisingly, higher tiers of government ignored brewing activity as a source of revenue until the mid-1800s. Indeed, brewers in the Province of Canada (the old union of Ontario and Quebec) got off scot-free until August 1858, when legislators levied the first excise on beer. Interestingly, the duty came largely at the behest of the province's resentful distillers, who had been paying excise taxes since 1793. Initially set at one cent per wine gallon in 1858, the tax stood at three cents per wine gallon on the eve of Confederation.

With the passage of the British North America Act in 1867 — the constitutional statute by which the Dominion of Canada was created — powers of excise taxation fell under federal jurisdiction. In late 1867, Ottawa rescinded the gallonage duty and placed a tax of one cent upon each pound of malt manufactured in the country. For the rest of the century, the malt duty remained in place. The only substantial changes to this excise tax were incremental jumps in its rate. Brewers grudgingly worked these increases into their wholesale and retail prices.

THE LONDON CUSTOM HOUSE, CIRCA 1875
This building housed the London Division office of the Inland Revenue Department. Inspectors based here collected malt taxes from brewers throughout Middlesex. Courtesy, J.J. Talman Regional Collection

later opened his own brewery "over Blackfriars Bridge" in 1847. To lure a successor to Rich, Grant advertised that his brewery could turn out a respectable 24 barrels of malt liquor per week during the brewing season (equivalent to nearly 400 cases of 24 in today's terms). In the summer of 1850, Grant sold the brewery at auction. At the time, it was leased to an unnamed tenant until January 1, 1851. Exactly who bought the brewery property remains a mystery. Perhaps, another local brewer successfully bid on the tools and appliances so he could add them to his own business. On the other hand, we do know that Leonard Perrin Jr., a baker by profession, bought the brewery building at the public sale. Not quite three weeks after the auction, Perrin purchased the brewery lot directly from Grant for £166. The baker soon converted the old brewery to suit the requirements of his trade. Interestingly, the remodelling did not spell the end of brewing at the downtown site. In the mid-1850s, Perrin began brewing ginger beer as a sideline to his baking business.

BEER LORE — In 1881, Guinness of Dublin turned out 1,000,000 barrels of stout, an amount three times greater than Canada's entire beer output that year. Indeed, the Irish brewery was so colossal that it had its own narrow-gauge railway system.

AD FOR JOHN GUMB'S BREWERY FROM THE LONDON TIMES OF APRIL 21, 1848
The wonderful thing about this "for sale" notice is that it gives us a rare peek into a mid-nineteenth-century brewery. (computer enhanced)

BREWERIES OUTSIDE LONDON DURING THE 1840S & EARLY 1850S

Three breweries operated outside London's boundaries during the 1840s and early 1850s. Like Grant's and Dimond's breweries, none of them wielded a particularly profound influence upon the local brewing economy. Still, as breweries in their own right, these modest enterprises do merit mention.

THE BLACKFRIARS BREWERY

In the early spring of 1847, Richard Rich opened the Blackfriars Brewery on the west side of Wharncliffe Road just south of Oxford Street in what was then the village of Petersville. Rich's two-storey brewery measured 60 by 30 feet, was supplied by a "never-failing spring, rising from 20 to 25 feet high" and, with a capacity of ten barrels per day, was more than twice as productive as the brewery he had previously leased from James Grant. For unknown reasons, he left the trade and rented the brewery to R.J. Balfour & Company in February 1853. Two months later he announced his intention to sell the business altogether. Rich either did not find a buyer or only temporarily relinquished ownership of the Blackfriars Brewery, as tax assessment records and newspapers references have him back in control of the brewery during the mid-1850s.

JOHN GUMB

The site of Englishman John Gumb's brewhouse is a mystery. Indeed, the only extant reference to his brewery is a for sale ad that ran in the London Times during the spring of 1848. Besides giving a cursory description of his works, Gumb noted that his brewery stood "within a quarter of a Mile of the Town of London." Whether or not he found a buyer is also a mystery. Census and tax assessment records from 1851 to 1854 show that Gumb ran a brick works on the north half of lot 25 in the broken front of Westminster Township (just north of where Wellington Road makes its dog's leg turn south of the Thames River). This location was about a quarter mile from what was then the southern boundary of London. Did Gumb convert his brewhouse into a brick factory? Or did his brewery stand somewhere else? The answers to such questions will likely remain hidden in the past.

SAMUEL HOCKING

The 1851 census lists thirty-eight-year-old Samuel Hocking as a brewer living in West Nissouri Township. A paucity of earlier or later commentary about Hocking makes it impossible to determine where or for how long this Englishman brewed in the township. Then again, he may have simply worked as a brewer at the Shanly distillery, which stood on the northwestern outskirts of present-day Thorndale.

CHAPTER FIVE

Steaming into the Railway Age, 1853 to 1872

THE RAILWAY — THAT great conqueror of time and space — affected virtually every aspect of life in Victorian Canada. Indeed, railway tracks belted together a new country and dramatically accelerated the pace of Canada's economic development. In Middlesex, an expanding rail network afforded area brewers access to wider markets and it was during the early railway age that London confirmed its position as the focus of brewing in Middlesex and claimed prominence as a major regional brewing centre. Over this period, Carling and Labatt became household words across Southwestern Ontario. A host of other players also waded into the local game. Some stayed and some went, but from out of this mix Strathroy emerged as the county's other important brewing hub.

THE GARRISON LEAVES & THE RAILWAY AGE ARRIVES

Until the mid-1850s, local brewers chiefly sought to slake their neighbours' thirst. However, two events occurred in 1853 that sparked profound changes in the dynamics of the county's beer business. The first was the withdrawal of the military garrison from London. The second officially puffed into the same place on December 15 that year. In many ways, the positive effects of the latter eased the negative consequences of the former. Although London's brewers sorely missed the soldiers' pay packets, the economic and population booms triggered by the arrival of the Great Western Railway quickly made up for the loss of British troops. More significantly, the Great Western's arrival urged local brewers to look far and wide.

BREWERY AGENCIES

As we have seen, shipping beer to distant markets was not unheard of before the railway age. However, railroads, with their relative speediness and power to overcome the seasonal difficulties of muddy roads and ice-packed waterways, were

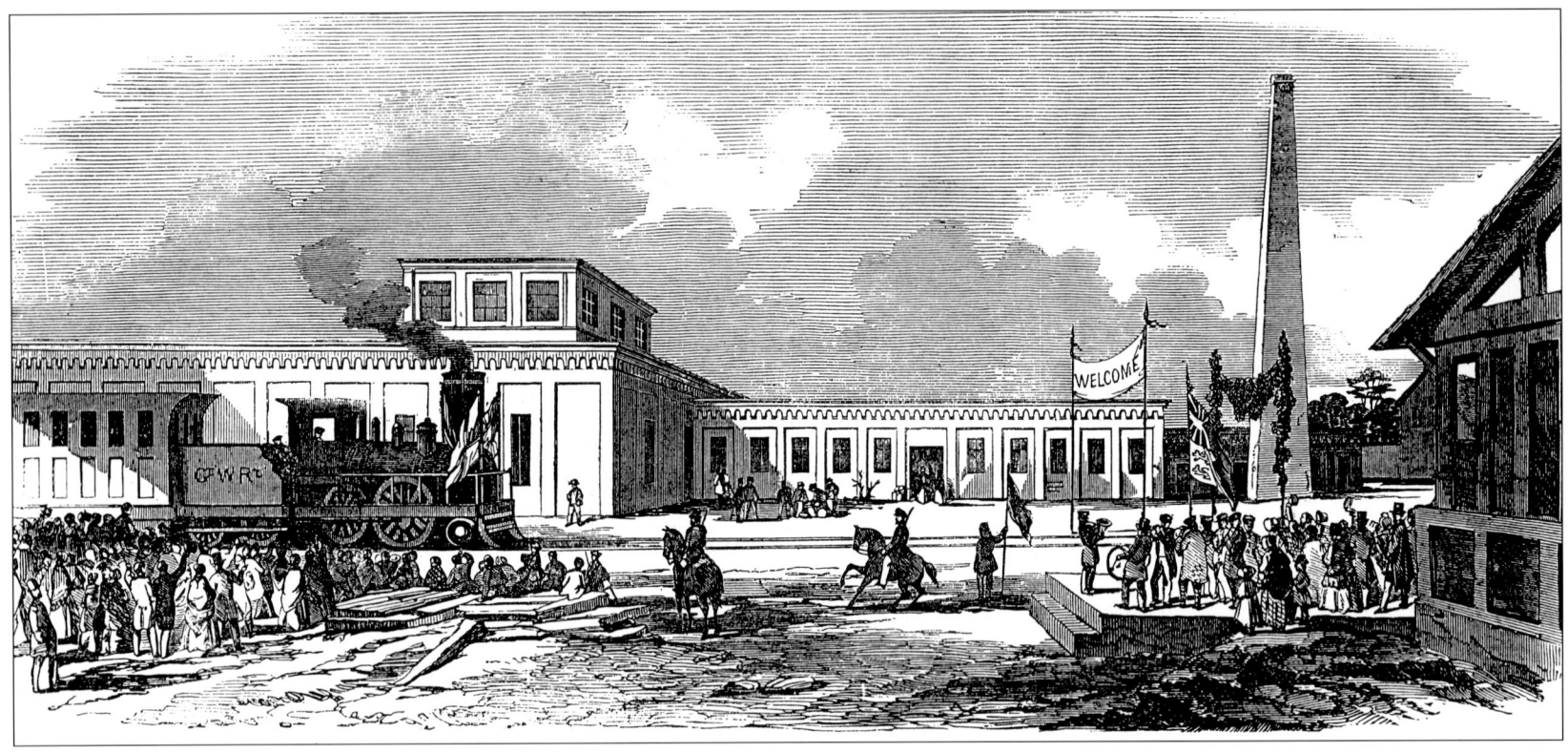

THE ARRIVAL OF THE INAUGURAL GREAT WESTERN
RAILWAY TRAIN AT LONDON, DECEMBER 15,
1853 FROM THE ILLUSTRATED LONDON NEWS OF
JANUARY 21, 1854
*The dawn of the railway age in London-Middlesex
forever changed the area's overall economy. For brewers,
the railway promised great opportunities for enhancing
fame and fortune. Courtesy, William P. Moran*

far superior to wagons, stagecoaches and boats. Brewers quickly recognized the
blessings of train transport and they consequently initiated a vigorous new era of
agency creation.

On this score, it should be emphasized that the railway significantly widened the
gap between small and large breweries. In short, modest brewers lacked what their
more prosperous competitors enjoyed — the capital and the economies of scale
necessary for establishing and maintaining large agency networks. Tying up money
in barrels, bottles and product shipped to sales representatives was expensive and
thus beyond the financial means of small operators. Compounding matters of
capital strength, agency beer had to compete with the price of locally made beer.
Therefore, only large breweries could produce malt liquor cheaply enough so that,
even after transportation costs were added, they could still vie with the price of
malt liquor made and sold in distant markets. Those brewers who could afford to
supply a string of agencies were generally able to enhance their manufacturing
advantages even further. In other words, increased sales ultimately gave them
access to greater capital from which they could finance plant improvements to

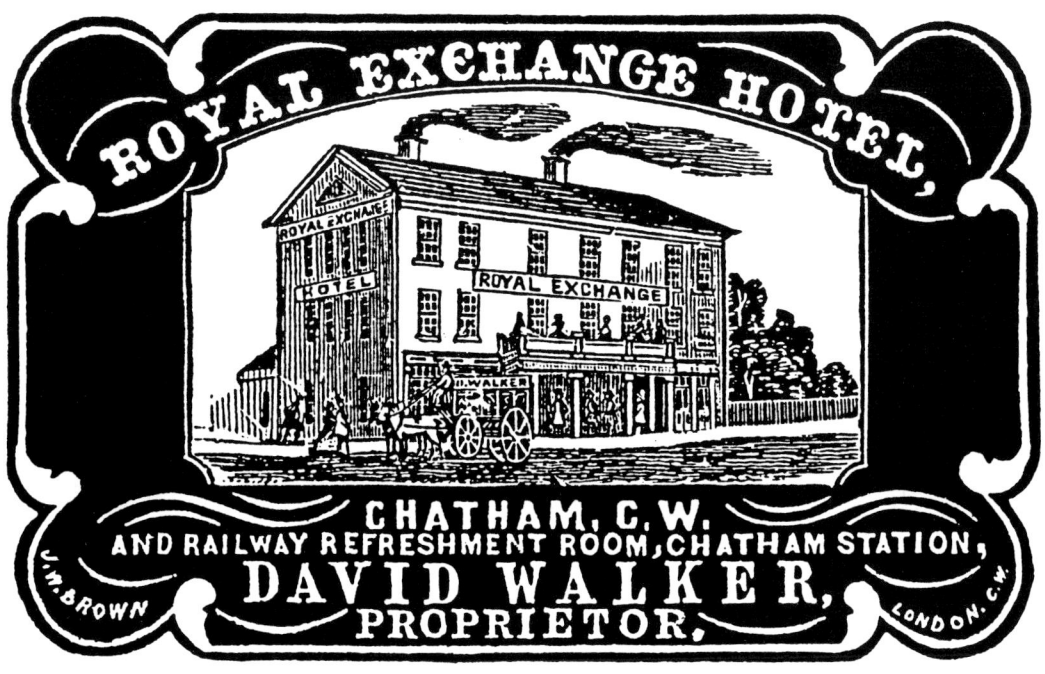

WOODCUT OF DAVID WALKER'S ROYAL EXCHANGE HOTEL IN CHATHAM FROM THE *CANADIAN ILLUSTRATED NEWS* OF DECEMBER 12, 1863
Most brewery agents were licensed liquor merchants. David Walker, the Chatham agent for W. & J. Carling from the mid-1850s until the mid-1860s, was somewhat unique in that he was a hotelkeeper. Nonetheless, he still functioned like a typical brewery agent of the time. Receiving consignments of malt liquor by rail, he wholesaled Carling beer to others in the local trade and retailed it directly to the public.

boost their production efficiencies and thereby make their beer even more price competitive. This circular process directly contributed to the remarkable drop in the number of Ontario breweries from 155 in 1862 to sixty-two in 1901.

CARLING & LABATT LEAD THE AGENCY CHARGE

Given the financial imperatives of agency operation, only the county's two largest brewers, Carling and Labatt (Eccles & Labatt until 1855), were able to organize and maintain sizeable agency networks during the third quarter of the nineteenth century. By doing so, they transformed themselves into major regional players within the overall Canadian brewing industry. Logically enough, the Londoners initially recruited liquor merchants in the region around London. In December 1858, for example, John Kinder Labatt, displaying a keen entrepreneurial spirit, ensured that the first Great Western train to steam into a breweryless Sarnia carried an agency consignment of his "celebrated" ale and porter. Besides Sarnia, Carling and Labatt raced each other into Ingersoll, Woodstock, Galt, Brantford, Hamilton, Toronto, St. Thomas, Strathroy, Watford, Forest, Thedford, Petrolia, Glencoe, Newbury, Bothwell, Chatham, Windsor, Lucan, Ailsa Craig, Parkhill, St. Marys, Stratford, Exeter, Seaforth, Clinton and Goderich. Every place was important in this great battle to dominate the region.

BEER LORE — In 1995, a bottle originally used during the 1850s by a Toronto brewer of ginger beer fetched nearly $4,500 at an antique auction. This rare artifact was unearthed at a building site in the Ontario capital. It cost the lucky construction worker· who found the bottle absolutely nothing to stoop down and pluck it from the soil.

LABATT AGENCY AD (UPPER) FROM THE GREAT WESTERN RAILWAY DIRECTORY FOR 1861-62 AND CARLING AGENCY AD (LOWER) FROM THE COUNTY OF OXFORD DIRECTORY FOR 1862-63
Blessed with sufficient venture capital, the Carling brothers and John Kinder Labatt used the railway to supply agency networks. Many agents took it upon themselves to advertise these popular sellers. Courtesy, J.J. Talman Regional Collection

Unfortunately, an imperfect archival record makes it virtually impossible to discover how much revenue Carling and Labatt derived from out-of-town sales. Nonetheless, sustained agency development clearly demonstrates that the Londoners found such outlets profitable. In what stands as the only contemporary estimate in this regard, a somewhat perturbed editor of the *Chatham Tri-Weekly Planet* calculated that his townspeople spent $5,000 on London beer in 1861. Of course, Carling and Labatt hardly neglected local beer drinkers. Ever anxious to sew up the local trade, they also distributed their ales, porters and stouts to a host of city vendors.

PRODUCTION SOARS

In absolute and relative terms, the new sales strategies adopted by W. & J. Carling and John Kinder Labatt propelled great leaps in production at their breweries. From January 1, 1860 to June 30, 1867, annual output at Carling's had nearly tripled from 112,416 gallons to 295,613 gallons, while yearly production at Labatt's had more than doubled from 74,813 gallons to 145,194 gallons. The figures for 1867 absolutely dwarfed output at most other breweries in Canada West (the industry average was 21,820 gallons). Indeed, the Carling brothers accounted for one-tenth of all provincial production. In 1870, Carling and Labatt respectively turned out $70,000 and $39,655 worth of beer, then the second and seventh highest returns posted in Ontario. Clearly, London had evolved into a very important brewing centre. It is also interesting to note that, according to municipal tax records, the Carling brewery proudly stood as the city's third largest business by 1859. With an assessed value of $4,646, the brewery was only bested by the Great Western Railway ($8,303) and the wholesale/retail hardware firm of Adam Hope & Company ($7,443).

EXPANSION

Naturally, rising sales brought about plant expansion. Around 1858, Labatt added a second malthouse and, in 1863, a five-storey brick tower brewhouse replaced the old stone brewery built two decades earlier. In the thick of the fall brewing season for 1865, the *London Prototype* described Labatt's brewery in glowing terms:

> J.K. Labatt, Esq., the present proprietor, is a gentleman favorably and popularly known. He is a whole souled Irishman, with all the genial

VIEWS OF LABATT'S BREWERY, CIRCA 1860 (UPPER) AND CIRCA 1870 (LOWER)
Brisk sales dramatically boosted production at Labatt's brewery during the ten years following 1853. So much so, that Labatt replaced his old brewhouse with a five-storey brick one in 1863. Courtesy, Steve Peters and Labatt Archives respectively

BEER LORE — Martin Luther, who nailed his ninety-five theses to the door of the church in Wittenberg, Germany, thus beginning the Protestant Reformation, was very fond of beer. Of all beer drinkers the world has ever seen, he is perhaps the one who has wielded the greatest influence on human history.

THE WESTERN WING OF THE CARLING BREWERY, CIRCA 1870
Anticipating a boom in business during the first years of the local railway era, William and John Carling expanded their brewery in the early 1850s. Still, agency sales growth encouraged the brothers to make minor plant additions over the 1860s. The fanciful nature of this drawing belies the true size of the Carling brewery at the time.

BEER LORE — Mary Queen of Scots, although not terribly fond of the English, thoroughly enjoyed their beer.

qualities incidental to the country from whence he hails. The London Brewery is now a big pile of brick, solidly and compactly built. It is five stories high, and comprises two malt houses, and the same number of kilns, four stock cellars, and a bottling cellar. In one of the stock cellars are six large vats, capable of holding 200 bushels each, and in which are stored pale brown stout. An extensive engine-house and wood-shed, a cooper and carpenter shop adjoin the brewery [along with] office houses and other apartments necessary for such an establishment. . . Mr. John Labatt, jr., is the brewer of the establishment, and his skill and ability in the duties of his office are such that to him, in a large measure, is due the high character and good name and celebrity which Labatt's ales and beer have attained throughout the Western Province [Southwestern Ontario].

Another major addition to Labatt's was constructed in mid-1866. Although the Carling brothers had greatly enlarged their City Brewery in anticipation of the railway age, they, too, found a need for improvement. Aside from a bottling room built in the early 1860s, the most notable effort in this regard was aimed at cooling their brewery. Just before Confederation, the Carlings lined their brewhouse with a wide verandah to shade its walls from the sun. A year later, *Anderson's London & Middlesex Directory* marvelled at the Carling brewing plant, then the county's biggest:

CITY BREWERY. — This extensive establishment. . . has been enlarged and improved from year to year, to meet the requirements of the increase of business. The main building, of brick, now measures 240 x 74 feet, with an addition of 74 x 40 feet, used chiefly as the bottling department. The whole building is two storeys high, with a basement. There are two malt kilns, with a capacity of 12,000 bushels each, being about one-half the amount required for the extent of business done. A ten horse-power engine is used, and from 25 to 30 hands kept constantly employed in the manufacture of ale and porter, the superiority of which is well established throughout Canada. The bottling department is kept well stocked with the several past years' manufacture. The cellars are excellently arranged, and well adapted for stock ale and porter.

AN ENVIABLE POPULAR REPUTATION
Bigger numbers and more bricks are not the only standards by which we can measure

London's growing brewing prominence. Another notable emblem of renown came in the form of media applause for the city's beverages. For example, the usually pro-temperance editor of the *London Prototype* returned this positive verdict in 1859:

> LONDON, C.W. BEER. — The London beer only requires its virtues to be known to render it as famous in Canada as the Burton ale is in England. It is the opinion of Englishmen — and who will question their judgment on beer — that the nutritious liquid [made] by both our worthy brewers [Carling and Labatt] is not to be beaten in the province. And thereby hangs a tale. A gentleman who is a resident of this city was sometime since in a town at this side of the lines near Detroit, when a friend asked him to have some beer. Our friend complained that he couldn't get a good drop of the beverage in _____ [detail not given — original underscore intentional]. Nonsense, replied the other, who was also a lover of the drink that Cobbett called liquid meat; come into _____ tavern, and I'll be bound you'll get it. The London man consented, and both had their beer, the excellence of which was at once admitted, much to the chuckling satisfaction of the _____ man. Our Canadian Cockney, however, took the liberty of inquiring from whom the host got the beer, when the latter replied, "from Mr. Labatt, of London!"

While local boasting was to be expected, outsiders also puffed the city's beer. For instance, the editor of the *Chatham Tri-Weekly Planet* introduced a Carling agency advertisement by pointing out that Carling's Celebrated Pale Ale was "pronounced by judges to be a superior beverage of its class." A few years later, the same journalist remarked: "In the London District, Carling's Ales stand very high in public estimation, as they do indeed throughout Western Canada [Southwestern Ontario]. One but needs to test this Ale to be fully satisfied of its merits." Significantly, such praise came from a scribe who had once implored his readers to forego Carling and Labatt products and patronize M.D. Wood's Chatham North Brewery. Chatham residents, however, evidently preferred London beer. In early January 1862, Wood's failed brewery was put up for sale.

CHANGING OF THE GUARD AT LABATT'S

Amidst this exciting era of rapid growth, sixty-three-old John Kinder Labatt died from heart trouble on October 26, 1866. Having enjoyed an immense popularity, he was mourned by many. As the *London Free Press* noted of his funeral: "This event

ELIZA AND JOHN LABATT, 1894
This mother and son team respectively formed the senior and junior partners in the firm of Labatt & Company. Eliza Labatt, the widow of John Kinder, later served as banker to her son John. John began his business life as a clerk in the grocery and liquor store of Edward Adams & Company, but jumped at the chance to learn the brewing trade as an apprentice brewer in Wheeling, West Virginia. Courtesy, Labatt Archives

GEORGE W. SMITH & JOHN LABATT

Although he never operated a brewery in the county, George Weatherall Smith, a native of Lincolnshire, England, holds an interesting place in Middlesex's brewing history. Smith first emigrated to North America in 1819, when his family settled in Syracuse, New York. Upon his father's death the next year, Smith returned to England, but was back in the United States by the mid-1820s. At various times, he worked as a supercargo along the Mississippi River and as a brewmaster in New York, Albany and possibly Pittsburgh. In 1833, he moved to St. Thomas, Upper Canada, where he established a brewery with William Peacey.

While in St. Thomas, Smith became acquainted with a number of local residents, including the Eccles and Labatt families. Interestingly, Smith may have actually known Samuel Eccles since his brewing days in New York (Eccles had also worked as a brewer in the same city during the mid-1820s). In any case, Smith married Samuel's sister, Mary, on December 2, 1833. Shortly after Mary's death a month later, Smith returned to the States. By 1835, he was

SMITH'S BREWERY, WHEELING, CIRCA 1860 *Courtesy, Thaddeus Podratsky*

running a brewery in Pittsburgh and another in Wheeling, Virginia by 1847. Besides turning out Kennett, pale and bitter ales, porter and brown stout, George W. Smith also produced one fully trained brewmaster of some renown.

In 1859, John Kinder Labatt arranged a brewing apprenticeship under Smith for his third oldest boy, John. Since he did not stand to inherit the family business — third sons rarely did — young John eagerly seized the chance to enter the trade elsewhere. Well schooled in the "art and mystery" by Smith, Labatt returned to Canada in 1863 to assume duties as brewmaster at Smith's Prescott brewery. The next year, Labatt returned to his father's brewery. With him, the junior John Labatt brought a recipe for pale ale that he had learned from his mentor. In 1876, the formula proved its worth beyond words, when Labatt's India Pale Ale captured a gold medal at Philadelphia's Centennial Exhibition. It was just the start for Labatt. In future, Smith's former apprentice would claim many more prizes for his quality brews.

took place on Sunday last, being one of the most numerously attended that we have seen for years. Upwards of eighty-five carriages joined in the procession, the funeral cortege being accompanied besides by a large number on foot."

Aside from leaving a trust for the education of his five daughters and minor son, the brewer's will directed that the brewery business "shall be continued by my wife Eliza Labatt for the benefit of herself and my children." If his widow declined, then "preference shall be given to my son John Labatt to be purchaser or tenant." And

GEORGE W. SMITH, PRESCOTT & THE "OTHER" LABATTS

John Kinder and Eliza Labatt had four boys who reached their adult years — Robert, Ephraim, John and George. As things stood, the oldest son, Robert, was to inherit the family business. It would appear that John Kinder believed that the London Brewery could neither support four owners nor survive any potential four-way squabbles over its management. Nonetheless, a war radically altered the inheritance plan.

With the outbreak of the U.S. Civil War, Labatt family friend, George W. Smith, had a few problems on his hands. One, the uncertainty of war soured the overall commercial climate. Two, military demand for grain forced the price of barley to skyrocket. Three, war always came with the possibility of property destruction. And four, Smith sympathized with the rebellious South and he consequently ran into sales troubles in the generally pro-Union northwestern counties of Virginia (these counties

LABATT'S PRESCOTT BREWERY, CIRCA 1870

separated from Virginia and joined the North as West Virginia in 1863). Sensing life would be better elsewhere, Smith liquidated his assets in Wheeling and established a brewing business at Prescott, Canada West. His young brewmaster, John Labatt, accompanied him.

When matters calmed in West Virginia, Smith returned to Wheeling in time for 1864's fall brewing season. He offered to lease the Prescott brewery to John Labatt. John could not afford it, but his brothers, Robert and Ephraim, could. The older Labatt boys ran the brewery in partnership until Ephraim died in 1867. Not long after Ephraim's death, Robert bought out Smith. In 1875, Robert and George Labatt, along with a number of others, formed the Prescott Brewing & Malting Company, Limited. Two years later, Robert passed away in England, leaving George in effective control of the business.

George's guidance was a mixed blessing. He was a fine brewer, and he even won several medals for his brews at the Colonial and Indian Exhibition in 1886 and at the Columbian Exposition in 1893, but he was not the ablest financial manager. In the mid-1880s, his older brother, John, bailed him out and became a silent partner in the business. After George's death in 1906, John converted the Prescott brewery into a warehouse and distribution facility for his London beer.

The most interesting dimension to this story is as follows. Had the U.S. Civil War not lured Smith to Prescott and had Smith not lured Robert Labatt to the same place, then Robert Labatt would have inherited his father's brewery in London. Now, think about that for a moment. Today, we might be drinking beer from Robert Labatt Limited instead of John Labatt Limited!

if John Jr. declined, then John Kinder Labatt's other sons, Robert Pritchard, Ephraim and George Thomas — in that order — were to be offered the London Brewery. At any rate, Eliza Labatt exercised her option to own the brewery and

GRAND TRUNK RAILWAY.

Advice Note, *London* _____ Station, *Sept 26 1864*

TO *Thomas Renier*

The undermentioned Goods, consigned to you, have arrived here this day; we will thank you to send for them as soon as possible, as they remain here at YOUR RISK AND EXPENSE.

Received the sum of $ _____

Date _____

For the GRAND TRUNK RAILWAY COMPANY.

FROM.	No. of Way Bill.	SENDER.	No. of Pckgs.	SPECIES OF GOODS & MARKS.	Paid on $ c.	Weight in lbs.	RATE in cents ₩ 100 lbs	TOTAL. $ c.
Stratford	204	C Dean		3 Brls Ale		900	12	1 08

NOTICE.—No portion of a consignment of Goods to be delivered until the Freight on the whole is paid. The Directors require the Carriage to be paid on delivery. The above named Goods will not be delivered unless this note be produced.   ☞ See conditions at the back hereof.

ABOVE RIGHT: GRAND TRUNK BILL OF LADING FOR THREE BARRELS OF ALE, SEPTEMBER 26, 1864
Charles Dean, the Stratford agent for the Hamilton brewing firm of Grant & Middlewood, was just one of many who shipped beer into Middlesex via a rail link, proving that the railway could be a double-edged sword for county brewers. By the way, the surname of the hotelkeeper who received this consignment of ale was properly spelled Rance and not Renier. Courtesy, J.J. Talman Regional Collection

ABOVE LEFT: T.J. MCDONOUGH AD FROM THE LONDON FREE PRESS OF AUGUST 3, 1869
As this announcement reveals, two other giants in Canada's beer world — Molson and Dow — were sure to use the railway to ship beer into mid-Victorian London-Middlesex. Ironically, T.J. McDonough was a personal friend of both the Carling and Labatt families.

control of the London Brewery passed to Labatt & Company. Eliza was the "Labatt" in the firm and her son, John, was the "Company." It is difficult to determine exactly what motivated this partnership arrangement. Perhaps, Eliza simply wanted a chance to run the business herself — after all, she had surely helped her late husband behind the scenes. However, it appears that she ultimately intended John to have the brewery anyway. On August 15, 1872, Labatt & Co. was formally dissolved and John Labatt acquired the brewery. It is not known how much the son paid his mother, but it was probably somewhere in the neighbourhood of $20,000 to $25,000.

THE INFLUX OF OUT-OF-TOWN BEER

Although rail connections afforded Carling and Labatt expedient means to ship their brews out of Middlesex, the same tracks also permitted out-of-towners to funnel their beers into the county. This continuous invasion of malt liquor came from as near as "just down the line" to as far away as the other side of the Atlantic

Ocean. For instance, Dundas brewer Robert Holt, taking advantage of his town's Great Western link to London, recruited a London agent for his "Celebrated Bottled Ale." Meanwhile, Charles Dean, Stratford's rep for Grant & Middlewood of Hamilton, used the Grand Trunk to reach S. & T. Rance, proprietors of the Arkell Hotel at King and Richmond. Further afield, Montreal giants Molson and Dow secured a host of local merchants to carry their brands. Even more distant, British, Scottish and Irish brewers, such as Abbott, Allsopp, Bass, Blood, Guinness, Hibbert, McEwan, Muir and Younger, channelled their old-country beers to Canadian wholesalers, who, in turn, forwarded them to dealers in Middlesex.

OTHER BREWERIES OF THE ERA

While the railway carried Carling and Labatt to greater heights, several other brewers appeared on the local scene. These arrivals included a jumble of short-term players, one oddball, a few humble and yet persistent souls and the unsuccessful progenitors of what eventually became Middlesex County's third largest brewery. Those who established themselves in London and its suburbs were obviously drawn to the city's lucrative and growing beer market. Meanwhile, a handful of entrepreneurs tried their luck in outlying parts of the county.

THE ELEPHANT BREWERY

In the spring of 1860, Thomas Bryan bought the defunct Blackfriars Brewery from Richard Rich and rechristened it the Elephant Brewery. Not much is known about Bryan's brewing enterprise beyond what details can be gleaned from an article which appeared in the *London Free Press* on December 7, 1860:

> Early on Saturday morning a fire was discovered in a building in Westminster, over Blackfriars Bridge, known as the "Elephant Brewery," owned and occupied by Mr. Bryan. . . It appears that from suspicions entertained regarding certain parties, Mr. Bryan believed that the place would be set on fire. . . and about half-past three o'clock [a.m.] he discovered smoke around the building. On going out, a building used as a stable was found to be in flames. Assistance was speedily at hand, but in consequence of there being no water near, all efforts to arrest the progress of the flames were abortive. The value of the building and contents was $1,000. After the fire, a fight took place among some of the neighbors with regard to the origin of the conflagration. A man named Rich said that the party who fired the

BEER LORE — According to a bartenders' guide book published in 1862, the recipe for ale punch called for: "A quart of mild ale, a glass of white wine, one of brandy, one of capillaire [a mixture of sugar and Curaçao], the juice of a lemon, a roll of the lemon peel pared thin, nutmeg grated on the top, and a bit of toasted bread." Go ahead, give a batch a try.

KENT BREWERY!

BEST GENUINE ALE AND PORTER.

Hotels and Families Supplied.

JOHN HAMILTON,

Ann Street,   - -   **London, Ont.**

KENT BREWERY AD FROM THE LONDON CITY DIRECTORY FOR 1877-78
John Hamilton bought the virtually bankrupt Kent Brewery from F.L. Dundas in 1861. With due diligence and a Scotsman's thrift, Hamilton was able to turn the brewery's fortunes around. Courtesy, J.J. Talman Regional Collection

BEER LORE — In 1879, there were 22,278 small breweries in the United Kingdom

premises came from Haystead's [tavern]. One of the brothers Haystead, who was present, said that Rich was a liar, when Rich repeated the assertion, and Haystead knocked Rich over. A couple of women, connections of Rich's, then attempted an assault on Haystead, and a regular "scene" ensued. . . Haystead is a respectable man and beyond suspicion, and Rich's attempt to fasten the crime on him caused the assault.

Bryan ran the Elephant Brewery until about 1863, when he moved into manufacturing farming tools. This marked the end of brewing at the site. As for Richard Rich, he may have been the Rich who established a brewery at the hamlet of Warwick in Lambton County around 1864.

THE KENT BREWERY

In 1859, amidst a general depression, Henry Marshall and John Hammond bravely opened the Kent Brewery on the south side of Ann Street just west of Richmond. The brewery was so named because its brews were flavoured with hops imported from the renowned hop fields of Kent, England. Confronted by the prevailing economic climate and by strong competition from the city's two largest breweries, Marshall & Hammond went out of business within two years. Their successors, Francis L. Dundas and John Phillips were even less fortunate. In August 1861, after only six short months, Phillips dissolved his partnership with Dundas, who, unable to save the sinking enterprise from mounting debt, gave up the brewery three months later in favour of Scotsman John Hamilton. Under the Hamilton name (Hamilton & Morgan with Daniel Morgan as a partner during the mid-1860s), the Kent Brewery found some much needed stability. In 1870, the 8,000 gallons of ale and porter produced at the Kent Brewery netted Hamilton a tidy profit of $500 (at the time, the average working man earned less than half that per year).

JOHN ALLASTER

In 1861, another Scot, fifty-four-year-old John Allaster, opened the Middlesex Brewery in London East. Later renamed the Dundas Street Brewery, it stood on the south side of Dundas Street between Adelaide and Lyle (one block east of the city's present police headquarters). A curious early reference to the brewery appears in the *London Free Press* for May 10, 1862: "Depravity. A little fellow, aged about fourteen years, was charged by his father with being drunk and disorderly. He [the boy] stated that he had got the liquor at a brewery on Dundas street, near Adelaide. . . He was sentenced to twenty-four hours' solitary imprisonment." Fortunately for Allaster, most of his customers were neither minors nor committed to jail for their appreciation of his beer. In 1868, he turned out a respectable 250 gallons of ale and porter per week during the height of the brewing season. Two years later, the aggregate value of malt liquor manufactured at his brewery was $2,080.

However, a bizarre misadventure nearly ended the brewer's career in the autumn of 1871. As the *London Free Press* reported: "Yesterday afternoon, while Mr. Allaster, brewer, at the East End, was superintending the process of boiling, he accidently fell into the vat, and although immediately rescued, we are pained to hear, was severely scalded about the body, and lies in a precarious condition. Dr. Cattermole is in attendance upon the unfortunate sufferer." Thankfully, Allaster recovered from this horrible ordeal. He later operated a hotel in complement to his brewing business.

WILLIAM HUMPIDGE

A native of Gloucester, England, William Humpidge opened a very modest brewery in connection with his Bell Inn on Talbot Street in late 1861 or early 1862. Not much else can be found out about this venture, except that it came to an end about a year later, when Humpidge left London to establish a much bigger brewery down the Great Western Railway line in Strathroy.

WILLIAM T. ERITH

Although not a brewer of traditional beer, the wonderfully unorthodox William T. Erith deserves consideration in this book. Sometime during the early 1860s, Erith, a "professor of classical music, lecturer on ancient and modern sacred music, and a teacher of singing and piano forte," branched out into roasting coffee, selling medicinal herbs and roots, manufacturing patent porter, malt and homemade wines and brewing botanic beer. Amazingly, he did all these things from his residence on Bond Street (now Princess Avenue) near William. Little else can be unearthed about Erith's interesting and erratic career path, except that he left London in late 1869 or early 1870 and popped up in Vineland, New Jersey several years later.

Dundas Street Brewery

JOHN ALLASTER,

BREWER OF ALE AND PORTER!

ALSO, THE CELEBRATED HERB BEER,

FOR MEDICINAL PURPOSES

Opposite M. Anderson's residence, }   **LONDON, C. W.**
Dundas Street East,

The Herb Beer has obtained a deserved celebrity for the cure of Dispepsia, Liver Complaint, Billiousness, &c., and has proved highly beneficial to a large number of the most respectable citizens, and is also recommended for Strengthening the Stomach and Increasing the Appetite.

MIDDLESEX BREWERY AD FROM THE *MIDDLESEX COUNTY GAZETTEER & BUSINESS DIRECTORY FOR 1864-65*
Considering the booming strength of the Carling and Labatt breweries, London was a rather competitive beer market throughout the 1860s. Still, persistent newcomers, such as John Allaster, did make a go of things during the decade. Of course, a little showmanship always helped. Courtesy, J.J. Talman Regional Collection

BEER LORE — Charlemagne, the great Medieval French king, personally brewed his own beer.

VICTORIA BREWERY,

King Street West, London, C.W.

DAVID HAYSTEAD,

PROPRIETOR.

MANUFACTURER OF BEER AND ALE BY THE BARREL.

VICTORIA BREWERY AD FROM THE *LONDON AND MIDDLESEX DIRECTORY FOR 1866-67* (ABOVE) AND JOSEPH SIDDALL, 1905 (BELOW)
Hotelkeeper David Haystead conducted his Victoria Brewery in much the same manner as today's brewpub owners conduct their breweries — for reasons of self-supply. Meanwhile, Joseph Siddall's youthful venture into brewing was cut short by a limited local market.
Courtesy, J.J. Talman Regional Collection

THE VICTORIA BREWERY

David Haystead, a native of Norfolk, England and one of the hotelkeepers mentioned in Chapter Three, entered the brewing trade in 1866. A loyal Briton, Haystead called his new enterprise the Victoria Brewery and originally operated it in conjunction with his tavern business at the southwest corner of King and Ridout Streets. From all appearances, his brewery functioned much like a Victorian equivalent to the brewpubs we know today. In 1870, his hand-powered brewhouse turned out a modest 1,150 gallons of beer. Three years later, he moved the brewery side of his business to Petersville, but exactly where in the village remains unknown.

JOSEPH SIDDALL

According to the late Dr. F.T. Rosser, an historian of Welsh settlement in Upper Canada, Joseph Siddall built a carding mill and operated a brewery "below the grist mill at the Lobo-Williams townline near Carlisle." More specifically, directories put Siddall on lot 24 of Lobo Township's thirteenth concession. Although Rosser did not say when Siddall ran the brewery, *Lovell's Canada Directory for 1857* includes in its description of Carlisle one "Joseph Siddall, fuller, carder and brewer." Given that earlier and later sources do not identify him as a brewer, it is safe to assume that he only ran his brewery for a short time during the mid- to late 1850s. Undoubtedly, a marginal local market ended his foray into beer-making.

THOMAS JANES

Census and municipal tax records for 1861 identify fifty-year-old Englishman Thomas Janes as a brewer in Delaware Township near Kilworth. In particular, his brewery was located in a converted grist mill on gore lots B and C. Since previous and subsequent assessment rolls make no mention of a brewery in that part of the township, it appears that Janes' entry into the brewing trade was short-lived.

JOSEPH THOMPSON

In 1862 or 1863, Joseph Thompson, formerly proprietor of Newbury's Union Hotel, opened a brewery in the village. As with most other humble brewing efforts, not much else can be found out about Thompson's venture, except that its survival was momentary. Despite having seven taverns, Newbury could not support its own brewery and Thompson had abandoned brewing by February 1864. It would seem that Carling and Labatt had a tight grip on Newbury. After all, the London-to-Windsor branch of the Great Western Railway passed right through the place.

JOHN CARLING — THE BREWER-POLITICIAN

The youngest son of Thomas and Margaret Carling, John Carling was born in London Township on January 23, 1828. Although first apprenticed as a tanner, he entered the brewing business at age twenty-one, when he and his brother, William, bought their father's brewery. While the Carling name has long since been famous in brewing circles both domestic and international, John Carling's true claim to fame was his distinguished political career.

John's entry into politics began rather inauspiciously in 1850, when he successfully ran for the local school board. Obviously impressed, electors returned him as a trustee for fourteen more terms. School administration, however, was not enough for the ambitious Carling and he moved into municipal government in 1854, succeeding his father as alderman for London's St. George's Ward. He kept this seat until 1858.

While his natural charisma secured electoral success during these years, the rough and tumble nature of municipal affairs polished him into a mature politician. However, Carling's aldermanic experience did not turn him into a boorish, loud-mouthed public figure. In fact, it did quite the opposite and taught him the power of behind-the-scenes networking, the value of compromise and the prudence of managing heated debate with measured, logical and occasionally humorous language.

Local politics also taught Carling the importance of lubricating the electorate. As the suspicious editor of the *Canadian Free Press* coyly observed of Carling's election triumph in 1851: "[In a room adjoining the polling station was] a barrel of beer for the refreshment of the thirsty, conspicuously branded with 'J. Carling,' but whether as brewer or donor, or what influence the beer may have exercised in securing the head of the poll we do not pretend to say." Now, in all due fairness, Carling was hardly the only Victorian politician to use booze to swing votes his way — the technique was widely practised at the time. Still, his profession likely made him better at it than most anyone else.

Nonetheless, aspirations drove the brewer to bigger and better things. In 1857, the city's leading Conservatives, John Kinder Labatt among them, publicly courted Carling to run as the party's candidate in the upcoming provincial election. He gladly accepted the invitation. While he hit the stumps, his party friends handed out $2 to every voter who promised "to drink to Mr. Carling's health" on election day. Local Reformers (precursors to Liberals) were outraged with the bribery, but the big, bad Conservative machine just rolled along and landed Carling a victory.

Carling never looked back politically — except once, when he co-chaired London's waterworks board in 1878 — and, although his subsequent electioneering became less sudsy, he stayed in provincial politics until 1872. In 1862, he became Receiver-General for the Province of Canada. Five years later, he became Ontario's Commissioner of Agriculture and Public Works, a post he held until 1871. His most prominent accomplishment while in this office was establishing the Ontario Agricultural College (now the University of Guelph).

Ultimately, the brewer shone brightest in the federal arena. He sat as London's Member of Parliament from 1867 to 1874, 1878 to 1891 and 1892 to 1895. His first cabinet posting came in 1882, when he became Prime Minister Sir John A. Macdonald's Postmaster-General. Three years later, Carling assumed the agriculture portfolio. As Minister of Agriculture, he founded and developed Canada's system of experimental farms. Carling's sincere and keen interest in farm matters — something that came to him honestly owing to his rural childhood and because of brewing's obvious connections to farming — provided the ministry with progressive and imaginative leadership. Considering that Canada's economy then rested upon an agricultural foundation (as it still does), this was economically crucial. He continued as Minister of Agriculture until 1892 and remained in cabinet as a minister without portfolio until 1895.

John Carling first became a senator in 1891, when, after losing an election to his Liberal opponent, Charles S. Hyman, Sir John A. appointed him to the red chamber in a ploy to retain the brewer as Minister of Agriculture. Upon proving that Hyman had illegally won the contest, Carling was re-elected to the House of Commons. He consequently resigned his senatorship. In 1896, Prime Minister Mackenzie Bowell re-appointed Carling to the senate. This time, the Londoner entered the upper house as Sir John Carling, as he had been made a Knight of the Grand Cross of St. Michael and St. George (K.C.M.G.) by Queen Victoria three years earlier. By the late 1890s, he was spending most of his time back in London.

Throughout his provincial and federal careers, John Carling exercised his position and influence to benefit London. Most notably, he secured for the city a magnificent post office building, a new Custom House, the Asylum for the Insane (now the London Psychiatric Hospital), a military camp, Wolseley Barracks, an infantry school, the land that now forms Victoria Park, the Great Western Railway car shops (employed 300 to 600 hands) and the Ontario Car Company shops (employed 200 to 300 hands). He also made sure that the Canadian Pacific Railway ran its Southwestern Ontario branch line through London.

Carling was also locally famous for his raucous victory parties, which, given his record, were numerous. Held at London's various large hotels, they were attended by hundreds of well-wishers and began with formal dinners, replete with piles of good food, plenty of drink and lots of crowing over Liberal tears. The feasts invariably ended with rounds of singing, boisterous cheering and victory marches around the banquet room with the triumphant politician carried upon the shoulders of his supporters. Ironically, Carling never drank beer at these parties or, for that matter, at any other time. Beer reportedly plagued him with terrible stomach trouble. Imagine that!

SIR JOHN CARLING RESPLENDENT IN HIS KNIGHT-COMMANDER'S UNIFORM, 1896 *Courtesy, J.J. Talman Regional Collection*

THE DELAWARE BREWERY

In late 1870 or early 1871, forty-five-year-old Englishman Cordley Tupholme established a small brewhouse in connection with his Great Western Hotel in Delaware (about where the Royal Canadian Legion Hall now stands). The hotelier likely desired a fresh, regular and inexpensive supply of ale for his barroom. Still, it would seem that conducting a brewery in the small village was no easy task. In late 1873, a restless Tupholme left Delaware to manage Balkwill's Hotel in London. He disposed of his tavern and brewery to local farmer Robert Ollett. Ollett ran both enterprises until July 1874, when he sold the tavernkeeping half of the business to George Rawlings and the beer-making half to Smith Spence. Spence carried on the

Delaware Brewery for another year and a half. Apparently in want of a larger customer base, he closed the brewery at the end of the fall brewing season in 1875. This, however, was not the end of brewing in the village.

ROBERT GODDARD JR.

In late 1870, according to *Lovell's Province of Ontario Gazetteer and Directory*, Robert Goddard Jr., whose father had once worked at Carling's, operated a small brewery on his farm lot immediately next to Dreaney's Corners (near the southeast corner of today's Dundas Street and Crumlin Road). While the hamlet was home to a busy tavern that served as an important stopover for the travelling public, local beer sales were apparently insufficient to support Goddard's inauspicious effort. Since the 1871 census does not mention his brewery, we can safely assume that it had earlier closed. In 1874, Goddard departed Dreaney's Corners to manage a hotel in London.

HEINRICH REMMLE & ERNEST SWEISLEND

The 1871 census lists twenty-eight-year-old German immigrant Heinrich Remmle as a brewer and farmer in Ekfrid Township (period directories locate him a few miles northwest of Melbourne) and twenty-four-year-old English immigrant Ernest Sweislend as a brewer in Wardsville. Unfortunately, nothing else can be learned about their brewing activities, although the lack of historical documentation suggests that they did not brew for very long and that their breweries were hardly prominent.

STRATHROY'S FIRST BREWERY

Strathroy's emergence as Middlesex County's second most significant brewing centre was rooted in the fifteen-year economic boom triggered by the local arrival of the Great Western Railway in 1858. To the entrepreneur's eyes, a rapidly growing community shone brightly with opportunity. In late 1862 or early 1863, William

MAP OF THE VILLAGE OF DELAWARE, 1878
Cordley Tupholme was another member of Middlesex County's hotelkeeping fraternity to expand into brewing. His brewery was contiguous to his hotel on the southern corner of Delaware's King and Bridge Streets (both now forming Longwoods Road).

BEER QUOTE — "Good ale is meat, drink, and cloth."
John Ray, *English Proverbs*

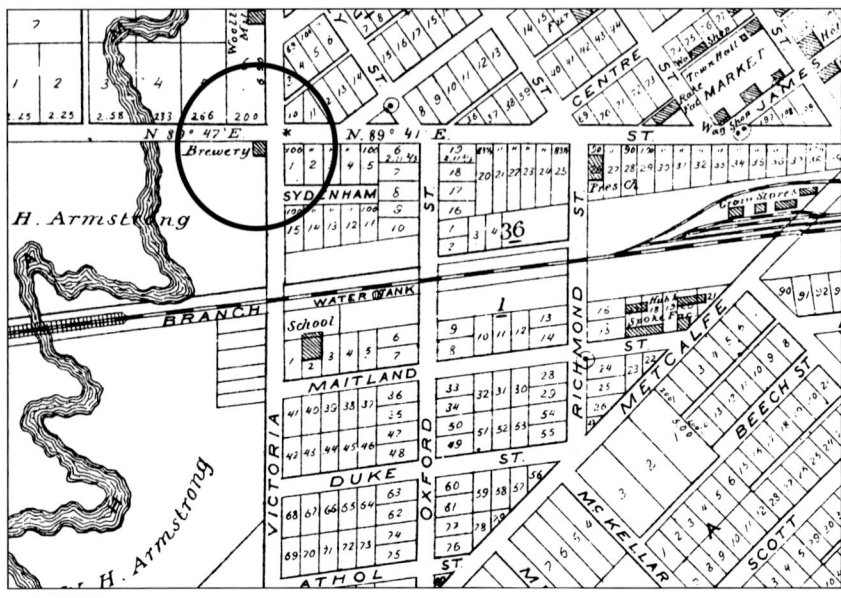

<small>DETAIL FROM A MAP OF STRATHROY SHOWING THE LOCATION OF THE WEST END BREWERY, 1878
Exactly where Strathroy's West End Brewery first stood remains a mystery. By the late 1870s, it was located on the southwestern corner of Victoria and Albert Streets.</small>

BEER LORE — In the seventeenth-century Dutch settlements scattered across what is now New York State, special courts composed of civic leaders convened to adjudge the worthiness of local beer. If a brewer's product was deemed inferior, his brewing license could be suspended or even revoked if the beer rudely offended the palate.

Humpidge, formerly a hotelkeeper and brewer in London, recognized Strathroy's potential and established an ale and porter brewery in the village's west end. According to *Page's Illustrated Historical Atlas of Middlesex County*, published in 1878, the brewery was situated on the southwestern corner of Victoria Street and Adelaide Township's fourth concession (now Albert Street), although it may have originally stood diagonally opposite this location during its first few years of operation (the historical record is unclear). In the fall of 1864, Thomas Snell Sr. joined Humpidge in a partnership styled Humpidge & Snell. Snell brought to the new firm several years' experience working for John Labatt. William Snell, another former employee at Labatt's, served as the firm's inaugural brewer.

As an interesting sidebar, it is quite likely that William and Thomas Snell were either brothers or cousins and belonged to the same Snell clan that had once operated breweries in London and Yarmouth Township during the 1830s and 1840s. Also, it should be pointed out that Victorian business directories usually confused Thomas Snell Sr. with his son and namesake, Thomas Snell Jr., and mistakenly listed the younger Thomas as the brewery's owner. The source of confusion may have been that Thomas Jr. worked at his father's brewery.

In 1868, Thomas Snell Sr. purchased William Humpidge's interest in the venture, when the latter left Strathroy to start a flour and feed business in Watford. Under Snell's ownership, the brewery remained a modest, yet steady one, with a workforce rarely greater than two or three employees. In 1870, Snell transformed 19,000 pounds of malt and 1,000 pounds of hops into 19,200 gallons of beer worth $4,000. The brewery's products enjoyed sufficient popularity in and around Strathroy that Snell ably withstood competitive pressures from local Carling and Labatt agents and from another brewery established in the village in 1870. To distinguish his brewery from this local rival, Snell subsequently billed his concern as the West End Brewery.

THE WESTERN STEAM BREWERY

Despite some rough times during its early years, Strathroy's second brewery became the community's most enduring and most famous. In mid-1870, Henry Large, in conjunction with a handful of silent partners, built a wooden brewery on the west side of Caradoc Street just south of the Sydenham River (near the site of today's

TSC Store). Named the Western Steam Brewery, the endeavour turned out its first brew in the fall of that year. The *London Free Press* commented upon its opening:

> These gentleman have erected a fine establishment and added thereto the latest improvements in machinery and general brewing apparatus. The senior proprietor, Mr. Henry Large, has had extensive experience in the technical routine of brewing [he had previously worked as a brewer in Detroit], and being a man of energy and enterprise, he will doubtless succeed in establishing a remunerative and satisfactory business.

The *Strathroy Age* also offered encouraging words: "The establishment has been fitted up regardless of expense and is now complete in every particular [manner]." All told, the new brewery building cost around $5,000 to construct.

WESTERN STEAM BREWERY !
CARADOC STREET,
STRATHROY, - ONTARIO.
H. LARGE & Co.,
PROPRIETORS.

CONSTANTLY ON HAND,
PALE ALE, AMBER ALE,
STOCK ALE, PORTER,
BROWN STOUT,
In quantities to suit purchasers.

☞ The Subscribers beg to say that their extensive facilities will soon enable them to compete with any Brewery west of Toronto.
They have spared no outlay in order to secure the best material and most approved machinery. ☞ Patronage Solicited.

H. LARGE & Co., Proprietors.

WESTERN STEAM BREWERY AD FROM THE CITY OF LONDON & COUNTY OF MIDDLESEX DIRECTORY FOR 1871-72
The decision of Henry Large and his partners to establish a brewery on Caradoc Street in Strathroy was a bold move in a regional market dominated by Carling and Labatt. Clearly though, a confident Large & Company had grand designs of competing "with any Brewery west of Toronto." Courtesy, J.J. Talman Regional Collection

EXPANSION & DOOM

Within two years of its founding, the Western Steam Brewery was expanded with the construction of a brick malthouse. However, Large and his partners required further investors to finance this improvement. In Victorian Strathroy, it was not uncommon for local merchants to channel their excess capital into local industries. Large's brewery was no exception and, by late November 1871, "Messrs. Fawcett, Robbs, Dewan, Beattie, Geary, H. Large, C. Grist, J. Noble, Hodginson, D. Decow, T. & R. Moyle, P. O'Keefe, D.B. Campbell, and several others" had invested in a company to assume the brewery's assets and management. Fully organized early the next year, the new business was named the Strathroy Brewing & Malting Company. A notable weakness of the company's ownership structure was that some of the firm's principals had divided their financial interests in potentially compromising

WANTED,
A　TRAVELLING　AGENT
for the
Strathroy Brewing & Malting Co.

☛ **An energetic man wanted. References
required. Apply to A. F. BEATTIE,
Sec. and Treas.**
Strathroy, Feb. 13, 1872. d-v

STRATHROY BREWING & MALTING COMPANY AD
FROM THE LONDON FREE PRESS OF FEBRUARY 13, 1872
*The Strathroy Brewing & Malting Company began with
a bang, but its name faded from the scene about a year
after its formation. (computer enhanced)*

BEER LORE — Nineteenth-century Canadians had
an equivalent to our "twist-off" beer bottle. Their
"twist-off" bottle sported a lip with an internal thread
into which a wooden stopper was screwed. However,
these closures were very expensive to manufacture
and were consequently rarely used by breweries of the
time.

fashions. This was especially so in the case of secretary and treasurer, Alexander F. Beattie, an insurance agent, auctioneer and investor in several manufacturing pursuits, including a brick yard and a woollen mill. Aside from subscribing shares, Henry Large also functioned as the company's brewmaster and business manager.

Most of the brewery's new proprietors appear to have been more interested in quick returns than in nurturing an infant business. When the Western Steam Brewery failed to become the gold mine once projected, the investor group dissolved the Strathroy Brewing & Malting Company and sold its assets to Alexander F. Beattie and James D. Dewan in January 1873. Since Henry Large continued on as brewmaster, it would seem that the firm of Beattie & Dewan was another speculative ownership vehicle, although Dewan, as a grocer and liquor merchant, would have undoubtedly found brewery proprietorship of some cost advantage in supplying his store. According to their declaration of partnership, the pair was slated to remain in partnership until January 7, 1876. This was not to be.

On July 1, 1873, a fire destroyed some $15,000 worth of wool manufactured and stored by Strathroy Woollen Company — a loss which precipitated a lengthy closure of the factory. Having invested $5,500 in the woollen company, Alexander F. Beattie found the conflagration especially devastating. Complicating matters, Beattie owed the St. Lawrence Bank $4,000 for a personal loan secured against the wool. Making things even worse for Beattie, J.D. Dewan, who saw the writing on the wall, bailed from the partnership two weeks after the fire. Ironically, Dewan began selling Carling and Labatt ale not long afterwards. Quickly spiralling into debt, Beattie was soon unable to meet his financial obligations. Consequently, the St. Lawrence Bank made an attachment against his only going investment, the brewery. To appease his creditors, the insolvent brewer assigned to J.B. Cummins, the local branch manager of the St. Lawrence Bank. As the Western Steam Brewery teetered on bankruptcy, the bank had some of Beattie's investment real estate auctioned off in October 1874. Seven months later, a few of the brewery's chattels, amounting to office fixtures, two carts, one sleigh, a Fairbank weighing machine and some other equipment, went on the auction block.

Although originally scheduled for May 25, 1875, the public sale of the brewery building and malthouse was postponed until October 14. With the final rap of the auctioneer's gavel, Matthew Bixel (also spelled Mathew, Matthias or Mattias and the surname sometimes written as Bixler), a brewer from Ingersoll, bought the defunct business for $7,000. Paradoxically, Beattie's downfall was the best thing to have happened to the Western Steam Brewery. Ambitious, experienced and clever, Bixel would soon turn the failed brewery's fortunes completely around.

THE BREWERS' HALL AT THE PHILADELPHIA CENTENNIAL EXHIBITION, 1876 (ABOVE LEFT), LABATT'S DOMINION OF CANADA MEDAL, 1876 (ABOVE TOP), LABATT'S AUSTRALIAN MEDAL, 1877 (ABOVE RIGHT) AND AN AD PROMOTING LABATT'S BRANDS AS MEDAL WINNERS, 1892 (RIGHT)

While his competitors looked on with envy, John Labatt parlayed the award-winning qualities of his brews into a most successful marketing recipe. The Londoner's extraordinary international prize record got its start in the building pictured above. Medals courtesy, Labatt Archives

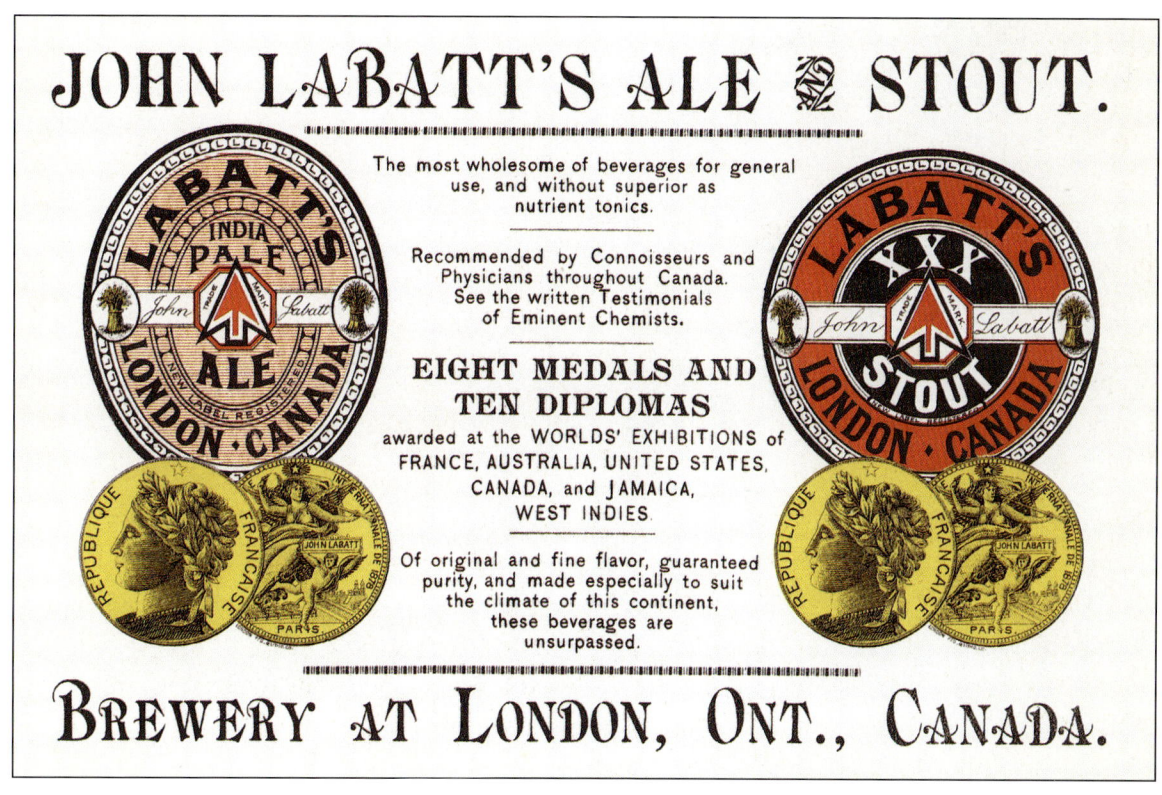

JOHN LABATT'S ALE & STOUT.

The most wholesome of beverages for general use, and without superior as nutrient tonics.

Recommended by Connoisseurs and Physicians throughout Canada. See the written Testimonials of Eminent Chemists.

EIGHT MEDALS AND TEN DIPLOMAS

awarded at the WORLDS' EXHIBITIONS of FRANCE, AUSTRALIA, UNITED STATES, CANADA, and JAMAICA, WEST INDIES.

Of original and fine flavor, guaranteed purity, and made especially to suit the climate of this continent, these beverages are unsurpassed.

LABATT'S INDIA PALE ALE — John Labatt — LONDON · CANADA — NEW LABEL REGISTERED

LABATT'S XXX STOUT — John Labatt — LONDON · CANADA

BREWERY AT LONDON, ONT., CANADA.

LONDON BREWERY

PALE AND XXX ALES

XXX STOUT AND PORTER

JOHN LABATT

W.A. Little Steam-Lith, Montreal.

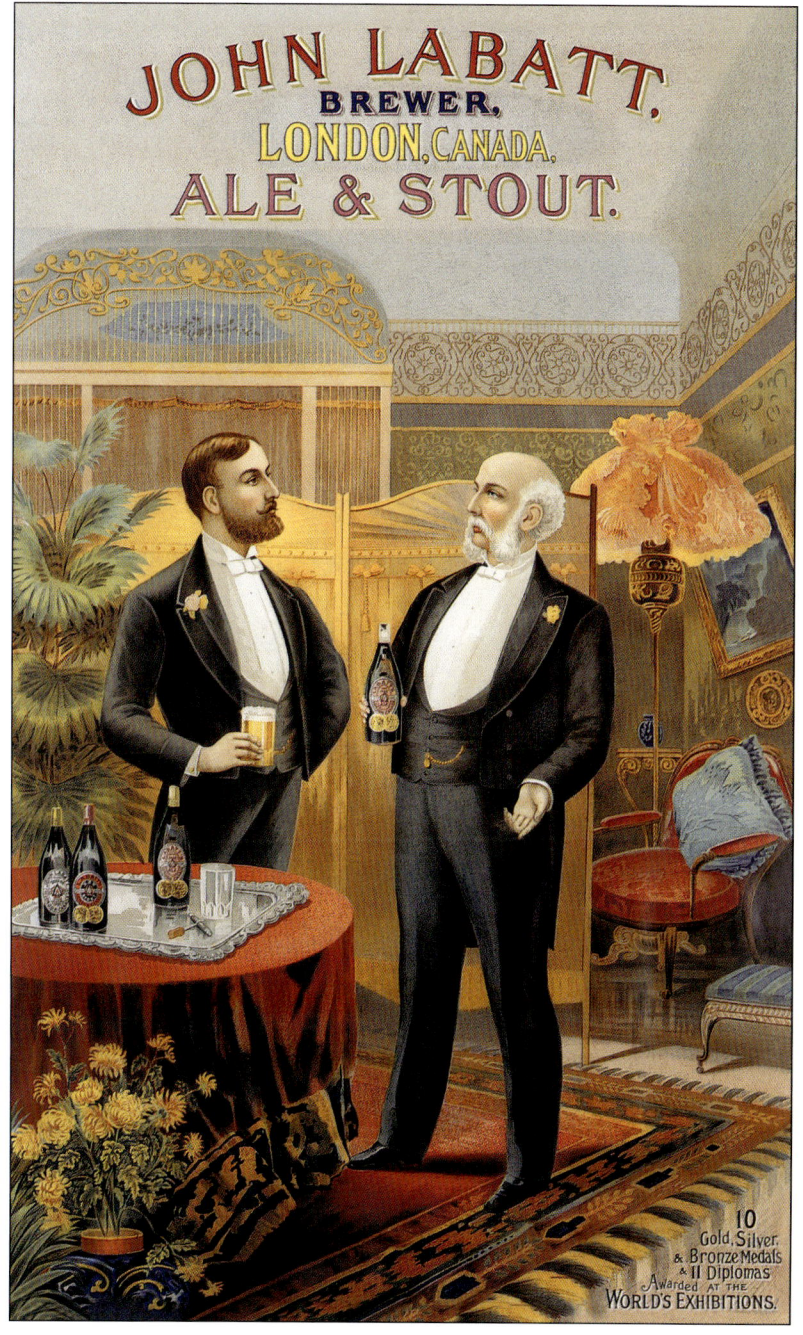

Labatt Advertising Posters, circa 1870 (opposite), 1894 (right) and circa 1900 (above)

John Labatt invoked themes of modernity and respectability for his advertising posters. To promote his brands as the best modern technology could provide, he relied upon the factory image, and he cultivated a respectable aura around his beers through his renowned "Two Gentlemen" concept. In and of themselves, these posters are truly amazing examples of nineteenth-century graphic design. By the way, of the three brands evident in the "Two Gentlemen" poster, I.P.A. was Labatt's Victorian bestseller by far. Introduced in 1867, the beer remained part of the brewery's product line-up until 1992. Courtesy, Labatt Archives and Paul Miller

BARRELS AND BOTTLES, CIRCA 1860 TO CIRCA 1900
Now much coveted by private collectors and museum curators, these artifacts were the two most common containers used to store, ship and sell beer during the nineteenth century. Time has aged these oak barrels from the Strathroy Brewing & Malting Company and Matthew Bixel with rich patinas. Meanwhile, the bottles shimmer with their crudeness and delightful flaws of manufacture. Courtesy, Jim Butler, Keith McCallum, London Regional Art and Historical Museums and Jim Maitland

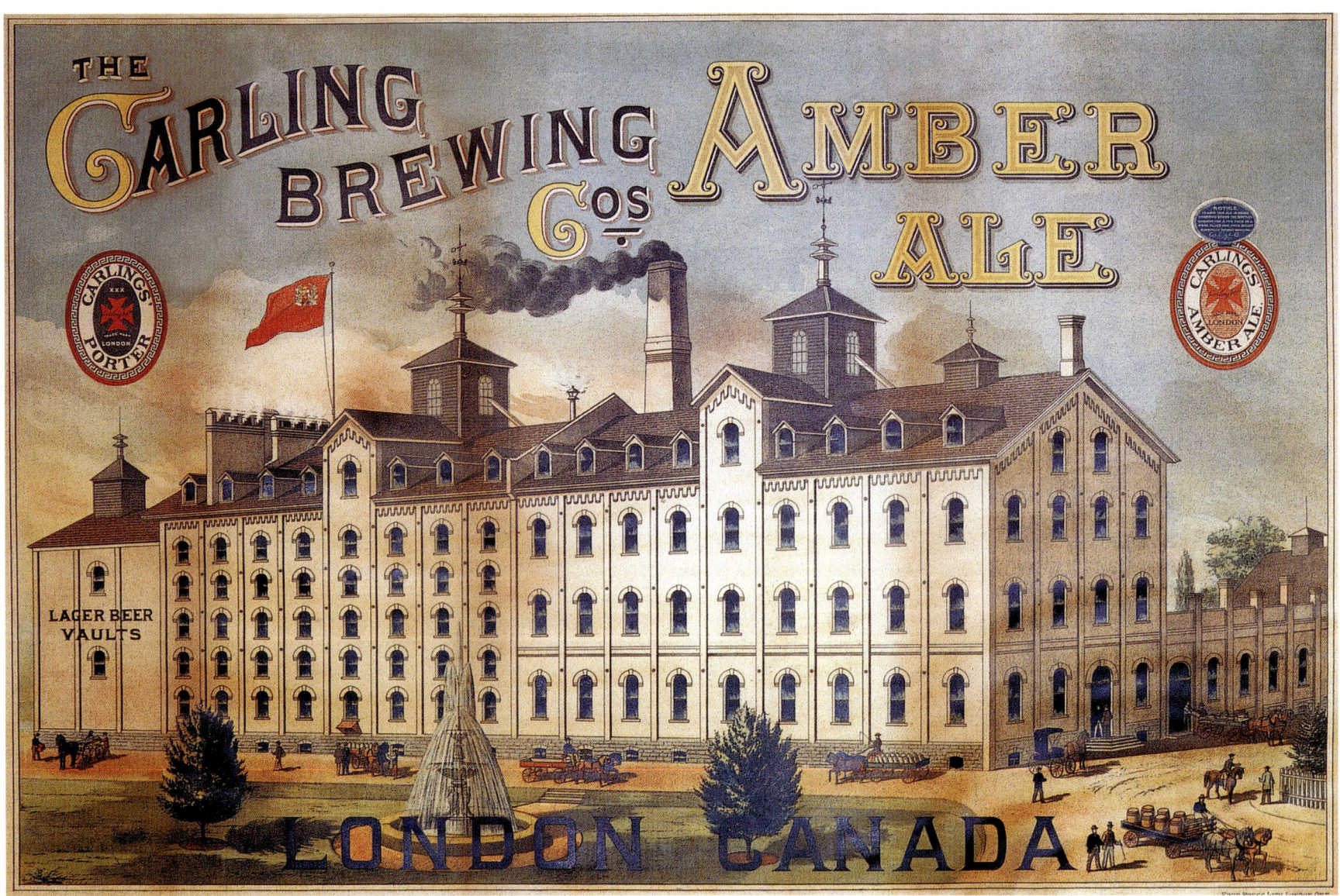

CARLING ADVERTISING POSTER, CIRCA 1895 (OPPOSITE),
PERSPECTIVE DRAWING OF THE CARLING PLANT, CIRCA 1900 (ABOVE
LEFT), JOHN CARLING, 1881 (ABOVE RIGHT) AND A CARLING AD,
1900 (RIGHT)

The Carling Brewing & Malting Company also presented a fresh and modern image through its advertising posters. However, such a public projection could be exaggerated upon occasion. For instance, the Carling brewery on Talbot Street, although massive, was never the seemingly endless monstrosity portrayed in the perspective drawing, which, incidentally, also shows mountains along the west bank of the Thames River. Interestingly, one cannot help but wonder whether John Carling based the promotional slogan, "The Old Name. The Old Fame. The Old Quality." on the slogan, "The Old Man, The Old Flag, The Old Policy," used during the federal election of 1891 by the Conservative Party in support of Sir John A. Macdonald, his loyalty to the Union Jack and his policy of tariff protectionism. Courtesy, London Regional Art and Historical Museums and J.J. Talman Regional Collection

LAGER BEER LABEL USED BY THE STRATHROY BREWING & MALTING
COMPANY, CIRCA 1900

*Matthew Bixel introduced lager brewing to Strathroy in the fall of 1876.
Thereafter, the German beverage served as the mainstay of the town's
brewing fortunes. Indeed, Bixel dominated Southwestern Ontario's lager
market for the next two decades. By the late 1890s, the brewery was
operating under the banner of the Strathroy Brewing & Malting
Company, whose successful Export Lager brand carried the enterprise
into the twentieth century. Courtesy, Jim Butler*

CHAPTER SIX

The Lager Invasion

A BOLD INTRUDER into a region dominated by ale, porter and stout, lager demands special treatment in these pages. First appearing in Middlesex at mid-century, the crisp and light German beverage rapidly surged in local popularity and convinced the thirsty to drink their beer in a revolutionary new way — ice cold. Lager, however, did not stop there and gave Strathroy the ticket to claim its place as the county's second major brewing centre.

LAGER'S EARLY YEARS IN THE COUNTY

The railway age brought an exotic foreigner to Middlesex. As German immigrant Louis Ernst announced in the *London Free Press* of September 10, 1856:

> A DELICIOUS BEVERAGE. LOUIS ERNST begs to inform his friends and the public that he has received several barrels of the best Buffalo Lager Beer, with which he is prepared to supply them at the Covent Garden Shades [his saloon]. As this is the first importation into London of this favorite beverage, L.E. strongly recommends it to the consideration of the public.

It should be emphasized that the saloonkeeper received his "Buffalo Lager" via London's Great Western Railway link to the American city.

Ernst's experiment proved a smashing success and the Teutonic arrival never looked back. By the 1860s, the beer had become a fixture in local saloons. William Hawthorn, for instance, stocked "Lager Beer of the best brands" at his Empire Saloon. Meanwhile, W.H. Rooks carried "Bauer's Lager Beer of superior quality" at his Beaver House and John White announced that he had "Huether's celebrated Lager Beer" at his Olympic Saloon. Not surprisingly, railway tracks linked London to Henry Bauer's brewery in Hamilton and Christopher Huether's brewery in Waterloo. More generally, a *London Free Press* reporter summed up the city's brisk lager trade in June 1870: "[The beer is] imported from the German districts of Berlin [Kitchener], Waterloo, and [New] Hamburg in quarter-barrels, and [is] had at most of the saloons and restaurants, the proprietors of which [make] large profits."

AN ICE-COLD BEVERAGE

Although it is rather difficult to account for changes in public taste, it would seem that lager's popularity was rooted in the fact that the beverage was traditionally served ice-cold. Now, imagine that you are a farmer in, let us say, the Lambeth area. The year is 1860 and it is the end of the August harvest season. After feeding your horses and yourself, you finally get your heavy wagon-loads of grain rolling towards London on the appointed day. As you make your way along the "Wharncliffe Highway," the intensity of the rising sun and a heavy blanket of humidity tell you that the month-long heatwave has no intention of surrendering its grip on your discomfort. The dusty road is no kinder. By the time you arrive at London's market, the temperature has risen to 85° Fahrenheit. After some hard bargaining with several penny-wise grain merchants, you at last secure your reward for a year's worth of sweat, backaches, frustration and constant weather worries. It is now early afternoon and the sun has baked the atmosphere to a wicked 99° Fahrenheit. At this moment, a beer or two would really hit the spot. Your thirst delivers you to Hawthorn's Empire Saloon where you are faced with a choice — a mug of heavy porter served at basement-temperature or, in the lingo of the saloonkeeper, a frosty "schooner" of ice-cold lager. The decision is obvious. The porter can wait until October.

Although fictional, the above portrayal faithfully embodies a very important dimension of lager's impact. As a chilled beverage, it was an ideal summertime refreshment. A *London Free Press* article from early 1878 aptly illustrates this:

> COOL AS ICE. — Our friend Campbell, of the St. Nicholas [Restaurant], is a decidedly cool man, and evidently intends to keep his customers cool through the heat of the summer. He has converted his large dining-room into a "Lager Beer Parlor," where his numerous customers can enjoy a nice "free lunch" with their lager every day from 11 a.m. until 1 o'clock p.m. . . . Everything Campbell serves is of the best quality the home and foreign markets produce. Carling & Co.'s Lager is the *only* lager served in this establishment.

Free lunches were common in London's competitive saloon trade and were invariably heavily salted to stimulate customers' thirst. The next year, the *London*

Free Press followed with a snippet of lager logic: "It is an incomprehensible fact, based on scientific principles, that as the sun grows warmer the lager grows colder."

Of course, barkeepers discovered that ale, porter and stout could also be served cold. Over time, more and more customers came to prefer chilled beer, regardless of its style. In this sense, lager, while never dominating the nineteenth-century beer market, had a most profound influence. Although the turn towards cool beer took decades to revolutionize the entire beer world, it is to Victorian lager saloons that we owe our current practice of sipping on not warm, but cold beer.

EARLY LAGER BREWING

Lager brewing had an rather inauspicious start in Middlesex. Nevertheless, honours for the county's first lager brewery belong to German immigrant Frederick Kompass (also spelled Friedrich Kompahs). In the autumn of 1860, Kompass opened a tiny lager factory in his saloon on King Street near London's market square. However, out-of-town competitors in the province's Germanic settlements humbled this venture. By early 1862, Kompass had abandoned the attempt. The void he left was not filled until 1869, when, amidst a notable surge in lager's popularity in London, W. & J. Carling inaugurated the beverage's production at their brewery. Although undoubtedly familiar with the principles of lager brewing, the Carlings hired "an experienced German brewer" from Buffalo to supervise the diversification project. A pleased *London Free Press* journalist observed that "now local demands can be supplied by the home product." However, the endeavour turned out to be a brief flirtation. For unstated reasons, the Carlings terminated lager-making sometime during the early 1870s. Perhaps, the planning and construction of a new brewery had diverted their attention. Sustained lager production finally arrived in Middlesex when Matthew Bixel breathed new life into Strathroy's Western Steam Brewery.

THE BIXEL STORY

The Bixel story in Canada actually begins in a politically unstable mid-nineteenth-century Europe. During the 1840s, calls for reforms, ranging from broader voting rights to outright revolution, sent waves of alarm coursing through the continent's royal palaces. In Württemberg, one of the more southerly German principalities, the general unrest of the era and fears about the militaristic posturing of neighbouring states compelled many to emigrate for a more stable life in North America. Among the thousands who fled Württemberg was the family of Maximus and Sophia Bixel, who settled in Oxford County in late 1847 or early 1848. Maximus, a brewmaster, was drawn to the area because of its hop fields (contiguous

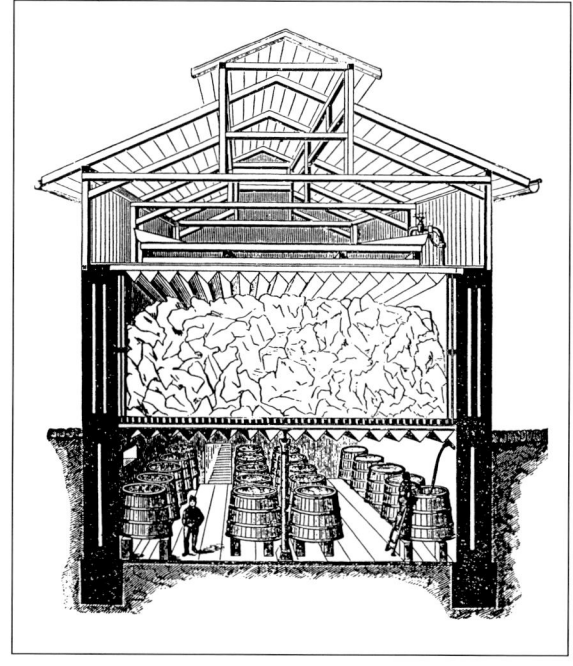

USING ICE STACKED ABOVE THE BREWERY CELLAR TO KEEP LAGER COOL, 1885
One of lager's attractions during typically hot and hazy Canadian summers was that it was served ice-cold — a thoroughly refreshing proposition. It was also brewed and aged at frosty temperatures. County lager brewers relied upon the above depicted method to cool their breweries.

OPPOSITE: LAGER SALOON ANNOUNCEMENTS FROM THE *LONDON FREE PRESS* ISSUES FOR (TOP TO BOTTOM) SEPTEMBER 6, 1869, MAY 5, 1879 AND OCTOBER 24, 1879
Competition amongst London's lager saloons was stiff. So much so, that price wars often flared up. By the way, it was commonly held in the nineteenth century that lager, as a crisp and lighter-tasting beer, was non-intoxicating. (computer enhanced)

MATTHEW BIXEL, CIRCA 1880
A native of Württemberg, Germany, Matthew Bixel came from a brewing family. He first settled in Ingersoll, moved to Brantford, returned to Ingersoll and then brought his energy and keen business sense to Strathroy in 1875. Courtesy, Arthur Bixel

OPPOSITE: MATTHEW BIXEL'S LAGER BEER BREWERY FROM PAGE'S ILLUSTRATED HISTORICAL ATLAS OF MIDDLESEX COUNTY, 1878
Bixel turned Strathroy's Western Steam Brewery into one of the province's busiest lager breweries. Sales of his lager dominated Southwestern Ontario and his success accorded Strathroy status as Middlesex County's second most important brewing centre.

to the large ones in northeastern Middlesex). One of the Bixels' sons, Matthew, a traditionally trained journeyman brewer, joined them later in 1848.

Upon his arrival, Maximus Bixel established a brewery in the village of Oxford (now Ingersoll). His beer was popular with bipeds and his brewery was a favourite hangout for bovine quadrupeds. At the village council meeting of January 1, 1852, Bixel complained that cows had made their way into his granary, feasted upon his barley stores and then rudely slept off their repast on his malthouse floor. About two years later, fire destroyed the brewery. Sometime thereafter, Bixel and his wife returned to their native land; however, at least two of their children remained in North America. After a brief move to the United States, Leonard (also spelled Leonhardt or Löwenhardt) settled in Plattsville, Canada West, where he conducted a cabinet and chair factory. Meanwhile, Matthew established a cigar-making business in Brantford. Another son, Antonie, may have also stayed behind or he may have returned temporarily to Württemberg with his parents.

In 1858, Adam Hunt built Ingersoll's second brewery, which he sold to a Mr. J. Dunn, who, in turn, sold it to Antonie Bixel in 1859. Antonie ran the Charles Street brewery for a year or two before selling out to his brothers, Leonard and Matthew. Antonie eventually wound up in Elko, Nevada, where he ran a brewery from 1874 until 1884. Leonard and Matthew remained partners until 1875, when, according to the recollection of Charles F. Bixel, Leonard's oldest son, they dissolved the firm of L. & M. Bixel because they could not get along. If such was the case, then the announced sale of Strathroy's defunct Western Steam Brewery was Matthew's convenient escape from an unworkable business relationship with his brother.

MATTHEW BIXEL

Just prior to Matthew Bixel's arrival in Strathroy, about one hundred Ingersoll gentlemen, chiefly business owners and civic officials, organized a complimentary dinner at the McMurray House hotel in honour of their departing friend, the brewer. The *Ingersoll Chronicle* reflected upon the town's loss:

> This purchase [of the Strathroy brewery] of course necessitated the removal of Mr. Bixel from among us, an event we are certain is much regretted by every person who knew him here. There can be no one acquainted with him without bearing the most friendly feelings towards him. Since he came to Ingersoll he has always been known as an honorable gentleman in the strictest sense, enterprising in his business, and always living and acting towards his fellow townsmen in such a manner as to be held in their highest esteem. Mr. Bixel was one of our

CYRUS BIXEL, CIRCA 1885
In late 1880, Matthew Bixel took his oldest son, Cyrus, into partnership. The new firm of M. Bixel & Son carried Strathroy's lager brewery to even greater heights. Courtesy, Arthur Bixel

BEER LORE — The world's most dreadful beer pun of all time appeared in the *London Free Press* in 1879: "Lager beer is more than a tonic; it is Teu-tonic." Groan!

very best citizens, and we can assure the people of Strathroy that their town gains largely by our loss. He will make business and friends in Strathroy as he has done here. We have no fears of his success anywhere. Therefore, although we are loath to part with a citizen of the stamp of Mr. Bixel, we are somewhat consoled by the fact that brighter prospects are in store for him at Strathroy than could possibly be expected here.

Hardly maudlin, the Strathroy correspondent for the *London Free Press* contentedly noted that the Western Steam Brewery was now "in experienced and able hands." Immediately upon arriving in Strathroy in late October 1875, Bixel put his new acquisition into running order. Since the fall brewing season was quickly coming to a close, he had no time to convert the brewery into a lager facility. Thus forced to put his master plan on hold, he instead settled for turning out ale and porter.

BIXEL'S LAGER

In the summer of 1876, Bixel at last found the time to refurbish his brewery. That autumn, lager brewing began for the very first time in Strathroy. Despite his training in the brewing arts, Bixel hired a Mr. Meyer, "one of the most celebrated brewers of Milwaukee," to oversee lager production. While Meyer filled the brewery's vaults with barrels of lager, Bixel concluded agency arrangements across Southwestern Ontario. Come the following spring, he would be set to take the market by storm.

In 1877, Matthew Bixel's genius and hard work paid off handsomely. As he funnelled his lager into taverns, saloons and licensed shops across the region, the health of the once bankrupt brewery blossomed. In the grand scheme of things, Bixel targeted nearby London as his primary market. He was sure to advertise in the city's newspapers and he was sure to get his beer into as many of the city's venues as he could. In late May, an astonished *London Free Press* commented upon the Strathroy brewer's success: "Lager beer is the popular beverage in London this summer. Nearly all the best houses [taverns and saloons] in the city run it, and Bixel's Strathroy lager is becoming quite a household word." The popularity of Bixel's lager continued into the next year and beyond. In mid-September 1880, an informal census of local businesses taken by the *Strathroy Western Dispatch* noted that the brewer employed eight workers — a number which ranked the brewery as the third largest in Southwestern Ontario. In all likelihood, Bixel's workforce grew bigger during the ensuing brewing season. A month and a half later, Matthew Bixel took his oldest son, Cyrus, into partnership. The new firm's name was M. Bixel & Son.

A Brief Return to Ingersoll

On March 27, 1881, Matthew Bixel's brother and manager of the Ingersoll Brewery, Leonard, died from a sudden heart attack. He was in his fifty-first year. With his passing, brewing came to a local end. However, it was not the last of Bixel lager in the Oxford County town. Several months later, Matthew either rented or bought his late brother's brewery and converted it into a bottling and distribution plant. He maintained this branch of his Strathroy-based business until sometime the next year, when the railway proved to be a cheaper means of servicing west Oxford.

Lager Reappears at Carling's

In 1877-78, Carling & Co. built a three-storey lager plant onto its new brewery at Talbot and Ann Streets (see following chapter for more about this brewery). The addition had an annual capacity of around 60,000 lager kegs (smaller than standard barrels) and its icehouse could hold 600 tons of ice piled twelve feet high. Such an artificial glacier chilled the fermenting room to between 35° and 40° Fahrenheit. By the early 1880s, Louis V. Ludwig, formerly of the Philip Best brewery in Milwaukee, was serving as Carling's head lager brewer. Ironically, Bixel's success had significant bearing upon the Carlings' return to lager brewing. Quite simply, Bixel's sales triumphs in London and throughout Southwestern Ontario proved the viability of large-scale lager brewing in what was traditionally an ale, porter and stout market. The Londoners could not resist such an opportunity. With Bixel and Carling & Co., Middlesex County became Ontario's third most significant lager region behind Toronto and Germanic Waterloo County.

Looking Southeast from the Oxford Street Bridge over the Thames River Showing the Rear of Carling's Brewery on Talbot Street, circa 1885

Carling & Company constructed a lager plant onto the western wall of their new brewery in 1877-78. It appears as the three-storey addition at the end of the main building to the left of this photograph. Courtesy, J.J. Talman Regional Collection

CHAPTER SEVEN

Still an Age of Ale, Porter & Stout, 1873 to 1884

ALTHOUGH LAGER HAD a profound impact upon the Victorian beer scene, we must place the beverage in context. Quite simply, owing to predominant consumer preference, ale, porter and stout still reigned supreme in the local and overall Canadian beer markets. An ad for Jimmy Smith's Albion Saloon in London forcefully spoke to this reality: "Lager Beer Nowhere! Bass, Molson's, Carling's and Labatt's Ale on draft. Only five cents per glass. Try it and Judge for Yourselves." While one might dismiss Smith's boldness as marketing bravado, he stood on the winning side of this beer war. The German newcomer still had a long march ahead. Indeed, the quick rise of Robert Arkell's new ale and porter brewery, plant expansion at Carling and Labatt, further agency creation by the same two London brewers, the rejuvenation of the Delaware Brewery and the development of ale, porter and stout brand names demonstrate the sustained popularity of British- and Irish-style malt liquors. Tellingly, Bixel and Carling were the only county brewers to manufacture lager during the last three decades of the nineteenth century. Labatt did not even bother with lager brewing until well after 1900.

THE KENSINGTON BREWERY

After careers in hotelkeeping and independent malting (see feature), Robert Arkell ventured into the brewing trade in the London suburb of Kensington (later London West) sometime in late 1872 or early 1873. His brewery, designed by London's foremost architectural firm, Robinson & Tracy, stood on the north side of today's Walnut Street just east of Forward Avenue. Convenient access to an unfailing spring of water dictated this hillside site.

Billed as the Kensington Brewery, Arkell's plant consisted of several outbuildings for storing grain, barrels and bottles and a four-storey main building for malting and brewing. To cool the brewery during the summer and thus permit year-round brewing, the architects cleverly incorporated the icehouse into the fermenting room's design. Since Arkell was not a trained brewer, his brewery was more of an investment rather than a "hands-on" operation. He hired a Mr. Townsend as his brewmaster and Joseph Stalker as his manager and travelling agent. While Townsend's background remains a mystery, we know that Stalker, formerly a long-serving travelling agent for Labatt's, was an experienced beer-seller. As the *London Free Press* noted: "In his hands there is every reason to believe that the interests of the Kensington Brewery will not suffer." Of course, this is not to suggest that Arkell had no idea about the brewing business. His previous involvement with malting was certainly an asset. More importantly, however, Arkell's broad experience as a hotelier blessed him with the knowledge of what most local beer-lovers desired — finely crafted ale and porter.

ARKELL'S RISING STAR

With a source of good water, a capable staff and an enticing product line consisting of East India Pale Ale, Amber Ale and XXX Porter, Arkell entered the field of competition well prepared to seize his share of success. And he did precisely that. Within weeks of completing his first batch, Arkell's brews had taken the market by storm. Indeed, the *London Free Press* gushed that ale from the Kensington Brewery was "All the Rage!" By mid-May 1873, Arkell, by turning out 100 barrels per week (1,600 cases of 24 in modern terms), had rapidly become a serious challenge to Labatt and Carling in the local arena. Naturally, such fortune brought about expansion, which came in the form of a new and much larger warehouse in the early fall of 1873 and an enlarged brewhouse the next year. In the spring of 1875, a grateful Arkell thanked the beer-drinking public:

> KENSINGTON ALE AND PORTER BREWERY. — Robert Arkell, proprietor, recognizes, with many thanks, the liberal support extended to him since his commencement. The increased demand for his "FINE ALES" and "GENUINE PORTER" establishes the gratifying fact that his efforts to produce a first-class article have proven a success. He feels much satisfaction in stating that the "PORTER" manufactured by him. . . is winning unusual favor, being acknowledged by consumers to possess all the exhilarating qualities and nourishing virtues for which the Dublin

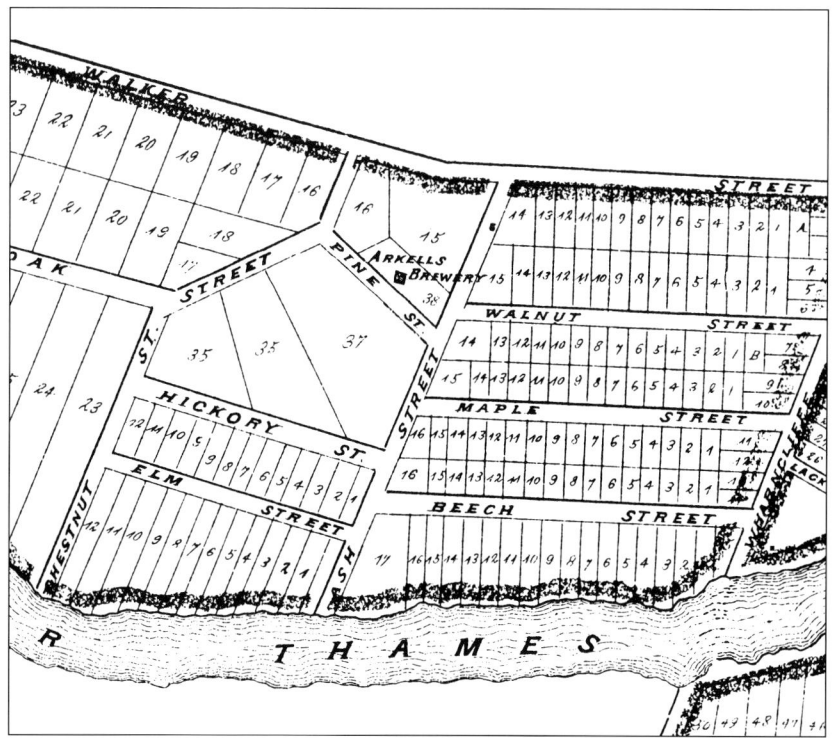

DETAIL FROM A MAP OF KENSINGTON VILLAGE, 1878
In order to access a never-failing source of spring water, Robert Arkell built his brewery upon a hillside site in the London suburb of Kensington Village. By the way, nearly every street appearing on this map has had its name changed. Today, we know Pine Street as the western extension of Walnut Street, Oak Street as Forward Avenue and Walker Street as Riverside Drive.

and London [England] stouts stand so highly pre-eminent. To this article he takes pleasure in inviting special notice, as being worthy of marked favor by all desiring a nutritious and pure malt beverage. To be had in bottle or wood. Also, fine Amber Ales.

A representative of Dun, Wiman & Company seconded Arkell's triumphant claims, albeit more neutrally and without the puff: "[He] is doing a good business and makes [good] on his transactions." The Dun agent further estimated Arkell's pecuniary strength to be around $15,000, an amount that was not far behind that of the county's second largest brewer, John Labatt. At the time, Arkell was stretching beyond London into such places as Mitchell, St. Thomas and Ingersoll. However, the Kensington Brewery's primary target continued to be the Forest City.

PROBLEMS CONQUERED

Despite his obvious success, difficulties posed by relative remoteness confronted Arkell in his wooing of London. Since physical presence was itself an excellent form of advertising, city brewers enjoyed a decided advantage simply by being in London. The Kensington Brewery, located beyond London's limits, might as well have been in Komoka when it came to having a face in Middlesex's most lucrative beer market. Compounding matters, since it was largely an age of travel by foot or horse, getting to his brewery was hardly convenient. To overcome these marketing dilemmas, Arkell was forced to recruit downtown city agents, whose establishments were central to Londoners. His first representative was W. Simpson Smith. From 1876 until 1881, Arkell's agency was next located at the Revere House, the hotel which he still owned but had lately leased out. Thereafter, the agency was housed in Longan & Company's liquor store on Dundas Street. Arkell also relied upon two other techniques to overcome his relative isolation. One, he ran daily advertisements in city newspapers. Two, he cultivated a large mail-order business by emphasizing in his ads that he would readily accept postal demands for his ales and porter. This measure made the Kensington Brewery only a postcard away.

Even if he had not adopted such an aggressive marketing plan, Arkell would have likely survived. After all, John Allaster, John Hamilton and David Haystead ran their small breweries without maintaining a strong public presence (not surprisingly, a strategy that limited the growth of these breweries). However, it is clear that a very ambitious nature drove Arkell and that he not only chose, but, more importantly, also knew how to be a major player on the local scene. Just as significant is the fact that Arkell opted to brew ale and porter and not lager. He

BEER LORE — From 1689 through to the 1710s, steadily increasing excise duties placed upon beer and malt helped to finance England's various war efforts against France. If it were not for these taxes, the sun might never have shone on the British Empire.

recognized that ale and porter brewing was his ticket to success.

THE UNTIMELY DEMISE OF THE KENSINGTON BREWERY

Unfortunately for Robert Arkell, his success did not last. On the early morning of January 26, 1882, flames were spotted rising from the Kensington Brewery. Witnesses called out the alarm and, within minutes, thirty to forty of Arkell's neighbours were valiantly trying to save the buildings and stock from the fire. At first, they were stymied by an uncooperative water valve that had been frozen shut by the cold winter air. Plain bad luck made things even worse, as thawing attempts broke the pipe that fed the valve. Unwilling to concede defeat, Arkell's army of friends organized a pail-and-bucket brigade, the only other alternative left to them in a village lacking its own fire department. However, it proved to be too little too late and the fury had nearly run its course by the time city firefighters arrived on the scene. When dawn's light hit the hillside, Arkell's brewery was in ruins. Of the main building, "nothing remained but a few crumbling walls, smoking ashes, charred machinery and broken bottles." Authorities fixed the total loss at $12,000, an amount hardly offset by Arkell's $6,200 in fire insurance coverage. Around $2,000 in cellar stock, the brewery ledgers and some office papers were the only things rescued. A defective stovepipe was later identified as the fire's cause, although Arkell personally believed that his brewery had been hit by an arsonist.

In spite of the fire, Arkell escaped overall financial disaster. He was a careful businessman, who enjoyed the benefits of considerable real estate investments and substantial savings (in June 1881, for instance, he sold his Revere House hotel for a reported $10,000). In addition, he still owned a profitable grain and produce wholesaling business. Nevertheless, for reasons that remain unclear, Arkell did not rebuild the Kensington Brewery. He lived out his remaining days with his wife, Maria, in their house next to the former brewery site. On July 16, 1883, fifty-four-year-old Robert Arkell died from apoplexy. Since the Arkells had no children, his estate was split amongst his widow, two sisters, five brothers and longtime Arkell family friend, Samuel Eccles. It is interesting to imagine to what heights Robert Arkell might have carried his brewery had it not caught fire.

KENSINGTON BREWERY AD FROM THE LONDON FREE PRESS OF JULY 11, 1877
To maintain a constant physical presence in London's lucrative beer market, Robert Arkell was a dedicated and often creative advertiser in the city's newspapers. (computer enhanced)

BEER QUOTE — "A quart of ale is a dish for a king." William Shakespeare, *Winter's Tale*, Act IV

THE NEW CARLING BREWERY, TALBOT STREET AT ANN, 1875

Taking two years to construct, the new Carling brewery building was the largest of its kind in Canada when it opened in mid-1875. The presence of a solitary scaffold, visible to the left of the rightmost cupola, suggests that this photograph was taken shortly before brewing began at the facility. Courtesy, J.J. Talman Regional Collection

CARLING'S NEW BREWERY

By the early 1870s, it had become clear to the Carlings that the jumbled assemblage of buildings and piecemeal additions that served as their brewery would limit their future ability to remain competitive. To be sure, W. & J. Carling was a major player in the Canadian industry, but, in order to stay that way, the firm required a modern, state-of-the-art facility. Consequently, the brothers commissioned David Roberts, a Toronto-based architect, to draw up the necessary plans. Meanwhile, W. & J. Carling acquired several acres of land on the west side of Talbot Street between Ann and Piccadilly. The presence of a powerful spring at the property dictated the location. The spring flowed at a rate of 60,000 gallons per day and its waters were a constant 52° Fahrenheit — perfectly suited to meet the brothers' requirements.

Construction started in 1873. Two years and 2,500,000 bricks later, a massive five-storey structure stood on the site. Measuring 150 by 250 feet — a ground-floor area nearly the size of a modern football field — and boasting an annual malting capacity of 80,000 bushels and an annual brewing capacity of around 70,000 barrels (2,500,000 gallons), it was then the single largest brewery building in Canada. With typical Carling foresight, these figures allowed plenty of room for future growth. The brewery's interior featured four Hughes' Patent malting kilns, a 400-bushel mash tun, a 9,000-gallon steam-copper (reputedly North America's largest) and eight 5,500-gallon fermentation vats. Complementing the enormity of these fixtures, steam powered the entire plant. Ultimately, the efficient, factory-like layout of the building and its heightened scales of economy blessed the Carlings with an enviable profitability. All told, the construction bill amounted to $100,000. Since it had dramatically sharpened the Carlings' competitive edge in the race to dominate Canada's beer market, it was a wise investment. In July 1875, brewing activity began in the new building. A lager brewhouse was added to the new brewery in 1877-78 (see preceding chapter). The addition was quite telling of the Carlings' bread and butter business. Ale and porter came first, while lager was an afterthought.

CARLING & COMPANY

A new firm inaugurated brewing at the new plant. On June 30, 1875, W. & J. Carling was officially dissolved. The next day, William Carling, John Carling, Joshua Dixon Dalton (John's brother-in-law and the Carling brothers' plant manager since the 1860s) and Thomas Henry "Harry" Carling (John's eldest son) formally joined together as Carling & Company. Under the terms of partnership, each partner received one-fourth of annual profits and was entitled to draw up to $200 per month against his profit share. However, the firm only managed the brewery and did not own its physical assets. Instead, Carling & Co. paid a yearly rent of $5,000 plus eight percent interest to William and John Carling, who maintained ownership of the plant and real estate. Still, by incorporating the next Carling generation — namely, twenty-four-year-old Harry Carling — into the brewery's upper management echelon, the formation of Carling & Co. should properly be considered as a mechanism of succession in what was essentially a family business. The partnership agreement also stipulated that each partner was to devote his full attention to the brewery and to no other business, except by consent of others in the firm. Needless to say, the others had no objection to John Carling pursuing his burgeoning political career (see feature). Indeed, in many ways, John's public life *was* brewery business.

THOMAS HENRY CARLING, CIRCA 1898
Popularly known as "Harry," T.H. Carling became a part-owner in the family business with the formation of Carling & Co. in 1875. He belonged to the third Carling generation to brew in London and his forte was production management. Courtesy, J.J. Talman Regional Collection

BEER LORE — Ancient Celts believed beer was a warrior's drink and the beverage of the gods.

THE CARLING BREWERY AFTER THE FIRE (ABOVE AND OPPOSITE), MID-FEBRUARY 1879
The sheer hollowness portrayed in the image above speaks volumes about the awesome effects of the Carling fire of February 13, 1879. Meanwhile, all that remained inside the great brewing landmark were its scorched copper and iron guts, contorted and convulsed almost beyond recognition. Incidentally, February 13, 1879 was not a Friday, but a very unlucky Thursday. Courtesy, J.J. Talman Regional Collection

THE CARLING BREWERY FIRE

Unfortunately, disaster struck the new Carling brewery within four years of its opening. Sometime during the wee hours of February 13, 1879, a malt kiln overheated and ignited a small fire, which, as the night-watchman busily shared some beer with friends, grew into a considerable blaze before being detected. Although seemingly tamed by firefighters, the fire later triggered an explosion which literally blew off the building's roof and engulfed its interior in an uncontrollable fury. An unmerciful wind only made matters worse. By eight o'clock in the morning, when the flames had burned themselves out, all but the brewery's northern bottling wing, cellarage space and walls had been destroyed. Moreover, as if to have salt rubbed into a most unkind wound, Carling & Co. had lost 100,000 bushels of barley and 800 tons of ice at a very crucial time of year — the eve of the spring brewing season. Insurance only covered $50,000 on the structure and $25,000 on the stock. All told, the conflagration left behind an estimated $200,000 in damages. A crestfallen John Carling returned from Ottawa the next day. A crowd of 400 met him at London's Great Western Railway station to offer sympathies. Kind words even came from his political foes.

Most sadly, the fire claimed something much more precious than physical property. The firm's senior partner and technical leader, William Carling, contracted pneumonia while fighting the blaze. He died from the illness two weeks later. All of London mourned William's passing and city residents turned out en masse to pay their respects to the departed brewer. Indicating just how warmly regarded he was, Carling's funeral cortege measured one and a half miles long. He willed the bulk of his estate, including his share of the business and brewery property, to his brother, John, and nephew, Harry.

REBUILDING

Despite their grief, the remaining partners had to carry on without William. Of immediate concern was finding an alternate production facility. Luckily, their former plant on Waterloo Street had yet to be sold or torn down. Grateful for the opportunity, the Carlings transferred their malting operations to the old quarters. For funding, John and Harry Carling negotiated a loan with the Bank of British North America. The amount was undisclosed, but it was likely substantial in order to meet the weighty cost of rebuilding. In return, the Carlings pledged the old brewery lands as security. To sweeten the deal, the Carlings threw in some bills of exchange and mortgage debts owed to them by other parties. These they sold to the bank for one dollar. In other words, the Carlings transferred some of their personal "accounts receivable" to their lender for a song. It was a desperate, but necessary concession. Meanwhile, Carling & Co. stepped up pressure on dealers and agents to remit monies owing to the brewery.

Since, much to his credit, the architect had designed the brewery's exterior walls to withstand the effects of fire, Carling & Co. was spared the agony of having to rebuild from scratch. In early March, local contractors, Christie & Green, began reconstruction in earnest. Time was of the essence and the

AN EXAMPLE OF THE "PHOENIX" ARTWORK, 1880
The rapid rebuilding of the burned-out Carling brewery was a triumph over horrible devastation. Carling & Co. appropriately adopted a phoenix motif to adorn company stationery. By the way, the fountain and garden were actually located to the east of the building and not to the south as pictured.

BEER LORE — In 1890, the combined production of beer in Germany, Britain, Ireland and the United States, then the world's leading beer producers, was 22,990,585,450 pints. If this amount was stored in the typical pint bottles of the era, and if those bottles were then arranged end to end, the resulting chain of bottles would be 3,628,565 miles long, a length that would wrap around the equator 145 and a half times!

builders posted performance bonds to have the work done by May 1. By the beginning of April, things had progressed so rapidly that John Carling headed back to Parliament Hill. Two weeks later, the lager plant was up and running. And two weeks after that, the rest of the brewery was completed. Costing upwards of $85,000, the whole project was nothing short of miraculous and it was as if a phoenix had risen from the pile of ashes. Indeed, such an image of resurrection later crowned the artwork appearing on company stationery.

Actual ale and porter brewing recommenced at 4 a.m. on April 29, but not before a very proud John Carling returned from Ottawa to host a grand banquet inside the rebuilt brewery. Attended by 150 guests, whose ranks included brewery workers, construction tradesmen and invited dignitaries, the celebration was marked by a bountiful meal, congratulatory speeches, lots of mirth and, of course, plenty of beer. The first toast was to "the health and future prosperity of Hon. John Carling," who responded by thanking everyone for their sympathy and help. Although mostly upbeat, he noted that the happiness of the day was marred only by the untimely passing of his brother. It was a sober reminder.

THE CARLING BREWING & MALTING COMPANY

On December 1, 1882, the Carling Brewing & Malting Company of London, Limited (Carling B. & M.) was constituted under a federal charter to assume the assets and operation of the Carling brewery. Middlesex's first incorporated brewing company, its initial capitalization stood at $200,000 divided into 2,000 shares with a nominal value of $100 each. The following individuals initially subscribed stock:

John Carling - 600 shares ($60,000 nominal value)
T.H. Carling - 200 shares ($20,000 nominal value)
John Beattie - 50 shares ($5,000 nominal value)
J.R. Minhinnick - 50 shares ($5,000 nominal value)
Robert Fox - 50 shares ($5,000 nominal value)
W.P.R. Street - 50 shares ($5,000 nominal value)

These six men also formed Carling B. & M.'s first board of directors, with John Beattie as president. Notable blocks of the outstanding shares were later taken up by members of the Carling family, Daniel Macfie and Josiah Blackburn, publisher of the *London Free Press* and a staunch political supporter of John Carling and the Conservative Party. It should be noted that one could not buy Carling shares on the open stock market — Carling B. & M. was a private entity.

On the face of things, it would seem that William Carling's death, Joshua D. Dalton's passing three years later and John Carling's growing political responsibilities brought about the incorporation. Then again, the inclusion of those outside the family into the ownership group reveals that the Carlings wished to broaden the brewery's management outlook, a prudent move if one wanted to compete on the rough-and-tumble national stage. John Rowe Minhinnick, a prominent oil refiner and dealer, understood the dynamics of distance shipping and how to market liquids both nationally and internationally. Since both commodities were distributed through agency arrangements, there was little essential difference between marketing oil and beer. William Purvis Rochfort Street, a senior partner in the legal firm of Street & Becher, possessed a wealth of knowledge about commercial and financial law. And John Beattie and Robert Fox respectively had extensive experience in the retail and financial services sectors. Still, Carling B. & M. remained very much a family business. Special clauses in the corporation's charter placed sharp restrictions on the sale and ownership of shares. Essentially, these terms guaranteed John and Harry Carling majority control of the company.

The manner in which John and Harry Carling transferred their joint ownership of the brewery over to Carling B. & M. suggests yet another reason lay behind the incorporation. The first step in this process called for the appointment of trustees to hold the physical and financial assets of the incorporated company. These trustees were Frank Smith of Toronto, Donald McInnes of Hamilton and Daniel Macfie of London. On behalf of Carling B. & M., the trustees purchased the brewery property and machinery from the Carlings for $150,000 — $75,000 up front and $75,000 payable through a six-year mortgage at a half-yearly interest rate of six percent. Of the first $75,000, the Carlings received $50,000 as soon as the brewery passed out of their hands on December 1. The remaining $25,000 was due three months later, but the Carlings were willing to accept $25,000 worth of stock in lieu of this amount. They probably ended up taking the stock. If an independent valuator estimated the brewery to be worth more than $150,000, then the overage was also due in cash to the Carlings (the valuation has been lost to time). Considering the sizeable up front cash payment and keeping in mind that the Carlings had previously taken out a large rebuilding loan, it would seem that the

CARLING & CO. AD FROM THE LONDON FREE PRESS OF APRIL 6, 1881
As this newspaper announcement attests, Carling & Co. needed about two years to recover completely from the brewery fire. To maintain trade, the firm advertised that product quality had not suffered in the least. (computer enhanced)

OPPOSITE: LABATT'S NEW BREWERY, LOOKING SOUTHEAST FROM TALBOT STREET NEAR SIMCOE, CIRCA 1875

A crippling fire forced John Labatt to rebuild in 1874. His new brewery, while not as large as Carling's, was still a marvel of technology and possessed an enviable capacity in its own right. Subsequent additions built to the east and southeast of this building further enhanced Labatt's production capabilities. Note all the venting. Courtesy, J.J. Talman Regional Collection

BEER QUOTE —
When neebors anger at a plea
And just as wud can be,
How easy can the barley bree
Cement the quarrel!
It's aye the cheapest lawyer's fee,
To taste the barrel.
Robert Burns

incorporation was also the Carlings' means of reducing or even eliminating their personal debts without losing control of the family business. In short, John and Harry Carling had sold their brewery and yet they had not. It was a clever scheme. To boot, it was above board and perfectly legal.

LABATT'S NEW BREWERY

John Labatt's decision to build a new ale and porter brewery was abruptly foisted upon him by the cruelties of fate. Between four and five o'clock on the morning of March 5, 1874, while his night-watchman soundly slept, a fire broke out in the engine room of Labatt's brewery. A passerby rang the alarm, but it would prove to be of little help. At the time, London's fire department was poorly equipped owing to municipal underfunding — a deplorable situation that had long caused considerable public outrage. As an inadequate water supply and bursting old hoses severely hampered the firefighters, the blaze spread throughout the entire brewery. By sunrise, Labatt's enterprise had been reduced to smoldering heaps of ash and charred rubble. Except a small portion of the cellar stock, everything — the engine house, malthouse, brewhouse, store rooms, drying kiln and icehouse — had fallen prey to the flames. Although reporters did not venture an estimate of total damages, Labatt's $21,000 in fire insurance policies did not even cover the $30,000 in malt lost that morning, let alone the rest of his destroyed property. Ultimately, the disaster presented John Labatt with two options — quit brewing or rebuild. Having spent so much time, energy and money growing a large agency trade across Southwestern Ontario, the plucky Labatt chose the latter course. His choice had its challenges.

The most immediate obstacle — finding money — stretched the brewer's financial resources to the limit. Most acutely, the quest for funds saw Labatt liquidate his personal savings and investments. Indeed, he even auctioned off the contents of his house! He also turned to his mother, the keeper of the family fortune, for a loan. Eliza, of course, responded favourably to her son's request. While Labatt may have approached corporate lending institutions, it would seem that no loans were ever granted, or at least not those secured either by a real estate mortgage or by a chattel mortgage (the fire, after all, had robbed Labatt of his chattels).

By the way, the subject of loans brings up two interesting urban legends that persist in London to this very day. The first is that the Carlings spotted Labatt a loan and the second is that Labatt returned the favour after the Carling fire. Neither of these scenarios is likely true for two primary reasons. Firstly, the Carlings

TYPICAL PRICES, 1873 TO 1884

RETAIL (not including deposit charges):
$1.00 per doz. bottles of Labatt's Ale in Goderich
$1.25 per doz. bottles of Carling's Ale in Walkerton
$1.30 per doz. bottles of Carling's Porter in Strathroy
$10.80 per barrel of Carling's Ale in Peterborough

WHOLESALE (including shipping charges):
$1.00 per doz. bottles of Labatt's Ale to St. Thomas
$1.00 per doz. bottles of Labatt's Stout to St. Thomas
$1.20 per doz. bottles of Labatt's Ale to Wingham
$1.50 per doz. bottles of Carling's Ale to Thunder Bay
$1.50 per doz. bottles of Carling's ½ & ½ to Thunder Bay
$1.50 per doz. bottles of Carling's Lager to Thunder Bay
$3.00 per firkin of Labatt's Ale to Brampton
$3.00 per firkin of Labatt's Porter to St. Thomas
$8.00 per barrel of Carling's Ale to Thunder Bay
$8.00 per barrel of Hamilton's Beer to London
$8.00 per barrel of Labatt's Ale to London
$8.00 per barrel of Labatt's Ale to Wingham

Note: Bottle sizes were not specified in the original documents, but they were probably quarts.

BEER LORE — In 1267, King Henry III of England established the Assize of Ale to fix the price of beer. Chronic offenders against the Assize's determinations were subject to the punishment of flogging.

were spending so much money building their new brewery that they probably had none to spare for Labatt. Secondly, still so pressed in 1879 that he had to borrow again from his mother to cover a financial pinch that year, Labatt probably had no funds to send the Carlings' way. Moreover, no registered mortgages were ever used by the parties to secure loans from one another and it is very unlikely that such cautious and practical businessmen would have lent money without the security of some sort of publicly registered record. In other words, despite the gentlemanly spirit which existed between the brewers (and it did exist) a paper trail most certainly would have been laid for any such loan.

The other challenge facing Labatt — time — undoubtedly tested his nerves. Unlike the Carlings, Labatt could not turn to an old brewery in order to save his season. Instead, he was forced to rebuild as rapidly as possible. Nevertheless, as a confident *London Free Press* reported, the brewer was equal to the task:

Mr. John Labatt is going energetically to work towards rebuilding the brewery which was destroyed by fire a few months since. Messrs. Robinson & Tracy, architects of this city, have had plans and specifications prepared for the new building, from which we observe that the structure about to replace the old one will be much larger, airy and commodious than the last, and indeed will afford double the capacity. The basement will be 150 feet long by 85 feet wide [nearly the size of a modern NHL ice surface] and laid out with the view of affording greater accommodation. It will contain a cellar 80 feet long by 40 feet wide, besides a fermenting room, wash-house, boiler-room, malt kiln, ice room and shipping room, all of which will be furnished with the newest and approved appliances and apparatus for prosecuting the business. The second flat will be divided into a malt-floor similar in size to the cellar underneath, a hop-room, cooler, a mammoth refrigerator, besides numerous grain bins, malt dust rooms, &c. The upper or third storey will be used exclusively as a grain storeroom. The building, when finished — and the stipulation is that it shall be completed and ready for occupancy by the 1st of July next [upcoming July], will be an ornament to the portion of the city in which it is located. The large malt house to be constructed in conjunction with the brewery will not be fully completed until the first of September next. In a very short time, then,

INDEPENDENT MALTING

The rise and fall of independent malting in Middlesex were tied to London's brewing success. In 1867, an unnamed party built a brick malthouse on the northwest corner of Ridout and York Streets. While the historical record does not yield the original owner's identity, the malthouse, with an annual capacity of 20,000 bushels, was undoubtedly erected with the intention of supplying malt to London's growing breweries. At the time, Carling's and Labatt's brewing capacities were outpacing their malting capacities.

By early 1868, Henry G. Lucas and Robert Arkell, styled as the firm of Lucas & Arkell, were running the malthouse. Lucas, an Englishman, was likely the same Henry G. Lucas who had been involved with malting and brewing in Cleveland, Ohio during the 1850s and early 1860s. Meanwhile, Arkell was one of London's most popular hotelkeepers. Exactly what prompted Arkell's move into malting is unclear, but his dealings with Carling and Labatt may have opened his eyes to their malt shortages. At any rate, Arkell left the partnership in late 1868 or early 1869. Lucas carried on producing pale, amber and roasted porter malt until the following summer, at which point commentary about him stops.

On August 4, 1869, James Slater bought the malthouse at public auction. As a produce and grain merchant, Slater, too, was connected to the local brewing scene. Under his guidance, the malting plant flowered. In 1871, a booming trade saw Slater enlarge the annual capacity of his works to 50,000 bushels. Shortly after Labatt's brewery fire some three years later, the maltster considered adding a brewery to his Forest City Malt House. It was a natural link, but he did not act upon the idea. Interestingly, had he done so he might have forced the fire-struck Labatt out of brewing.

Instead, the combined 165,000-bushel malting capacity of both the reconstructed Labatt brewery (1874) and the new Carling brewery (1875) ultimately spelled the end of Slater's malting endeavour. Indeed, in October 1879, Slater publicly announced that his malthouse was up for sale or lease. Landing neither a buyer nor a renter, Slater continued malting, but on a much smaller scale. So as not to waste capital tied up in the facility, he began to lease out the building's unused space. One of his tenants included the former lager brewer at Carling's, Louis V. Ludwig, who converted a portion of the premises into a vinegar and cider factory. In the late 1880s, malting operations ceased at Middlesex's only independent malthouse. Thereafter, Slater devoted his greatest energies to his produce and grain business.

Mr. Labatt will be able to resume business, and it is hoped that his energy, perseverance and determination to obliterate all traces of the devouring element [fire] will meet with a hearty response from his old customers, as well as many new ones, in the shape of increased orders.

Construction progressed rapidly and according to schedule. In mid-June, after the last brick had been laid, Labatt hosted the workmen and his employees at a "social" inside the building. Two weeks later, the brewer re-fired the kettle.

Standing on the site of the old brewery at the southern end of Talbot Street, the new Labatt plant was laid out on a factory plan and boasted advanced scales of economy. It had an extraordinary annual malting capacity of 85,000 bushels and an initial yearly brewing capacity of 30,000 barrels (1,080,000 gallons). Labatt's enviable malting capability, one that was beyond the needs of his brewery, signalled his desire to be a serious player in the overall malt trade. Indeed, within a few years,

BEER LORE — Forty-three breweries are recorded in Britain's legendary *Domesday Book*.

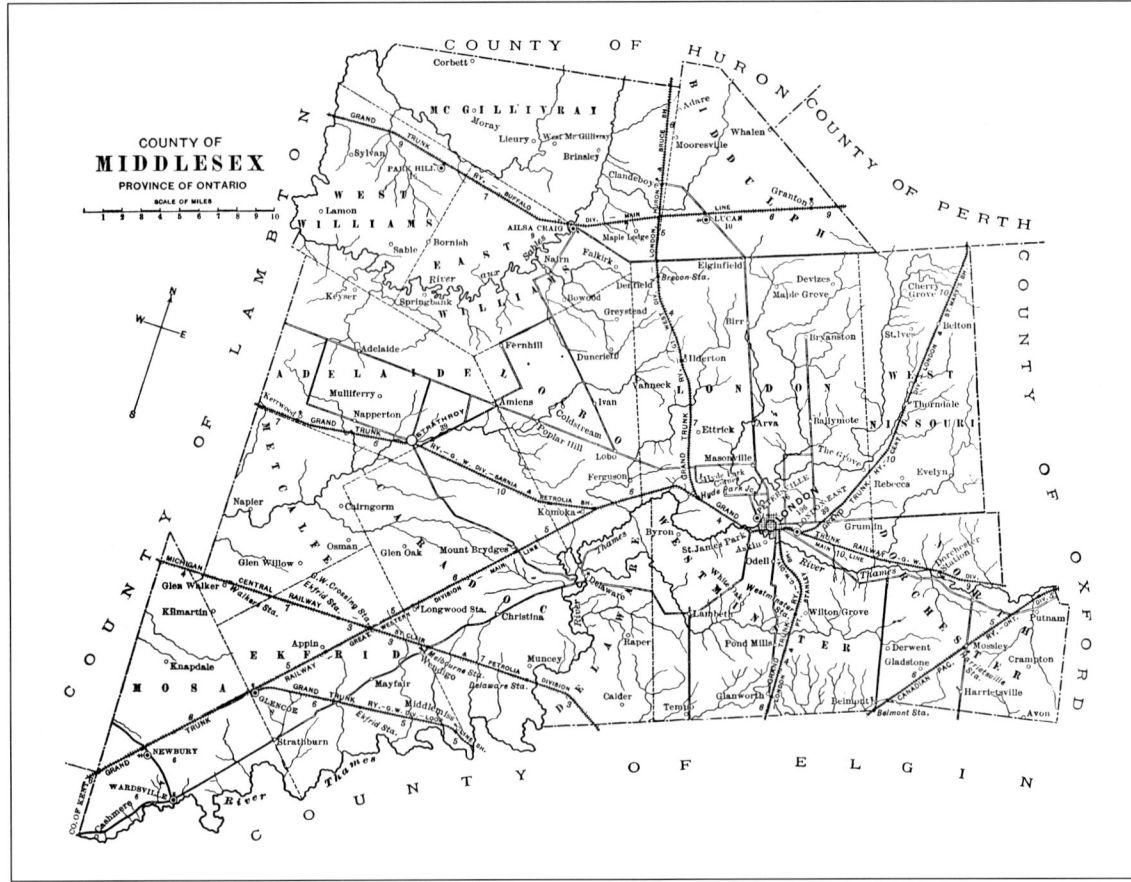

Labatt was selling malted barley across the country. His malt customers included Alexander Keith, the noted Halifax brewer. Subsequent plant additions in 1877-78, 1880 and 1881 cumulatively multiplied Labatt's brewing capacity by about thirty percent.

Ironically, the fire was a blessing in disguise, as it forced Labatt to build an efficient, streamlined facility at a time when his major competitors, including Carling, were expanding or rebuilding their breweries. Ultimately, the new brewery would allow Labatt to improve his market position quite dramatically. Still, for all too obvious reasons, not long after opening the plant, John Labatt signed a petition that demanded better equipment for city firefighters. His signature joined those of William and John Carling and dozens of other prominent locals.

MAP OF MIDDLESEX COUNTY FROM THE ONTARIO COUNTY GAZETTEER, 1885
With London as its hub, the county's railway network had reached its Victorian maturity by the mid-1880s. During the period 1873-1884 and beyond, Carling and Labatt utilized this web of track to reach customers across the breadth of the Dominion. Meanwhile, Bixel used the same lines to dominate Southwestern Ontario's lager market.

MORE AGENCIES & MORE COMMERCIAL TRAVELLERS

Increased capacity permitted Carling and Labatt to expand their agency networks beyond Southwestern Ontario and beyond the rail corridor leading to Hamilton and Toronto. Over the period from 1873 until 1884, the Londoners established sales outlets in such distant places as Walkerton, Collingwood, Peterborough, Ottawa, Montreal, Quebec City and Winnipeg. Carling even appointed a representative in Detroit, Michigan. Invariably, their agents proudly advertised that they stocked London beer. For instance, Best & Nettleton, an energetic liquor firm in Collingwood, proclaimed in the *Collingwood Enterprise*: "We are sole agents for Carling's Celebrated Amber Ales and Porters, which have been pronounced almost equal to Bass, this we sell either in Bottles, Kegs, half Barrels, Hogsheads or Puncheons, at brewery prices. All orders sent us by mail will have our prompt and careful attention." Another firm, John Wright & Brother, eagerly represented

Labatt in the same town. The Wrights' advertisements highlighted Labatt's prize record (see below) and noted that his beer was "Pronounced by all Ale Drinkers to be the best in Canada."

Whereas one or two commercial travellers sufficed in earlier years, Carling and Labatt each now maintained a team of these salesmen in order to service urban agencies and to reach every outlying hotel, saloon and licensed shop. Ultimately, the hotel trade loomed largest. The Victorian equivalent of the modern brewery rep, the typical traveller was either an industry insider or recruited from the hotelkeeping ranks. This selectivity was important, as such individuals generally understood the retail aspects of the beer business. For example, in Joseph Huggard, formerly a hotelier in Petrolia and Sarnia, Carling B. & M. had a very dynamic and talented salesman. On just one trip to the Georgian Bay district, he sold "$4,000 worth of beer in thirty days." While this may not sound astonishing today, consider that $4,000 was then around sixteen times greater than the average factory worker's annual wage!

However, bottling plants and commercial travellers were hardly exclusive to Carling and Labatt. Stiff agency competition confronted the Londoners wherever they went. For example, dealers representing William Dow & Company of Montreal, Canada's largest Victorian brewer, vied with Carling's and Labatt's sales outlets in Ottawa, Kingston, Toronto, Hamilton, Sarnia and Winnipeg. Moreover, sales reps from other breweries also crisscrossed the country in search of customers. Of course, all brewers in Middlesex, large or small, had to contend with external intrusions into their local markets. In mid-1881, for instance, the formidable Toronto Brewing & Malting Company established its Southwestern Ontario bottling plant in London. To manage this operation, the nervy Toronto concern lured salesman and former brewer Charles James away from Carling's.

Nevertheless, Carling and Labatt, armed with their new breweries, did exceedingly well at fighting for position in this dog-eat-dog beer world. A simple comparison of official excise tax records from 1873-74 and 1883-84 supports such a claim. In absolute terms, the amount of beer produced over this period in the London Revenue Division leapt by a whopping 225 percent from 733,765 gallons to 1,654,991 gallons. In relative terms, the former figure represented eight percent of overall Canadian output, while the latter represented thirteen percent. Significantly, this five-percent jump illustrates that the London brewers had grabbed a larger relative share of the market over the decade. True, production at other, much smaller breweries in the London Revenue Division was included in the aggregate returns, but the fact remains that Carling and Labatt overwhelmingly led the charge in the district.

TORONTO BREWING & MALTING COMPANY AGENCY AD FROM THE LONDON FREE PRESS OF SEPTEMBER 7, 1881
In the late summer of 1881, Charles James opened the Toronto Brewing & Malting Company's Southwestern Ontario agency at 139 Albert Street. A former Carling employee with considerable experience in the beer business, James deftly oversaw the Torontonian's invasion of London-Middlesex. So much so, that within two short years, James had to relocate his bottling vaults to much larger quarters at 338, 340 and 342 Clarence Street. (computer enhanced)

BEER LORE — William Penn, the Quaker founder of Pennsylvania, was, among other pursuits, a brewer of esteemed reputation.

ENGRAVED LIKENESSES OF THE MEDALS WON BY JOHN LABATT AT PHILADELPHIA IN 1876 (UPPER) AND AT PARIS, FRANCE IN 1878 (LOWER)
John Labatt's ale and porter did tremendously well at international exhibitions during the last quarter of the nineteenth century. His medal winnings added immeasurably to his fame and fortune.

LABATT'S MEDALS

While booming sales were certainly complimentary, the ultimate degree of critical praise for local beer first came in 1876. That September, John Labatt's India Pale Ale captured the gold medal for bottled ale during the brewers' competition at Philadelphia's Centennial Exhibition. He also won the silver medal for bottled stout. Since Labatt had outdone some of the continent's most renowned brewers, the triumph spoke volumes about the excellence of his brew and did wonders for his reputation. He had arrived! Three months later, the Canadian government echoed the Londoner's accomplishments at Philadelphia by awarding him further medals. Labatt, however, was hardly a flash in the pan and his attention to brewing quality stood him in good stead. By the close of the century, his beers had garnered a total of ten medals and twelve diplomas at international competitions. Besides Philadelphia, victories came at world's fairs and major exhibitions held in Sydney, Australia (1877), Paris, France (1878), London, England (1886), Jamaica (1891), Chicago (1893) and San Francisco (1894). Over the same period, the brewer also earned several awards at Ontario's regional fairs. Even more international glory came during the early twentieth century. His winning record undoubtedly boosted sales.

Carling was the only other county brewer to enjoy success at international taste-tests. Notably, the brewer took medals at London, England's Colonial and Indian Exhibition in 1886 and at Chicago's Columbian Exposition in 1893. While this record pales against Labatt's, it is not an entirely fair comparison to make. Quite simply, Carling did not enter most of the competitions that Labatt did. Then again, we will never know whether this itself was a concession to Labatt's superior flavour or a lack of interest on Carling's part to enter the fray.

THE DELAWARE BREWERY REVIVED

Under the shadow of London's excitement, another brewery returned to the local ranks. In the fall of 1881, Cordley Tupholme reopened the Delaware Brewery at a location slightly west of where it originally stood. The *Strathroy Dispatch* held out great hope for the revived venture: "Delaware now sports a brewery which produces ale of such a nectar, as promises to emulate the fame of Guinness. Under the management of Mr. Tupholme, it is doing finely and is turning out about ten barrels per diem." While it is impossible to know if Tupholme's beer truly rivalled the eminent Irish article, it is fair to assume that his production level surpassed the very modest demands of the immediate Delaware market. Consequently, it would appear that the rejuvenated Delaware Brewery enjoyed sales beyond the village.

However, Cordley Tupholme apparently preferred to focus his energies upon

CARLING'S CLEVELAND BRANCH

Victorian London, Ontario and Victorian Cleveland, Ohio shared two things. Each was nicknamed the Forest City and each was home to a Carling brewery. In the fall of 1880, Carling & Co., anxious for a go at brewing on the American scene, looked across Lake Erie to the burgeoning port of Cleveland and purchased John P. Haley's Forest City Brewery on the northwest corner of Canal and Seneca Streets. Then the fifteenth largest manufacturing centre in the United States, Cleveland was home to a dynamic beer market. The city's half dozen breweries annually manufactured over $1,200,000 worth of beer for a thirsty public who patronized over 1,100 local saloons (American licensing regulations generally permitted more watering holes per capita than did Canadian ones). Making the place even more enticing was the fact that it was home to thousands of expatriate Canadians, many of whom surely missed a refreshing tankard of Carling ale or porter.

The Carlings changed the name of their new acquisition to the London Brewery and installed Charles R. Stuart as plant superintendent. Stuart's previous experience as the brewery's local bottling agent gave him intimate knowledge of the city's beer trade. As the only ale and porter facility in a city dominated by lager producers, the Cleveland branch seemed destined for success within a promising niche market, but two events in 1883 convinced the Carlings otherwise. One, flames struck the brewery on December 17. Although only causing a slight loss that was covered by insurance, the blaze must have been quite unpalatable to the already fire-bitten Carlings. Two, and much more seriously, a senior employee at the branch skipped out with the brewery's cash receipts. Consequently, on December 29, John and Harry Carling sold the brewery to John S. Macbeth, a brother of George Macbeth, the business manager and corporate secretary for Carling B. & M. in London. Hugh Spencer, possibly the same Hugh Spencer who had once operated a brewery in Brantford back in the 1850s and 1860s, accompanied Macbeth to Cleveland and served as his brewmaster. By the way, it is possible that Macbeth and Spencer had been involved with the

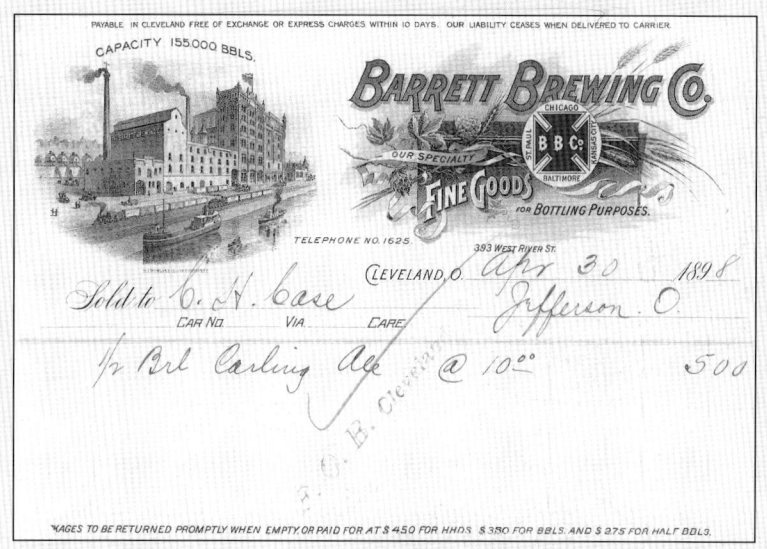

BARRETT BREWING COMPANY INVOICE, APRIL 30, 1898 *Note the price of Carling Ale. Courtesy, Carl Miller*

Cleveland branch since 1880.

However, this was not the end of Carling beer in America. Macbeth entered into an agreement with the Carlings to brew his ale and porter under the reputable Carling name. The international licensing arrangement was, perhaps, the first of its kind between brewers in the two countries. When Macbeth later enlisted the firm of Barrett & Barrett as his distributors, the Carling name spread to Chicago, Peoria, Kansas City, St. Paul, Baltimore and points in between. Success quickly found Macbeth and he moved to larger quarters at 393 West River Street in 1884. Seven years later, he sold out to the Chicago-based Barrett Brewing Company (an outgrowth of Barrett & Barrett), who retained Carling ale and porter as its flagship brands in Cleveland. Under the Cleveland & Sandusky Brewing Company, a combine which Barrett Brewing joined in 1898, the Carling name survived in the U.S. well beyond the turn of the century.

running the Queen's Arms Hotel in Delaware and his farm in Delaware Township. In 1882, he turned the brewery over to a twenty-seven-year-old relative, George. Under the younger Tupholme, the Delaware Brewery prospered as never before. While specific production figures for this era are elusive, tax records reflect George's hard work. During his first two years, the assessed value of the brewery nearly quintupled from $300 to $1,400. In late 1883 or early 1884, another Tupholme, William (according to Victorian directories), or more likely, Ernest Willard (according to Tupholmes still in Middlesex), joined George at the brewery.

THE BIRTH OF BRANDING

In the long run, the single most significant development to come out of the period 1873 to 1884 was not plant expansion, sales growth or even establishing an award-winning brewing reputation in and of itself. Rather, Canadian brewers started to think differently about their beers and the need to differentiate them in what had become a very congested marketplace. This revolutionary departure in thought was the natural consequence of mass production and stiff agency competition. It gave rise to branding and forever changed the brewing industry.

Prior to the mid-1870s, brewers generally used simple possessives to characterize their products. Quasi-generic names resulted. There was Carling's Ale, Labatt's Ale, Sleeman's Ale, Grant's Ale, Copland's Ale, O'Keefe's Ale, Davies' Ale, Calcutt's Ale, Brading's Ale, Dow's Ale, Dawes' Ale, Molson's Ale, Boswell's Ale, Keith's Ale and Oland's Ale, along with Carling's Porter, Labatt's Porter, Sleeman's Porter, Grant's Porter, Copland's Porter, O'Keefe's Porter, Davies' Porter, Calcutt's Porter, Brading's Porter, Dow's Porter, Dawes' Porter, Molson's Porter, Boswell's Porter, Keith's Porter and Oland's Porter. In taverns, saloons and liquor shops across the country, the bland assortment all sounded and looked pretty much the same.

So, in order to give their beers unique identities and thus distinguish them from the crowd, beer-makers adopted more sophisticated naming practices. This marked the birth of the brand name in brewing circles. For instance, Carling's Ale became Carling's Amber Ale, Carling's Porter became Carling's XXX Porter and, most creative of all, Carling's Lager became Carling's Bavarian Stock Lager. Importantly, these names conveyed greater meaning than just who brewed the beers. Amber Ale promised bright, golden deliciousness. XXX Porter guaranteed bold and strong flavour. And Bavarian Stock Lager offered carefully aged crispness in the best German tradition. Meanwhile, John Labatt called upon a different branding technique. Avoiding descriptives, he instead promoted his beers as the international prize winners they were. To accomplish this, he had likenesses of his medals included in the artwork for his bottle labels, advertising and business

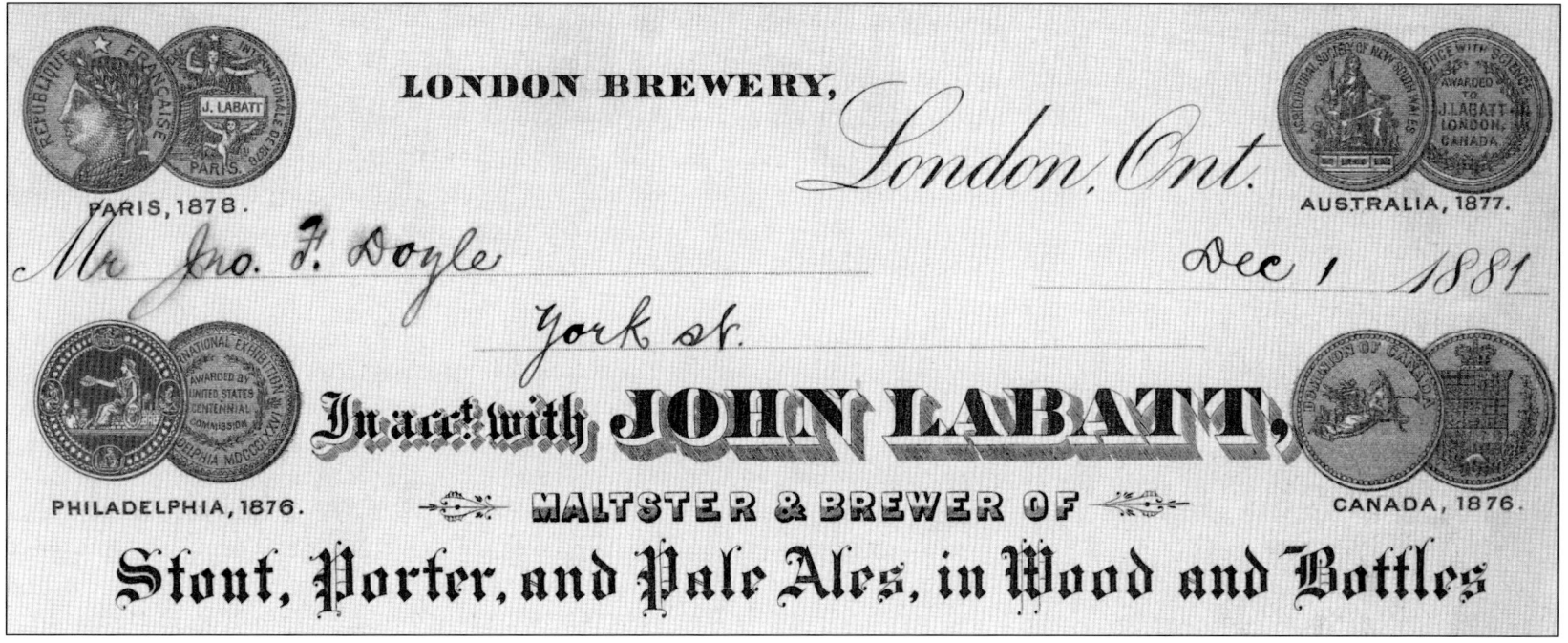

stationery. If Labatt's India Pale Ale and Labatt's Stout were quasi-generic names on their own, then they became true brand names once the association with the awards was made unbreakable in the consumer's mind. The move was as ingenious as it was simple.

Of course, branding had to be nurtured by mass advertising if it were to be truly effective. This promotional stage would begin in the mid-1880s (see Chapter Nine). Still, the foundations of beer branding had been laid. It was a profound Victorian commercial achievement and remains with us today. Indeed, as the universally understood meaning of the word Blue clearly attests, branding has become the dominant feature of modern beer marketing.

A THINNING OF THE RANKS

Despite the continued dominance of British- and Irish-style beers, a handful of Middlesex's ale and porter breweries passed away during the 1870s and early 1880s. The first to go was David Haystead's brewery. Strange to say, after he relocated the Victoria Brewery from downtown London to Petersville in 1873, comment about it just fades from the historical record. It would seem that Haystead stopped brewing shortly after the move. By 1877, he was running a hotel and grocery shop on the

LONDON BREWERY BILLHEAD EMBLAZONED WITH MEDAL IMAGES, DECEMBER 1, 1881
Quite understandably, John Labatt branded his beers with his remarkable prize record. Indeed, the association with the medals remains a marketing tradition at Labatt's to this day. Check out the label on your next bottle of Labatt 50. Courtesy, Jim Maitland

OPPOSITE: QUART CARLING BOTTLE SPORTING A BRAND NAME LABEL, CIRCA 1885
Branding became a key issue in Canadian brewing circles beginning in the mid-1870s. To compete in a marketplace clogged with all sorts of beers, brewers renamed their products with an eye to distinguishing them from the pack. Brand names, as opposed to quasi-generic names, became the rule of the day. Modern brewers follow this mid-Victorian practice albeit with the help of much more sophisticated design, print and broadcast technologies. Courtesy, Jim Maitland

southeast corner of Adelaide and Grosvenor Streets. The small brewery conducted in London East by David's son, John, also disappeared from the scene about the same time. Begun in 1872 and operated with a Mr. Spettigue as a partner the next year, the younger Haystead closed his brewery in 1874. Exactly what motivated the Haysteads to abandon their breweries is the subject of some speculation. Perhaps, low capitalization made it difficult to compete against the city's giants or maybe their beer simply was not up to snuff. Then again, other pursuits may have seemed more worthwhile financially.

The march of time also got the better of John Allaster's Dundas Street Brewery in London East and Thomas Snell Sr.'s West End Brewery in Strathroy. Allaster kept his brewery going until sometime during the late 1870s, when he closed it in order to concentrate upon running his hotel. He returned to brewing from 1881 until 1883, but whether on his own account or in someone else's employ, city directories do not clearly state. At any rate, seventy-seven-year-old John Allaster retired from all business activities in 1884. On April 13 of the same year, fifty-nine-year-old Thomas Snell Sr. died from heart failure. One of Strathroy's most popular citizens, his funeral was attended by many. With no heirs interested in carrying on the business and with strong prohibitionist agitation likely scaring off potential buyers, the West End Brewery subsequently shut down for good.

Meanwhile, John Hamilton of the Kent Brewery steamed merrily along, content with his modest, yet steady local trade. However, the most notable event to occur at his establishment during these years sadly had little to do with the brewing business. On July 21, 1875, Hamilton's brother and employee, William, committed suicide in the brewery's stable. A deeply troubled man with a history of alcoholism, William purposely ingested a solution of water and Paris Green (an garden insecticide). He suffered an agonizing death while his horrified brother and an attending physician, both unable to counteract the poison, looked on helplessly.

At the close of 1884, with a new century on the not-so-distant horizon, Middlesex County was home to five breweries. In order of size, they belonged to the Carling Brewing & Malting Company, John Labatt, M. Bixel & Son, John Hamilton and the Tupholme family. All but one would survive the test of local-option prohibition.

CHAPTER EIGHT

Banning the Bottle:
The Dry Crusade

NOT EVERYONE APPRECIATED the beer manufactured in London-Middlesex or anywhere else in Canada. Over the last two thirds of the nineteenth century, an untiring temperance army crusaded against John Barleycorn and King Alcohol. At first, drys used tactics of moral suasion in attempts to win drinkers over to the cause. However, wets proved quite unwilling to surrender their drink culture. In the face of such reluctance, temperance supporters turned to prohibition strategies. Their pinnacle of achievement in this regard came in the 1880s, when the local-option Scott Act swept across most of English-speaking Canada. The prohibitory law forced Middlesex's smallest brewer out of business and strongly influenced another to build a new brewery outside the county. Ironically, Carling and Labatt discovered that Scott Act prohibition was not entirely bad for business and they seized this opportunity to enhance their market positions even further.

THE GREAT TEMPERANCE CAMPAIGN
During the late 1700s and early 1800s, a great religious awakening swept across the English-speaking world. A significant theological feature of this revival was the widely held belief that the Bible commanded Christians to shape society in the image of Christly perfection. This, in turn, would pave the way for the Saviour's second coming. Notably identified as sins to be cleansed from the world were blasphemy, Sabbath-breaking, sexual immorality, slavery and drunkenness. In particular, efforts against the latter sin gave rise to the temperance movement.

   Organized temperance found its way to Canada in the late 1820s. In 1827, the very year that brewing got its start in London-Middlesex, the first Canadian temperance society was formed at Beaver River, Nova Scotia. The following year, the first such group in Upper Canada was established in, of all places, Bastard Township near Brockville. A year after that, the first temperance society in Middlesex was organized in West Nissouri Township.

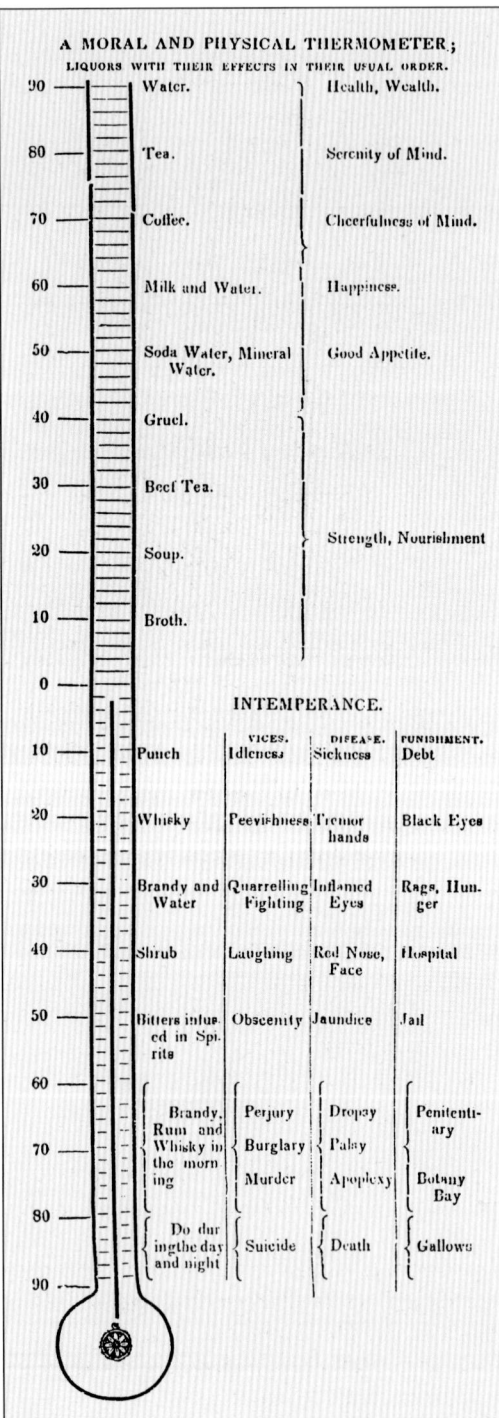

At first, temperance proponents were not necessarily against the consumption of fermented drinks. Indeed, since they believed in literally tempering their drinking habits, they thought of beer, wine and cider as ideal temperance beverages. Starting in the mid-1830s, however, many temperance supporters began to embrace the concept of total abstinence or teetotalism. A number of inter-related issues prompted this evolution. Firstly, it was held that the consumption of beer and wine led to the abuse of stiffer drink. Secondly, it was recognized that overindulgence in fermented beverages also brought on the sin of drunkenness. Thirdly, it was Biblically interpreted that beer did not exist during the time of Christ and that the wine of the era was nothing but unfermented grape juice; therefore, one could not drink at all if one were to live in Christly perfection. By the way, the term "teetotal," which denotes total abstinence, is rooted in the saying, "T for total abstinence," and not owing to abstainers' love of tea.

For the most part, those who joined the teetotal camp were from the middling classes and were evangelical Christians. Their ranks notably included Free Kirk Presbyterians, Methodists, Baptists, Congregationalists and some low church Anglicans. In general, Roman Catholics, most Anglicans, Old Kirk Presbyterians and more conservative Methodists remained outside the total abstinence fold. Politically, teetotallers gravitated towards the Reformers (now the Liberal Party). Naturally, exceptions to these demographic rules dot the historical record. For example, London sported a Catholic Teetotal Society during the 1850s, some Bixel brewery workers were Baptists and Free Kirk Presbyterians, and the staunch Liberal, Daniel Macfie, sat as the president of Carling B. & M. during the mid-1880s.

THE GREAT BATTLE BEGINS

The total abstinence movement required adherents to sign the teetotal pledge. However, the century's great dry crusade did not start in earnest until the late 1830s and early 1840s, when teetotallers, in keeping with their evangelical bearings, began to demand that their imbibing neighbours also give up drink. The new enemies in this phase of temperance reform became moderate drinkers and, most especially, those who manufactured and/or sold beverage alcohol, collectively known as the liquor traffic. More specifically, abstainers were convinced that moderate drinking set a poor example for others, inevitably led to backsliding and served as the vehicle by which an evil liquor traffic maintained its stranglehold on society.

In order to convince others to cease drinking, teetotallers sought to portray moderation as dangerous and to expose beer and wine as poisonous. As in wars before and since, the first casualty was often the truth. In the early 1850s, for instance, a columnist for the *Canada Temperance Advocate*, billing himself as

Medicus, argued that daily use of fermented beverages "stimulated to a morbid degree the organs of digestion, so that an excess of blood is generated from moderate quantities of solid food." The self-styled medical expert called this ailment Plethora and suggested that it led to fatal apoplexy (an effusion of blood serum in the brain), inflammations, gout and rheumatism. Medicus concluded that "in those of delicate frames [meaning women?], indulgence in moderate drinking induces obstinate dyspepsia, and functional diseases of the liver, accompanied by that degree of mental depression which may amount to hypochondria, and the tendency to commit suicide."

The editor of the same journal followed with another sincerely held, but unsubstantiated claim. Unfairly intimating that Canadian brewers were devious by nature, he argued that ale and porter contained infusions of "a variety of narcotic drugs and herbs," including "hops, a poisonous, narcotic herb." Besides such pseudoscientific denouncements, tales of social devastation and death caused by drink filled temperance literature of the era.

Evaluating the mid-century success of the temperance movement in purely numeric terms is virtually impossible. However, it is obvious that moral suasion and scare tactics had not worked their intended magic, as most Canadians had yet to join the teetotal flock. Indeed, brewing progress in London-Middlesex and elsewhere, for that matter, speaks volumes about drink culture's resilience.

Occasionally, drinkers voiced what they thought about their abstemious brethren. For example, "One Who Likes a Glass of Beer Now and Then," writing to the *London Free Press* in defense of responsible drinking, questioned the rants of a local teetotaller: "He is probably no more correct in his denunciations of the moderate drinkers than in his wholesale scorn for the [non-abstaining] clergy because they will not conform to his narrow views." Meanwhile, Colonel Thomas Talbot tersely dismissed temperance groups as "damned cold water drinking societies." Of course, the vast majority simply kept on raising their cups in silent opposition. Nonetheless, the battle lines had been drawn.

PROHIBITION BECOMES THE ANSWER

Impatient, intolerant and resolutely convinced of the righteousness of their cause, teetotallers resolved to impose their will on society by means of prohibitory law. This departure was a direct volley against brewers, distillers, licensed retailers and their customers. In August 1851, the Reverend R.D. Wadsworth, a leading light in temperance circles, succinctly, if arrogantly, explained the logic behind prohibition: "Some talk of moral suasion — pshaw! What effect will it have on many long in the [liquor] trade? Others talk of waiting for public opinion — I ask, how long? 'Tis

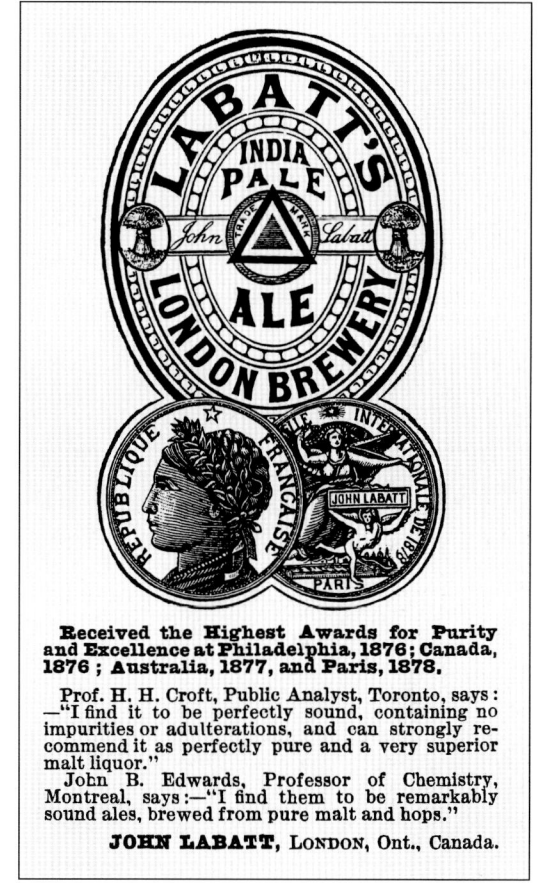

ABOVE: LABATT I.P.A. AD FROM *THE FARMER'S ADVOCATE* FOR JUNE 1886
Temperance proponents often claimed that beer was laced with all sorts of poisons. To refute such groundless pronouncements, John Labatt frequently employed written testimonials from legitimate scientific experts.

OPPOSITE: "MORAL AND PHYSICAL THERMOMETER" FROM THE CANADA TEMPERANCE ADVOCATE OF JULY 15, 1850
Although perhaps laughable to our twenty-first-century eyes, early temperance attacks on beverage alcohol could be quite creative. The "Moral and Physical Thermometer" highlighted the dangers of strong drink. Where do your liquid pleasures rank?

STOP THE DEATH FACTORIES!

ANTI-LIQUOR TRAFFIC CARTOON FROM THE GRIP,
OCTOBER 30, 1886
*Drys in mid-Victorian Canada sincerely believed that
hotels, saloons, distilleries and breweries were essentially
death factories and were responsible for the economic,
social, moral and spiritual ruin of countless souls.
Moreover, temperance supporters associated the sale of
booze with Satan's work. This sketch by the famous
Canadian political cartoonist, J.W. Bengough, himself a
prohibitionist, reflects these doctrines. Note the Devil in
the background.*

nonsense! We have waited long enough. The axe must be laid at the root — THE TRAFFIC! And the blow must be struck by Government."

Around the time Wadsworth delivered his impassioned declaration, the State of Maine passed North America's first comprehensive statute of prohibition. The Maine Law, as it became known, gave hope to temperance advocates across the entire continent. In 1852, Malcolm Cameron, another prominent dry crusader and a Clear Grit member of the provincial legislature, vowed before a Sons of Temperance gathering in London that "he would sustain the introduction of the Maine Law in his place in parliament." The politician remained true to his word, but a coalition of brewers and distillers, through a paid lobbyist, stymied the passage of both Cameron's bill and a similar one which appeared before legislators in 1854. Needless to say, teetotallers were furious.

TEMPERANCE REFORM IN LONDON-MIDDLESEX

Meanwhile, a whole raft of temperance organizations had sprouted in London-Middlesex. Active throughout the rest of the century and beyond, they bore such names as the Sons of Temperance, the Daughters of Temperance, the Cadets of Temperance, the Good Templars of Temperance, the Young Men's Prohibition Club, the Red Ribbon Club, the Blue Ribbon Club (our practice of wearing "cause" ribbons is inherited from the temperance movement), the Woman's Christian Temperance Union and the Western Ontario Temperance and Prohibitory League. Detailing the particular activities of each and every temperance group in Middlesex is well beyond the scope of this book. Suffice it to say, they spread the good word, strove to convert the masses, lobbied against the licensed trade and worked to achieve prohibition. It should also be noted that county temperance workers, despite the best lobbying efforts of such renowned brewers as John Carling, often succeeded in persuading local politicians to place caps on or even reduce the number of municipally issued liquor licenses.

THE DUNKIN ACT

On the larger stage, what appeared to be a significant legislative triumph came with the passage of the local-option Dunkin Act in 1864. Named after its parliamentary sponsor, Christopher Dunkin, the statute empowered any county, city, town, township, parish or incorporated village in Canada West and Canada East to enact a by-law to prohibit the local sale of intoxicating beverages in quantities of less than five gallons. Before the Dunkin Act could come into effect, electors in a given municipality had to vote for its adoption in a local plebiscite. Although not a law of all-out prohibition, the act still buoyed drys with great hope. However, because the wider public preferred their liquid cheer, the Dunkin Act failed to find popular acceptance.

By the mid-1870s, Canadian temperance advocates had become quite dissatisfied with the progress of their movement. They had been pushing the dry agenda for two generations and yet had not achieved that exalted goal of banishing King Alcohol from society. Indeed, rising production figures clearly proved that brewers, distillers and beverage retailers had ably weathered nearly five decades of temperance attacks. Moreover, the general population had largely resisted or abandoned prohibition in the form of the Dunkin Act. For instance, in Ontario, Canada's supposed hotbed of temperance fervour, only fourteen of the thousand or so municipalities covered by the Dunkin Act were dry under the statute in 1875. In short, drink culture was far too entrenched to be dislodged.

THE MONTREAL CONVENTION

Temperance workers naturally found this reality completely and utterly unacceptable. In order to initiate a remedy, 260 drys gathered at a convention in Montreal on September 15, 16 and 17, 1875. Among them were such luminaries as George W. Ross, West Middlesex's Member of Parliament and a rising young star in the movement, Malcolm Cameron, dean of Canadian prohibitionists, and Alexander Vidal, the senator from Sarnia whose eminence in temperance circles saw him elected as convention president. Invited foreign dignitaries included Neal Dow, father of the Maine Law, and T.H. Barker, secretary of the United Kingdom Alliance. The meeting was an important turning-point with important ramifications.

Had the conventioneers honestly evaluated the progress of their movement, they would have concluded that the wider public still needed to be won over by means of moral suasion and not through legal coercion. However, they opted for the latter course and resolved to lobby for a federal law of all-out prohibition. By again choosing to impose their will upon their recalcitrant neighbours, the actions of the Montreal delegates reveal just how unbending Canadian temperance soldiers could be. To carry out their plan, the conventioneers appointed a committee to establish

GEORGE W. ROSS, "PROMOTER AND CHAMPION OF PROHIBITION," FROM THE CANADIAN ILLUSTRATED NEWS, OCTOBER 2, 1875
A native of Middlesex County, George William Ross owed much of his political success to his strong prohibitionist leanings. When he attended the great Montreal temperance convention, Ross was the Liberal M.P. for West Middlesex. He later became Ontario's Minister of Education. While holding this portfolio, he instituted temperance instruction as a regular part of the province's elementary school curriculum. Ross ended his career in elected politics as Ontario's premier from 1899 until 1905.

a national temperance organization. In mid-February 1876, this body came into being as the Dominion Alliance for the Total Suppression of the Liquor Traffic.

THE CANADA TEMPERANCE ACT

Formidable in name and action, the Dominion Alliance served as an umbrella association for Canada's various and sundry temperance groups. As such, it pressed Ottawa for the enactment of national prohibition. In the Liberal prime minister, Alexander Mackenzie, the Dominion Alliance had someone sympathetic to the cause; however, Mackenzie was also a political realist who believed that the overall Canadian populace was not prepared to accept total prohibition. Upon consulting the prime minister, the Dominion Alliance retreated to pushing for a local-option statute. The drys were granted their wish in the dying days of the Mackenzie administration, when the Hon. R.W. Scott tabled a prohibitory bill in the senate (the upper house then played a much more active legislative role). The bill received royal assent on May 10, 1878 and became known officially as the Canada Temperance Act (CTA) or, more familiarly, as the Scott Act after its parliamentary sponsor.

The Scott Act functioned at either the city or county level. The statute specified that a petition praying for a municipal referendum on local CTA adoption had to be presented to the Governor General in Council. To be valid, a petition had to bear the signatures of at least one-fourth of a municipality's qualified electors. A plebiscite then followed a properly executed petition. If the majority of voters opted for the act, then the local sale (not the manufacture or private consumption) of beverage alcohol, except for medicinal, sacramental or industrial purposes, became illegal upon the expiry of the current license year. The act remained in local effect for a three-year term, after which another municipal referendum took place. Penalties under the statute included the seizure of contraband liquor, a $50 fine for a first offence, a $100 fine for a second offence and imprisonment for a third offence.

CHALLENGING A MOST UNWELCOME LAW

Quite obviously, the CTA was bad news for those in the liquor traffic and their customers. Hardly a passive lot themselves, wets attacked the very existence of the statute by challenging its constitutionality and lobbying for its repeal. Unfortunately, the liquor trade lost both battles. The constitutional challenge failed because the crusty old Law Lords of Britain's Judicial Committee of the Privy Council (then the highest court in the British Empire) concluded that the CTA fell within the right of Canadian Parliament to enact laws for "peace, order and good

BEER QUOTE —
While beer brings gladness, don't forget
That water only makes you wet.
　　　Harry Leon Wilson, *The Spenders*, Page 237

government." And the appeal to the recently restored prime minister, John A. Macdonald, failed because, despite his drinking habits and the presence of John Carling in his cabinet, "Old Tomorrow" recognized the political advantage of relative inaction. For all intents and purposes, those in the trade and their customers were left to fend for themselves.

THE SCOTT ACT ERA

The CTA stirred a new sense of purpose within the Canadian temperance movement. Under the guidance of the Dominion Alliance as national co-ordinator, local Scott Act Associations across the country orchestrated the necessary petition drives and plebiscite campaigns. By the mid-1880s, their zealous efforts had carried the law into force over much of the Maritimes, parts of Quebec, most of Ontario and two counties in Manitoba. In Southwestern Ontario, prohibitionists had persuaded voters in St. Thomas and in the counties of Brant, Bruce, Elgin, Huron, Kent, Lambton, Middlesex, Norfolk and Oxford to adopt Scott Act prohibition. Only Brantford and London and the counties of Essex, Grey and Perth remained as wet islands in a sea of dryness.

In the Middlesex referendum of 1885, county electors adopted the Scott Act by a margin of 3,375 votes (5,745 for and 2,370 against). It stands as the largest pro-CTA majority ever recorded in Victorian Canada. However, this mark and the Scott Act sweep are rather misleading about prohibition's popularity. Voter turnout in every Scott Act contest, including Middlesex's, was quite low. It seems that most electors did not care about the issue one way or the other. Interestingly, London, with its dominant population of drinkers, never even hosted a Scott Act vote.

THE SCOTT ACT IN MIDDLESEX

On May 1, 1886, Middlesex County's Scott Act regime officially began. Even so, the day hardly saw the end of drinking in local saloons and taverns, as barkeepers across the county defiantly flouted the prohibitory law. Some openly served the thirsty, while others resorted to tactics of stealth, such as concealing liquor supplies and confining drinking to secret rooms. However, the authorities were not always outfoxed. For example, during the year ending December 13, 1887, police magistrate James Noble of Strathroy, the judicial official responsible for CTA

COL. VIDAL'S CAMP, ROSSEAU, ONTARIO, JULY 1895
Proving just how small Victorian Canada could be, this friendly gathering of cottagers includes John Labatt, the London brewer, T.J. McDonough, the London liquor merchant, and Colonel Beaufort Henry Vidal, a cousin of Alexander Vidal, the president of the Dominion Alliance for the Total Suppression of the Liquor Traffic. Left to right — Colonel Vidal, T.J. McDonough, John Labatt, Milly Harris, Maurice ? and Miss Vidal. Courtesy, J.J. Talman Regional Collection

BEER LORE — Brewers William and John Carling once owned a large business block in downtown London. During the early 1860s, one of their tenants was, quite ironically, the local Sons of Temperance chapter, which rented space in the building for use as a meeting hall. Who do you think laughed hardest about this, William or John?

hearings in Middlesex, tried 275 cases under the statute, returned 225 guilty verdicts, imposed $12,800 in fines ($9,445 of which was collected), sent two offenders to jail for two months each on third offences and committed twelve others to jail for nonpayment of fines. Notable defendants that year were Matthew and Cyrus Bixel, who were mulcted to the tune of $350 plus costs on convictions for three first offences and two second offences (the type of Scott Act charge was discretionary and not based upon the number of prior convictions).

Scott Act policing in Middlesex owed its relative efficiency to the dedication and diligence of license inspectors charged with the law's enforcement. For instance, D.H. Williams, the inspector for East Middlesex, was an ardent prohibitionist and sat as president of the East Middlesex Temperance Alliance (conflict of interest was not a well-developed concept in the Victorian age). Besides applying his abstemious principles to his job, Williams, like other local license inspectors, routinely called upon private citizens, who were warm friends of the cause, to operate as "whisky detectives" in the effort to catch bartenders red-handed. Much despised by the liquor traffic, these undercover agents would order drinks at area hotels, have charges pressed against the offenders and then testify at ensuing CTA trials. Whisky detectives rotated from one circuit to the next in order to preserve their anonymity.

A MOST UNDIGNIFIED CONTEST

Scott Act prohibition brought out the worst in people on both sides of the temperance debate. Above all, passions threw the criminal justice system into disrepute, as perjury tainted many a CTA trial and violent resistance marked the law's overall administration. Not surprisingly, drinkers summoned as witnesses in Scott Act cases often gave false testimony to shield their favourite hotelkeepers from conviction. Indeed, it seems that many imbibers in Middlesex either were extremely forgetful or simply loved to drink nothing but soda pop. However, perjury was hardly a one-way street. Many whisky detectives also stretched, bent or otherwise distorted the truth in order to secure guilty verdicts.

Blackmailing liquor sellers was just as pernicious to the administration of justice. On this score, Middlesex's most notable Scott Act blackmailer was, of all people, the Reverend John Stonehouse of Adelaide. The reverend's game of extortion involved targeting a given hotelkeeper with an anonymous letter, wherein the hotelkeeper was advised that a CTA case had been worked up against him. But, if the hotelkeeper forwarded $25 to an address in Toronto, the evidence would not be turned over to the authorities. Stonehouse successfully blackmailed several hoteliers in West Middlesex until early 1888, when Wesley Prangley of Strathroy refused to pay, discovered the minister's identity and pressed charges of his own.

Upon arrest, the con artist in a collar protested that his object was merely to secure from the offenders "an admission. . . that they had broken the Act." Once done, the clergyman claimed that he intended to turn the money and written evidence over to the proper officials. A local reporter dismissed this plea of innocence as "the gauziest excuse ever offered, but is on par with the tactics of the average informer and blackmailer — after arrest." However, it was a moot point. The disgraced minister absconded to the United States and never faced a Canadian judge. By the way, Stonehouse wound up running a hotel in Michigan later that year. The *London Free Press* wryly commented upon such irony: "And the hotelkeepers feel aggrieved to think that their business has been degraded by the acquisition of such a character into their ranks."

VIOLENCE

Unfortunately, tempers flared over CTA enforcement in Middlesex. Understandably upset with watching prohibition threaten their livelihoods and angry about what they perceived to be the underhanded techniques of whisky detectives, hotelkeepers sometimes lashed out violently. An excellent case in point occurred in Strathroy on April 11, 1887, when an angry crowd gathered at the town's railway station and viciously attacked a witness whose testimony had just secured the convictions of six county hoteliers. According to one newspaper account:

The party [of witnesses] got on the train for London, but instead of going inside, Irwin, one of the informers, a man upwards of 60 years of

"NOT A UNIT!"

I MAY TELL YOU PLAINLY, THAT ON THIS QUESTION (THE SCOTT ACT) THE CABINET IS NOT A UNIT.— *Sir John to the Anti-Scott delegation.*

THE REVEREND WILLIAM MCDONAGH, CIRCA 1881
A native of Enniskillen, Ireland, the Reverend William McDonagh distinguished his forty-four-year career as a Methodist preacher with a pronounced evangelical outlook. In particular, he chose the temperance cause as his mission in life and he condemned the liquor traffic with almost obsessive zeal. Courtesy, United Church of Canada/Victoria University Archives, Toronto

age, stood on the platform to light his pipe. Here Thomas Richardson, whose case had been enlarged, pounced upon him, and tried to drag him from the train. Irwin clung to the railing, and in this position he was struck a terrible blow in the face by Richardson, who cut Irwin's nose badly. Another party kicked him in the hand, and still another in the stomach, and Irwin would undoubtedly have been dragged from the train and badly beaten had it not fortunately for him commenced to move, and his assailants were forced to desist.

Richardson was subsequently convicted of assault. Later that year, a gang of men attacked a party of Scott Act informers in Parkhill. Despite such brutality, Middlesex County was actually quite tame in comparison to some other jurisdictions. For example, a wave of anti-CTA arson fires swept Huron County and a hotelkeeper dynamited the home of a prominent Scott Act supporter in Sarnia.

BIXEL VERSUS MCDONAGH

Perhaps one of the most interesting CTA struggles to unfold in Middlesex was the one fought in Strathroy between the lager-making Bixels and the Methodist minister William McDonagh. If two parties were ever predestined to tangle, they were the ones. The Bixels were brewers' brewers and, as we have seen, had few compunctions about disobeying the detested CTA. Meanwhile, McDonagh presided over the West Middlesex Scott Act Alliance and vociferously opposed such vices (or pleasures) as dancing, card games, billiards and, of course, drinking. It should come as little surprise that the beer-makers and the preacher did not like each other at all.

On December 2, 1888, at the height of the Scott Act era in Middlesex, matters between them came to a head. While delivering one of his usual fire-and-brimstone sermons in Strathroy's Front Street Methodist Church that Sunday, the good reverend just happened to mention that the Bixels made their lager beer from the filthy water of the Sydenham River. Nothing could have been further from the truth and Matthew, Cyrus and Oscar Bixel slapped McDonagh with a $5,000 slander suit the following day. Now, since it was quite rare for a man of the cloth to find himself in such a predicament, the story made big news. In mid-May the next year, the Bixels won their case, but received only $30 in compensatory damages. Even so, McDonagh appealed the judgement and the parties later settled out of court for an undisclosed sum. Thereafter, the reverend gentleman chose his words much more carefully.

THE SCOTT ACT & BREWING IN LONDON-MIDDLESEX

Besides the headaches brought on by slanderous temperance speeches, the CTA affected the local brewing scene in other significant ways. Most obviously, it immediately harmed sales. Indeed, George Tupholme understood this all too well, as the Scott Act instantly eroded most of his already small local market. He closed the Delaware Brewery for good not long after the CTA came into force.

Initially, at least, Carling and Labatt also saw business fall off with the start of prohibition. After all, just as the Scott Act adversely affected the brewers' trade customers, so it affected the brewers themselves. To make matters worse, the nationally oriented Londoners suffered this effect not only in Middlesex, but everywhere else that the CTA came into standing. A further complication was the fact that financially pinched hotelkeepers in Scott Act regions often had trouble paying their brewery accounts. The pressing need to compensate for this soured environment undoubtedly prompted Carling and Labatt to speed up their agency programs in cities whose large populations of beer drinkers held Scott Act forces at bay. Interestingly, the Kent Brewery, which enjoyed most of its sales in a thoroughly wet London, largely escaped the harmful consequences of the CTA.

BIXEL'S BRANTFORD BRANCH

The Scott Act also threatened the regionally oriented Bixel brewery. As a concerned *London Free Press* reporter remarked: "What troubles Mr. M. Bixel, of the Strathroy Lager Beer Brewery, is who is going to reimburse him the $35,000 he has invested in his business there? Possibly some of the temperance cranks will put their hands in their pockets (or somebody else's) and pay Mr. Bixel. It was they who brought the humbug into life." However, the Bixels refused to bow before the Scott Act and they resolved to establish a branch brewery at Brantford in order to bolster their business.

The resourceful Strathroy brewers did not settle upon the Telephone City by accident. During the mid-1880s, the place was the only Ontario city without a functioning brewery of its own. (This state of affairs had arisen chiefly because Brantford's brewery operators of the late 1870s and early 1880s had failed to build agency networks to brace themselves them against the deluge of beer which poured into the city from a host of outside brewers, including Carling and Labatt of London.) Also making the city attractive was the fact that Brantfordites who liked to raise a glass of cheer had rebuffed the advances of their Scott Act toting neighbours. In sum, Brantford was a breweryless, yet beer-thirsty city. It stood as a ripe market for the Bixels to exploit and use as a base in west-central Ontario. Just as enticing was the bonus that Brantford bordered the southern edge of the

BEER LORE — The modern word booze is a variant of the Middle English word *bouse*, which meant to drink deeply or for the sake of fellowship and enjoyment.

BIXEL'S BRANTFORD BREWERY, CIRCA 1895
Scott Act pressures in Middlesex convinced the Bixel family to build a branch brewery in Brantford, Ontario. The success of this new venture later saw the Bixels abandon their brewing operation in Strathroy. The old White brewery, which Matthew Bixel converted into a malthouse, appears to the right. Courtesy, Brant County Museum and Archives

province's lager-drinking nexus in Waterloo County and was a hop, skip and a jump away from Guelph, Hamilton and Toronto. As an interesting aside, the expansion was also a return to the place where Matthew had once operated a cigar factory back in the 1850s.

As the site for their new brewery, Matthew and Cyrus Bixel purchased George White's defunct brewery property at 1 Alfred Street. Incidentally, Joseph Luke & Sons, the Tillsonburg brewers, had recently used the building as their Brantford bottling agency. Wilhelm Griessen, the famed lager brewery architect of Chicago, designed the branch facility and the Cooper family of Strathroy built it. To oversee

the building project, which began in earnest in September 1888, Matthew Bixel took up temporary residence in Brantford. Meanwhile, the old White brewery was converted into a malthouse.

In early April 1889, Bixel's Brantford lager made its debut. As the *Brantford Expositor* raved: "The bars of this city have been supplied with the first output of beer from Bixel's new brewery. The quality of this beverage is said to be exceedingly good." Oscar Bixel, a graduate of New York's School of Brewing and recently employed "in some of the largest breweries in the States," served as brewmaster and production manager, while his younger brother, Arthur, functioned as business

STEREOSCOPIC VIEW OF THE CARLING BREWERY, CIRCA 1882
Taken on the cusp of the Scott Act era in Middlesex County, this photograph gives us a rare peek at the rear of Carling's plant. Belonging to a popular series of London and area stereoscopic views, this artifact reminds us that not everyone in the great temperance age despised breweries. Courtesy, John Saddy

manager. The Bixel boys worked well together and the branch's smashing success would later see the brewing Bixels leave Strathroy in favour of Brantford.

A SILVER LINING IN A DARK CLOUD

If the Scott Act initially harmed London's brewers, strange to say, it proved beneficial in the long term. For instance, the wet city became a Mecca for drinkers from Scott Act communities. They still wanted beer and they made frequent pilgrimages to London to quench their thirst. Naturally, their demands materially boosted local beer sales and, in a relative sense, this twist especially benefitted the Kent Brewery. Similarly, and despite the hopes of prohibitionists, demand for beer did not evaporate in dry municipalities. In fact, as breweries shut down in such Scott Act places as Simcoe, Woodstock, St. Thomas (one of two closed), Delaware and Sarnia, calls for beer in those localities became even more acute. London's brewers were more than happy to oblige. As John Labatt later testified before the Royal Commission on the Liquor Traffic: "I made more money during the Scott Act time than I ever did since or before. . . If anyone came to buy ales from us, I did not care whether it [the order] was from a Scott Act county or not, I would sell." Quite ironically, by closing or weakening breweries elsewhere, the CTA ultimately strengthened the market positions of the two London giants.

THE SCOTT ACT REPEALED

By and large, the CTA was a failure. Drinkers knew it, brewers knew it and even the drys themselves knew it. If anything, the Scott Act demonstrated the unworkability of prohibition. Moreover, the law's administration and enforcement had pitted neighbour against neighbour — sometimes violently so — and this result was a far cry from the temperance movement's original goal of attaining Christian peace on earth. By 1889, the CTA had been repealed across Ontario and in most other jurisdictions elsewhere in Canada. In the Middlesex plebiscite, locals banished the act by 5,530 ballots to 2,992. This majority of 2,538 votes was the second largest repeal margin recorded anywhere in Victorian Canada.

In the immediate post-CTA era, the temperance camp regrouped and, forgetting (or, perhaps, because of) the lessons learned during the local-option Scott Act years, began to push for all-out national prohibition. They did not achieve anything of consequence until the early twentieth century. Meanwhile, brewers, hotelkeepers and beer drinkers, much relieved, gladly welcomed the return to normalcy.

BEER LORE — Otto von Bismark, Germany's Iron Chancellor, had an enormous appetite for food and drink. In fact, he used his legendary capacity for beer to outmanoeuvre diplomatic opponents who were more readily besotted.

CHAPTER NINE

Marching Towards a New Century, 1885 to 1900

THE LAST DECADE and a half of the nineteenth century formed the pinnacle of Victorian advertising achievements. During this period, vital commercial concepts, such as brand-driven marketing, the creation of brand images and the development of company identities, rose to prominence in the business world. In particular, these strategies forever changed the ways in which brewers, big and small, promoted their beers. Amidst this new climate, brewery agencies and the hotel trade remained as important as ever; however, increasing market integration forced Carling and Labatt to place greater emphasis on "big city" sales. The Hamiltons also adopted brand-driven marketing techniques, but in a more reactive fashion in order to keep their Kent Brewery viable. All told, only Strathroy's brewery experienced a notable decline during these years, but not until after the Bixels had stopped brewing in the town.

THE ADVERTISING REVOLUTION

The period from 1885 to 1900 witnessed the zenith of Victorian advertising. As new technologies revolutionized the delivery of the message, new thought revolutionized the message in the delivery. Ever anxious to succeed in a rough-and-tumble marketplace, Canadian brewers readily warmed to such change. The goal of the new game was to broadcast one's name as widely as possible and, in a world without television, the printed word was the only way to accomplish this.

Advances in graphic design and typesetting radically changed the appearance of print-advertising. A comparison of Carling and Labatt ads from the 1850s and 1880s reveals just how remarkable this transition was (see next two pages). The earlier ones are far from inspiring. The type is plain, rigidly laid-out and distinguished solely by bolded headlines. In addition, both notices, each measuring one column wide by about an inch deep, were easily lost in a forest of other ads. Reflecting progress made in the printing sciences, the later ads exude design

LONDON BREWERY.

JOHN K. LABATT,
(LATE LABATT & ECCLES,)

BREWER and Malster, Dealer in Barley, Malt and Hops, London, C.W. Ale and Beer in Barrels and Bottles.

London, September 8, 1855.   d108-ly

W. & J. CARLING,
BREWERS,
LONDON, CANADA WEST.

A STOCK of their CELEBRATED ALE and PORTER, in Bottle and on Draught, always on hand.–Orders solicited.

London, Sept. 15, 1859.   D1323-ly

LABATT AND CARLING ADS FROM THE 1850S (UPPER AND LOWER) AND 1880S (OPPOSITE)

Although typical design examples of their time, the mid-nineteenth-century brewery ads shown above were hardly imaginative. Meanwhile, advances in printing technologies and the dictates of brand-driven marketing combined to lend a much more sophisticated look to brewery advertising later in the century. What does your eye notice first in the ads appearing opposite? Incidentally, John Kinder Labatt's partnership with Samuel Eccles was properly known as Eccles & Labatt. (earlier ads computer enhanced)

sophistication. They dance with different typefaces and line weights and their display size makes them hard to miss. Of course, the label images jump right off the page (more about this very shortly).

Other advancements widened brewers' advertising options. Improvements in lithography gave rise to ads, business stationery and postcards adorned with finely executed artistic details. The march of lithography also greatly reduced the production costs of full-colour trade-cards, posters and calendars. Brewers freely gave these away by the thousands. Meanwhile, progress in porcelain-working, metal-stamping and screen-printing saw the proliferation of outdoor porcelain and sheet metal brewery signs and a myriad of promotional giveaways, including bottle openers, key chains, watch fobs, ashtrays, tip trays and serving trays. Naturally, these freebies were emblazoned with beer advertisements.

BRAND-DRIVEN MARKETING

If advances in ad design and printing techniques changed the delivery of the message, then the turn to brand-driven marketing brought about a new message. A natural outgrowth of the branding developments discussed in Chapter Seven, brand-driven marketing entailed the reworking of advertisements so that they highlighted specific brands of beer. This simple, yet clever innovation proved valuable in the struggle to distinguish beer in highly integrated markets. In other words, it was the focused advertising support used to promote brands before the public. In this respect, brand-driven marketing was also the product of an emerging consumerism.

Again comparing our ad specimens from the 1850s and 1880s reveals the sophistication of brand-driven marketing. The earlier ads truly say quite little about the brewers' beers, besides the fact that they were generics available in the two conventional vessels of the day. Indeed, the Labatt insert devotes considerable attention to products — barley, malt and hops — which most consumers were unlikely to ever want. The later ads far outclass their uninformative predecessors. Above all, they emphasize the brewers' flagship brands by instantly drawing the eye to the label facsimiles. (If you can honestly resist this intended effect, then yours truly will treat you to a pint of your choice.) Importantly, such striking features ensured product recognition and kept the ads from disappearing into the page. Moreover, statements of quality assurance and prize winnings have prominently replaced the wasteful and unnecessary references to secondary brewery products. Ultimately, there was no mistaking exactly what was being promoted, who manufactured it and that it was a worthwhile buy — the essential themes of brand-driven marketing.

By the way, John Labatt pioneered the use of label images as a regular feature of

brewery advertising. He initiated the practice in December 1885 and made it a consistent feature of his ads thereafter. O'Keefe of Toronto and Carling appear to be the next Canadian brewers to have adopted such a measure, but trailed the enterprising Labatt by about a year and a half.

THE NEW FLAVOUR OF ADVERTISING
During the last fifteen Victorian years, the branding ethos expressed itself in countless imaginative ways. In 1887, for instance, a series of rotating Carling B. & M. ads featured general claims of quality, seasonal angles, favourable comparisons to old-world standard-setters, and the targeting of specific consumer groups: "Carling's First Prize and Gold Medal Ale and Porter Are the Purest and Best in the

CARLING BREWING & MALTING AD FROM THE
LONDON FREE PRESS CHRISTMAS NUMBER FOR 1889
*Striking in its detail, this advertisement impressed upon
consumers the virtues of Carling's brand line-up. In
particular, the brewery illustration conveyed an image of
modern, factory-made beer to a Victorian populace
obsessed with industrial progress. This ethos stands in
sharp contrast to current beer marketing practices.*

Market — Try Them!" "Carling's Milwaukee Lager is the Finest, Purest & Best Drink for Summer Weather." "Carling's Old and Superior Stock Ale. . . equal in every respect to Bass' XXX." "For the Use of Invalids [then meaning weak, undernourished people] and Ladies Our Porter is. . . guaranteed by us to be made from the same malt as Guinness' Dublin Stout, and equal to it in every respect." On December 27, 1900, the London brewer finished the century on a very brash note: "If there is any better Ale than Carling's it has yet to be introduced to civilization."

John Labatt was just as creative. In 1893, for example, he promoted his I.P.A. and XXX Stout as "The most wholesome of beverages for general use, and without superior as nutrient tonics. Recommended by connoisseurs and physicians throughout Canada." Quite understandably, he also highlighted his brands' growing prize-record. After victories at Chicago's Columbian Exposition, for instance, he triumphantly declared that his brands were "Surpassing all Canadian and United States competitors in every respect." A more elaborate claim, this time for Extra Stock Ale, came in April 1900: "Brewed with exceptional care and watchfulness until just the right body and flavor are obtained. Its flavor is the true flavor of good malt and hops. No substitutes used. At the proper age it is bottled, and consumers are offered an absolutely pure, sparkling and delicious beverage — tonic and refreshing to the body and quenching to the thirst. One case in your home will demonstrate to your entire satisfaction that it is the best table ale brewed." Labatt concluded the century by boldly asserting that his brand of brands, I.P.A., was "free from the faults of Lager and heavier brands of Ale and has the virtues of a pure beverage."

THE LABATT CAMPAIGN

John Labatt's late Victorian print-advertising campaign was then Canada's most spirited. Wide-ranging, demographically savvy and quite pioneering, it deserves special mention. Notably, Labatt stands as one of Canada's first brewers to see the value of always keeping his brand names before the public eye. To reach the broadest swath of consumers, he placed ads in newspapers, magazines and directories across the country. In particular, Labatt identified newspapers, great and small, as his best bet. In keeping with this philosophy, he promoted his flagship brands in journals that ranged in size from small community sheets, such as Gore Bay's *Algoma Conservator*, to widely circulated metropolitan dailies, such as the *Toronto Empire*.

Another notable Labatt promotional innovation was that he was the first brewer in Ontario, if not all of Canada, to advertise on a sustained basis in demographically targeted periodicals. To capture the notice of particular beer-loving audiences, he turned to such market-specific serials as *The Farmer's Advocate* (Canada's foremost agricultural journal), *The Labor Advocate* (official organ of the Knights of Labor), *The Irish Canadian* (held a large Irish-Catholic readership), *The Sentinel and Orange and Protestant Advocate* (held a large Irish-Protestant readership), *The Week* (a current affairs paper), *Saturday Night* (an upscale variety magazine) and, of course, periodicals aimed at the licensed trade.

Although Labatt's advertising strategy might seem rather unremarkable in light of modern beer marketing, one must understand that the fundamentals he laid down are still with us. Have a hard time believing this? Then consider that Labatt recently outbid Molson for the sponsorship rights to *Hockey Night in Canada* chiefly because most of the program's viewers also happen to love beer. The logic behind landing the television deal traces its origins to John Labatt's choice to advertise in the audience-specific journals of his time. Just as the Victorian brewer went after Irish beer-drinkers in Irish-interest newspapers, the modern brewer is now going after Canadian beer-drinkers of all ethnic backgrounds through a hockey show. The only real difference between then and now is the medium of communication.

In any event, Labatt's promotional creativity was undoubtedly expensive. More

JOHN LABATT, 1900
This clever brewer kept his finger on the pulse of Canada's ever-evolving society. Most importantly, he understood that increasingly sophisticated promotional techniques were needed to reach an increasingly sophisticated public. Indeed, Labatt's late Victorian advertising campaign was pioneering in several important respects. Courtesy, J.J. Talman Regional Collection

OVERLEAF: LATE NINETEENTH-CENTURY BOTTLE OF CARLING'S EXPORT INDIA PALE ALE
Carling B. & M. entered the world of India Pale Ales around 1898, when its Export I.P.A. came on board. It was a heavier variety of this beer style and was premium priced for a premium market. Courtesy, Jim Maitland

importantly, however, it also paid off handsomely. According to the Mercantile Agency, over the last two Victorian decades, the value of Labatt's business quadrupled from around $50,000 to more than $200,000. Given this phenomenal leap, it can be rightfully said that Labatt's advertising blitz was his masterstroke.

NEW BRANDS

While brand-driven marketing became a fact of life in the beer world, Carling and Labatt rechristened some of their brands. In 1886, Labatt's Stout became the stronger-sounding Labatt's XXX Stout. Meanwhile, Carling changed Bavarian Stock Lager to Milwaukee Lager in a move to associate the beer with the continent's most famous lager city. In 1895, Milwaukee Lager became Imperial Club Lager. This intentionally, although quite ironically, lent a British cast to the Germanic drink. Entirely new brands also came on board during the era. In 1889, Labatt introduced Extra Stock Ale and Carling added Export India Pale Ale about ten years later.

Interestingly, these new brands, whether reincarnated or freshly developed, were aimed at niche markets. As Labatt's Toronto rep noted of Extra Stock Ale: "This special brand is extra heavy; brewed from the very best malt (English and Bavarian hops used in every brew), and is equal, if not superior, to any imported ales." Carling's Export India Pale Ale was similarly heavy. Both brands were premium priced and directed at a burgeoning market for premium beers. At the other end of the scale, Carling's Imperial Club Lager was a low-octane, low-priced brand. As one ad proclaimed: "This delicious beverage is suitable for family use, containing only about 2½ percent of alcohol." In 1896, a mere sixty cents could get you a dozen quarts of Imperial Club Lager on the retail market. This was about a third the cost of twelve quarts of regular alcohol beer. Now, to think that modern brewers take full credit for coming up with the concepts of premium, light and economy beers!

IMAGE MARKETING

As strange as it may seem to our twenty-first-century sensibilities, modern brewery advertising has not incorporated a single new basic premise since the late nineteenth century. To be sure, radio, television and the Internet lend a fresh and sophisticated ring to modern ads, but the raw psychological themes — namely, the association of beer with modernity, friendship, social popularity, health, good times, the good life, athletic prowess, sexuality and, of course, the superior taste experience — were all worked out before 1900. Put another way, only the manner of presentation has changed and not the substance. In any case, at the heart of things lay the selling of an image, which, in turn, sold beer.

Carling and Labatt particularly sought to portray their brands as the finest modern technology could provide. To understand why they chose this route is to understand the Victorian mind-set. In a nutshell, Victorian Canadians were obsessed with material progress and they fancied goods produced in the most up-to-date manner. (They sound a lot like us, do they not?) Consequently, they associated top product quality and reliability with that ultimate industrial symbol of their age, the large smoke-stacked factory. To lend a factory-made image to their brands, the London brewers incorporated handsome drawings of their plants into their advertising posters (for examples, see the Colour Plates). Given that Carling and Labatt did, in fact, operate factory-like breweries, the association was not an unfair one. John Labatt, however, did not stop with projections of modernity. Most notably, he blended themes of friendship and the good life in his famous "Two Gentlemen" poster (see Colour Plates). To boot, this brilliant advertisement also conveyed an image of respectability as a clever counter to the smear tactics of the temperance lobby.

LABEL FOR LABATT'S I.P.A. WITH THE FAMOUS ARROW TRADEMARK, CIRCA 1887
Trademarks were fundamental to building an overall brewery identity in late Victorian Canada. In the mid-1880s, John Labatt adopted a red triangle as his first trademark. However, Bass, the English brewing giant, had a few problems with the Londoner's choice, since it had long used a red triangle as its trademark. Not wishing a legal battle, Labatt reworked his triangle into an arrow. All things considered, the new shape was much more animated and appropriately symbolized his upwards climb. By the way, "Ask your Grocer for the Arrow Brand" was one of Labatt's popular advertising slogans.

BUILDING BREWERY IDENTITIES

Late Victorian brewers, ever sensitive to outward appearances, also cultivated public identities for their breweries. This development, the forerunner of today's corporate image building, both grew from and fed into brand-driven marketing. Most obviously, the very act of advertising brand names gave breweries an identity. For instance, John Labatt's promotion of his brands as prize winners had the added effect of blessing his brewery with a prize-winning reputation. More concretely, perhaps, symbols and stylized artwork also contributed to public image. For example, Carling's Maltese Cross and Labatt's arrow, both trademarks adopted in the mid-1880s, were strong identifiers of their breweries. Incidentally, Labatt always described his mark as an arrow and not a spearhead as has often been assumed. In the late 1890s, the Londoners began to distinguish their very names with custom letterings.

"BIG CITY" AGENCIES

Integration in the Canadian beer world reached its Victorian peak during the period from 1885 to 1900. A combination of increased production capacity and greater scales of economy at newly built breweries, the expansion of rail networks and the proliferation of refrigerated railway cars (perfect for non-winter transport of beer) saw suds flow from everywhere to everywhere. Lessons learned from the Scott Act era also came into play, as many brewers sought sales far and wide just in case that horrible little bugaboo — local-option prohibition — ever returned.

CARLING B. & M. CORPORATE LOGOS, CIRCA 1895 (UPPER) AND CIRCA 1900 (LOWER)
In the mid-1880s, Carling B. & M. chose a Maltese Cross as its trademark and thereafter "The Mark that Means Quality" distinguished the company's stationery, advertising, label artwork and custom bottle designs.

Not surprisingly, agency competition was furious during these years and Middlesex's two brewing giants, Carling and Labatt, constantly strove to outdo each other on the grand national stage. In this race, Canada's biggest cities claimed special importance, as funnelling beer into large urban places was the least expensive way to reach the greatest number of thirsty consumers. However, intense rivalry made things tough in big cities. The state of affairs in Toronto is an excellent case in point. Besides Carling and Labatt, large breweries in Montreal, Lachine, Port Hope, Hamilton, Guelph, Waterloo, Brantford, Owen Sound and Walkerville (now part of Windsor), not to mention Toronto's own beer-makers, also courted public favour in the Ontario capital. In short, the city was absolutely awash in beer from all over. The same can be said about Canada's other major centres.

Ultimately, fighting for position in big urban markets demanded a new agency strategy. Prior to the mid-1880s, Carling and Labatt relied upon the time-honoured plan of having licensed grocers and liquor dealers represent them in large cities. While these retailers had intimate local knowledge, their commercial energies were divided every which way. How could an agent effectively promote Carling's Amber Ale when he was also selling lettuce, tomatoes, flour, eggs, sugar and meat? Or how could an agent effectively promote Labatt's India Pale Ale when he was also selling scotch whisky, rum, gin, brandy, champagne, O'Keefe's Lager, Dow's Porter and even Carling's Amber Ale? Such logic was not lost on Carling and Labatt. Unwilling to lose out, the ever ambitious Londoners shifted control of their "big city" agencies to aggressive specialists, who could devote sole attention to their brands. Significantly, this move was a crucial part of brand-driven marketing. Since Carling and Labatt first organized specialized sales branches in Ottawa and Montreal, it is worthwhile looking at developments in these cities.

CARLING'S OTTAWA AGENCY

During the late 1870s and early 1880s, Ottawa sales of Carling's beer languished under a string of liquor merchants. To rectify matters, Carling's directors placed the agency in custody of a specialist in 1884. The person they entrusted with the job was George A. Mace, formerly a grocer in Exeter, Ontario who was known to the London Carlings through the Huron County Carlings. Living up to expectations, Mace quickly built up a brisk trade. Indeed, blossoming sales under his direction saw the agency move from 30 O'Connor Street to successively larger quarters at 48 O'Connor and then at 142-144 Albert Street. Tellingly, the Albert Street facility was the largest brewery sales branch in Canada from the time it opened in 1888 until well after 1900.

In 1889, the Carling board rewarded the diligent and competent Mace with the rejuvenation and management of the Carling agency in Ontario's most lucrative beer

COMMUNITY INVOLVEMENT

To say the least, the county's Victorian brewers displayed tremendous community spirit. Most notably, many of them occupied some sort of political office at one time or another. For instance, John Balkwill, Alexander F. Beattie, John Carling, Thomas Carling, J.D. Dewan, John Dimond, Samuel Eccles, John Kinder Labatt, John Labatt and Thomas W. Shepherd all sat on various civic boards and councils. Indeed, Balkwill was the early Victorian equivalent to the mayor of London in 1845 and Dewan became Strathroy's first mayor in 1872. By the way, Balkwill was occasionally asked to leave council meetings owing to his beerful indulgences. It is not clear whether he was just acting as a walking endorsement for his brewery or whether boredom with civic politics simply got the better of him! At the time, the municipal scene was deadly dull. It did not begin to liven up until the mid-1850s. (John Carling's storied public life appears in an earlier feature.)

Incidentally, an interesting urban myth has become associated with John Kinder Labatt's aldermanic career. To this day, many Londoners credit him with originating the Victoria Day holiday. Now, while it might seem appropriate that a brewer, of all people, came up with the idea for Canada's famous May Two-Four weekend, he simply did not. At the root of this legend is a motion that Labatt the alderman put forward to organize a local celebration of the Queen's birthday. He was neither the first nor the last London councillor to do so. Moreover, credit for the national holiday properly belongs with the federal government. Nonetheless, feel free to enjoy this tale over some cold ones next Victoria Day!

Brewers also devoted time (and money) to purely economic community pursuits. The most prominent of these concerned transportation. For instance, the Carling brothers and John Kinder Labatt were principals in the formation of the Proof Line Road Company, the legacy of which is the Richmond Street/Highway Four northerly route out of London. The road was designed to enhance London's regional dominance and the connection between the road's development and selling beer should be painfully obvious. The same logic saw the brewers become involved with the establishment of railways, such as the London & Port Stanley and the London, Huron & Bruce. Despite issues of self-interest, such ventures were still of wider public importance.

Business interests were channelled even farther afield. For example, John Carling, Harry Carling, John Kinder Labatt, John Labatt, Robert Arkell and James Slater were active in London's Board of Trade. John Labatt particularly involved himself with enterprises outside his brewery. He was a vice-president of the London & Western Trust Company, director of the Huron & Erie Loan & Savings Company (a forerunner of Canada Trust), a member/director of the Ontario Investment Association, an investor in the Bank of London in Canada, a president of the Bennet Furniture Company (London East maker of church and school furnishings) and a principal of the North American Agricultural Implement & General Manufacturing Company. However, not everything Labatt touched turned to gold. For instance, the defaulting of the latter enterprise cost him dearly.

When it came to charity, local brewers could be exceedingly generous. Beer money particularly found its way to church causes. For instance, John Kinder Labatt's munificence virtually built Glanworth's Anglican Church and John Labatt liberally contributed money to Anglican missionary efforts. Brewers and their families also financially supported sports associations, schools, hospitals, homeless shelters and funds in aid of fire sufferers.

Furthermore, beer-makers offered their time and experience to a wide variety of local organizations and institutions. The Bixels devoted considerable energies to Strathroy's Masonic lodges. John Labatt was an executive member of the Church of England Young Men's Association, the Irish Benevolent Society and the London Baseball and Athletic Association. And John Carling presided over the London Horticultural Society and the Victoria Rifle Association and sat as the honourary president of the Yorkshire Society of Ontario, the Country Club of London and the Sons of England. The dynamic Carling was also a patron of the London Football Club and a trustee of London's Protestant Home for Orphans, Aged and Friendless.

BEER BARONS & THE GOOD LIFE

As one might expect, sizeable brewery profits permitted the Bixels, Carlings and Labatts all the trappings of the Victorian good life. First and foremost, they lived in stately homes that just oozed affluence. Outside, these mansions radiated with the grandiose architectural features that were so typical of the time. Inside, they were done up in true Victorian fashion, replete with parquet floors, Persian carpets, carved-oak panelling, elaborate wall hangings and decorations (which some today might dismiss as horribly gaudy), fine silver sets, tons of Eastlake and Second Empire furniture and bric-a-brac galore. Domestically, the wives ruled the roost and managed household staffs that included house maids, parlour maids, gardeners, stable boys, laundresses, cooks and wet nurses.

Socially, beer barons and their families were invited to all the best parties and fancy-dress balls. Moreover, their weddings were grand affairs with guest-lists that read like the who's who of the local establishment. Interestingly, Carlings routinely attended Labatt weddings and vice versa. Beer money also allowed the Bixels, Carlings and Labatts the luxury of annual vacations to such far-flung places as the Maritimes, New England, Britain and Continental Europe. They also frequented cottage resorts in Port Stanley, Muskoka and along Lake Huron's shoreline. In particular, Muskoka was a favourite destination of the Labatt family.

HANNAH CARLING, WIFE OF JOHN CARLING (LEFT), APRIL 1889 AND SOPHIA LABATT, SECOND WIFE OF JOHN LABATT (RIGHT), CIRCA 1885
Courtesy, National Archives of Canada and J.J. Talman Regional Collection

In addition, Middlesex's wealthy brewers could afford private educations for their children. In 1893, for instance, one of the award-winning scholars at Trinity College was John Sackville Labatt, the oldest son of John Labatt. John S. later became a beer baron in his own right and so did his younger brother, Hugh Francis.

BEER LORE — University students in sixteenth-century Germany had a notorious reputation as ill-behaved over-imbibers of beer. When it comes to university students, it would seem that some things never change!

---

market, Toronto. In typical Victorian fashion, Mace, upon the eve of his departure from Ottawa, received "a gold watch and chain" from his replacements, John Alexander Carling and Frederick William Carling, respectively John Carling's second and third oldest sons. J.A., or Jack as he was popularly known, had come to Ottawa from Montreal where he had reorganized that city's Carling agency in partnership with Thomas F. Mace (likely related to George A. Mace). Meanwhile, F.W. had joined Jack at the capital in order to be schooled in the retail beer trade. The firm of Carling Brothers ran the bottling outlet until the mid-1890s, when F.W. assumed its management on his own account. He carried the agency into the next century.

LABATT'S MONTREAL AGENCY

John Labatt's brands found immediate favour in Montreal. This was partly owing to the brewer's French surname and partly owing to his fortunate recruitment in 1878 of J.B. Richer as his initial Montreal agent. A wholesale/retail grocer at the corner of Lagauchetière and St. Charles Borromée Streets, Richer was considerably experienced at distributing goods throughout the city and had valuable contacts in the local licensed trade. Richer approached his new task with zeal and consequently moved great volumes of Labatt's beer.

Despite his vigour for the suds business, the grocer still had other commercial responsibilities. As growing sales began to outpace the capabilities of Richer's food business, Labatt recognized that enjoying the greatest potential of the Montreal market required a more specialized agent. In 1886, he transferred the agency to the recently formed Victoria Bottling Company. The move, however, was not intended as a slap against Richer. Indeed, the fact that the Victoria Bottling Company initially operated next to Richer's store strongly suggests that the grocer was somehow involved with the company's formation. Sometime during 1887 or very early 1888, for reasons that remain hidden by those pesky gaps in the historical record, Victoria Bottling became the sole property of P.L.N. Beaudry.

Beaudry immediately relocated the concern to much larger quarters at 20-26 St. Dizier Street, an address in the heart of Montreal's wholesaling district. Having dropped all other lines, Beaudry devoted his fullest energies to promoting Labatt's India Pale Ale and Labatt's XXX Stout. Within four short years, the dynamic rep had so greatly elevated sales that another relocation had become necessary. This time, the agency moved into a specially constructed building which stood prominently on De Lorimier Avenue near St. Catherine Street. Boasting 10,000 square feet of floor space, "fully supplied with every convenience, etc., and [employing] quite a large number of men and several [delivery] teams," the new two-storey facility was one of the largest of its kind in Canada. Evidence suggests that John Labatt financed construction and thereafter retained ownership of the building. Meanwhile, Beaudry owned and managed the distribution side of the

PERSPECTIVE DRAWINGS OF LABATT'S BREWERY AND AGENCIES IN TORONTO, MONTREAL AND OTTAWA, 1900
"Big city" agencies were key in the struggle for national dominance. If one did not have them, then one did not have the slightest chance of being a major player in the Canadian game. By 1900, the ever-aggressive Labatt and Carling had established sales branches across the entire country. By the way, the brewery view looks southeast from the intersection of Simcoe and Talbot Streets. Courtesy, J.J. Talman Regional Collection

HENRY "HARRY" WEIDMAN, CARLING'S AGENT IN
BRANTFORD, 1888
*Harry Weidman became the Brantford agent for Carling
B. & M. in 1886. Well-connected, jovial and genial, he
built up a brisk trade in the Telephone City and, despite
the workings of the Scott Act, in a supposedly dry Brant
County as well. In the summer of 1889, George Sleeman
of Guelph successfully courted Weidman as the Brantford
rep for his Silver Creek Brewery.*

business under the Victoria name. Montreal sales of Labatt's beer prospered under
Beaudry's direction into the twentieth century.

Interestingly, Labatt's Montreal triumph brought about some unusual and
certainly unwanted attention. During the 1880s, A.C. Dionne, a Montreal liquor
dealer, sold bottled beer using faked Labatt labels. Dionne's labels were not precise
duplicates, but were close enough that they were fraudulent or at least laughable.
In place of "Labatt's / India Pale Ale / London Brewery" and "Labatt's / XXX Stout
/ London Brewery" the liquor merchant substituted "Albert's / India Pale Ale /
Nonlon Brewery" and "Albert's / XXX Porter / Nonlon Brewery." In addition, John
Labatt's signature appeared as "John Albert" on the forgeries. Although Dionne's
labels were cut in the same shape and bore the general colour scheme of real Labatt
labels, some of their design features differed slightly. For instance, the arrow
trademark, the barley sheaf emblems and the Paris medal images used on the
genuine article were respectively replaced with a diamond trademark, tree-like
emblems and altered medal likenesses. (For a comparison with legitimate Labatt
labels, refer to the first page of the Colour Plates.) It is an age-old saying that
imitation is the highest form of flattery. Quite understandably, however,
John Labatt was far from flattered and he called upon the law to stop such
audacious piracy.

OTHER "BIG CITY" AGENCIES

Carling and Labatt used the critical knowhow acquired in Ottawa and Montreal to
re-organize or establish agencies across country on the exclusive plan. Every major
city stood as an important battleground in this late Victorian contest for market
share. By the 1890s, the Londoners had nurtured specialized sales outlets in such
regional hubs as Halifax, Saint John, Quebec City, Montreal, Ottawa, Kingston,
Toronto, Hamilton, Brantford, Winnipeg, Regina, Calgary, Edmonton and
Vancouver. In general, "big city" agents were paid a basic salary plus a percentage
commission on sales to encourage productivity. To fund agency expansion during
this era, Labatt, still feeling the financial consequences of the 1874 fire, borrowed
money, while Carling appears to have used retained earnings.

An idea about the significance of these agencies comes from the fall of 1886,
when the *London Free Press* glowingly noted that Carling & Mace had "built up a
trade of something like ten carloads per month" within a year of putting Montreal's
Carling agency on the principle of exclusive representation. By the way, to
jumpstart business, Jack Carling and Thomas Mace had friends fan out into
Montreal's tavern community and demand Carling beer. When unable to secure

their delight, they would kick up a fuss and assure barkeepers that Carling's was the best on the market. A few days later, Carling and Mace would call around and solicit business. Not surprisingly, orders anxiously poured forth. Many other "big city" reps were just as aggressive and creative.

AGENCIES IN SMALLER PLACES

The brewers' battle for market share continued to lend importance to smaller cities and towns, especially in Ontario. In keeping, Carling and Labatt maintained agencies in Simcoe, Woodstock, St. Thomas, Chatham, Sarnia, Windsor, Stratford, Goderich, Walkerton, Collingwood, Orangeville, Guelph, Galt, Brampton, Peterborough, Cobourg, Trenton, Belleville, Picton, Brockville and points in between. While success in large centres dictated the move to specialists, the Londoners had to compromise this philosophy elsewhere. Quite simply, dealers in smaller places did not enjoy trades big enough to make exclusive agency arrangements worth their while. The end result was that Carling and Labatt had to settle for agents who stocked other products and other beers. Still, something was better than nothing.

DETAIL FROM A CARLING AD APPEARING IN THE *LONDON NEWS* ANNIVERSARY ISSUE FOR 1897
The most remarkable feature of this advertising example is that it boasts the custom-designed typeface that Carling B. & M. adopted to craft its public image even further. Note the Maltese Cross.

FOREIGN AGENCIES

The county's two largest breweries also cast eyes beyond Canada's borders. John Labatt wanted a slice of the American pie, particularly in the mid-western states. By the mid-1890s, the brewer had established agencies in Chicago, Omaha and Kansas City. Carling was also present in the United States with an outlet in Detroit and through a licensing agreement with a Cleveland brewery (see feature). More amazing, perhaps, is that Carling B. & M. even looked to the Pacific Rim for customers. Beginning in the late 1880s, Carling used the Canadian Pacific Railway to reach Hong Kong of all places! Once every year, several railcars full of Carling's Amber Ale and XXX Porter would leave London and head for Vancouver via the "Great Red Route" that belted together the British Empire. Upon arrival at the western port, the beer was loaded aboard a steamship and carried across the ocean to a representative in the fabled Anglo-Chinese city.

BEER LORE — As Canada's Minister of Agriculture, John Carling was in charge of organizing the country's exhibits at the Indian and Colonial Exhibition at London, England in 1886, the International Exhibition at Jamaica in 1892 and the Columbian Exposition at Chicago in 1893. At these three international fairs, John Labatt's beer out-prized Carling's beer. Talk about irony!

THE LOCAL MARKET STILL UNDER SIEGE

To revisit another recurring theme, agency integration in the local market also attained its Victorian peak during the period from 1885 to 1900. At liquor stores

LONDON'S MASONIC TEMPLE, NORTHWEST CORNER OF KING AND RICHMOND STREETS, CIRCA 1882
During the mid-1890s, this building housed Ed Shea's liquor store. Who was Ed Shea? Well, he was London's late Victorian equivalent of The Beer Store of our century. Besides local brands from Carling, Labatt and Hamilton, he also stocked Bott's Malt Stout and a slew of beers from Bass, Guinness, Sleeman, Walkerville Brewing and all the big Toronto concerns. In 1900, Shea moved to larger quarters at 173 Dundas Street. Courtesy, J.J. Talman Regional Collection

and hotels throughout the county, the parched could find relief with beer from dozens of Canadian breweries. Prominent Ontario intruders from outside Middlesex included British American Brewing (Windsor), Walkerville Brewing (Windsor), Rudolph & Begg (St. Thomas), Luke (Tillsonburg), Bernhardt/Otterbein (Woodstock), Devlin & Steele (Stratford), Rau (New Hamburg), Kuntz (Waterloo), Huether (Waterloo), Rock Brewery (Preston), Bixel (Brantford), Sleeman (Guelph), Holliday (Guelph), Grant (Hamilton), Taylor & Bate (St. Catharines) and Copland, Cosgrave, Davies, Dominion, O'Keefe, Reinhardt and Toronto Brewing & Malting (all Toronto). Quebec names included Boswell (Quebec City), Dawes (Lachine) and Molson and Dow (both Montreal). Those who preferred an old-country taste could still rely upon the usual familiars, such as Guinness and Bass, and those who wanted something new and American could turn to Anheuser-Busch, whose famous lager arrived on the scene during the late 1880s.

TRAVELLERS & HOTELKEEPERS

In the grand scheme of things, hotel sales still loomed very large in Canada's late Victorian beer world. Thanks to a much broader historical record, we can paint a fairly clear picture of the relationship between London's brewers and hotelkeepers during the years 1885 to 1900 (although what happened during this period was likely the case before the mid-1880s).

Travelling brewery reps continued to come primarily from the brewing and hotelkeeping trades and, unlike earlier times, a national railway network allowed them to roam the entire country from the Maritimes to Vancouver Island. In Ontario, Carling and Labatt travellers serviced sales territories scattered from Windsor in the southwest to Cornwall in the east to Sudbury and Thunder Bay (then Fort William and Port Arthur) in the north. No stone was left unturned! Orders were forwarded by mail or telegraph back to London for fulfillment by rail and/or wagon. Occasionally, a rep might send a request to the nearest urban agent. Still, direct dealings with the home brewery were preferred and intentionally kept agents hungry enough to hunt up their own sales.

Relaying orders, however, was easy — landing them in the first place was the trick. Commercial travellers had to engage all of their charms and wits to bring in sales. Jack Carling, for instance, recalled that, in order to keep every hotelkeeper happy in a small town, he had to buy his drinks from one, purchase his meal from another, get his overnight lodgings from yet another and so on and so forth. In the face of thick competition — a situation which gave hoteliers a great deal of bargaining power — brewery reps had to offer clients a whole raft of inducements to cultivate and maintain customer loyalty. First and foremost, hotelkeepers were extended generous credit terms. Depending on the scale of their bar businesses and their financial standings, they could order from $200 to $500 worth of beer without having to make good for three months. Moreover, Carling and Labatt allowed hoteliers to honour their obligations through regular monthly payments or through lump sums returned every few months. Rebates were sometimes granted once an account was squared. Carling B. & M., for instance, refunded fifty cents per half-barrel in the 1890s.

Other inducements included budging on "one-price-for-all" policies, waiving freight charges on fulls sent out and on empties sent back and waiving deposit charges on bottles, cases, barrels and pump and tap sets. However, such charges were levied on unreturned or damaged property. Incidentally, deposit fees were quite hefty and were typically as follows: 50¢ per dozen quart bottles, $1.00 per wooden bottle case, $1.25 per quarter-barrel, $1.75 per half-barrel, $2.25 per standard barrel, $4.50 per hogshead and $10.00 per pump and tap set. In addition, the abovementioned advertising giveaways sweetened many a deal with hotelkeepers.

TYPICAL PRICES, 1885 TO 1896

WHOLESALE (including shipping charges):
$0.50 per doz. quarts of Carling's Bavarian Stock Lager to Dunnville
$0.79 per doz. pints of Carling's Amber Ale to London
$0.89 per doz. pints of Labatt's I.P.A. to Port Arthur
$0.89 per doz. pints of Labatt's XXX Stout to Port Arthur
$0.90 per doz. quarts of Carling's Amber Ale to Dunnville
$1.00 per doz. quarts of Carling's Amber Ale to Massey
$1.00 per doz. quarts of Carling's XXX Porter to Massey
$1.13 per doz. pints of Labatt's I.P.A. to Petrolia
$1.64 per doz. quarts of Labatt's I.P.A. to Port Arthur
$1.64 per doz. quarts of Labatt's XXX Stout to Port Arthur
$1.75 per firkin of Carling's Bavarian Stock Lager to Dunnville
$2.00 per doz. quarts of Labatt's I.P.A. to Petrolia
$3.50 per kilderkin of Carling's Amber Ale to London
$7.50 per barrel of Labatt's I.P.A. to Petrolia
$7.50 per barrel of Labatt's XXX Stout to Kingston
$8.00 per barrel of Carling's Amber Ale to Gore Bay
$8.00 per barrel of Carling's XXX Porter to Massey
$8.00 per barrel of Carling's Amber Ale to Massey
$14.00 per hogshead of Carling's Amber Ale to London
$15.00 per hogshead of Carling's XXX Porter to London
$15.00 per hogshead of Carling's Amber Ale to Picton
$15.00 per hogshead of Carling's Amber Ale to Sandwich
$15.00 per hogshead of Labatt's I.P.A. to Kingston

DRAWBACKS

The hotel trade was not without its headaches, however. Most notably, travellers maintained constant vigils against the use of their taps for other beer. Accounting discrepancies complicated matters, while point-blank refusals to pay up, customer insolvencies and absconding debtors made things even worse. Of course, routine accountings, regular communication, compromise, tact and skillful negotiation went a long way to solving problems. For example, to accommodate a customer who had fallen upon hard times, credit terms could be further extended or debts even discounted or forgiven in very special circumstances. Upon rare occasion, Carling and Labatt accepted property mortgages and transfers of hotel ownership to settle sorely past-due accounts (hotels were subsequently sold off).

CRIMES AGAINST THE BREWERY

If outward Victorian appearances gleamed with moral uprightness, then the era's dark closet was filled with a whole raft of swindlers, robbers, break-in artists and sundry felons. These crooks stole everything and anything that they could lay their hands on, including what breweries in London-Middlesex had to offer. For instance, a burglar once made off with one of Robert Arkell's brewing instruments, while an even bolder thief or thieves audaciously stole a delivery cutter and horse from a duo of Carling brewery teamsters who were on a wintertime hotel run. The same fate befell a set of barrel skids used by some Labatt employees while on another winter delivery trip.

Naturally, beer was the most coveted prize of all and some criminals went to amazing lengths to claim it. Indeed, one drunken fool even tried to roll a full barrel of ale right out the door of Carling's warehouse! Another intoxicated thief, a soldier with the Royal Artillery, was caught trying to break into Labatt's brewery. Not wishing to offend London's wider community of beer-drinking military personnel, a forgiving John Kinder Labatt declined to press charges. Beer barrels were also favoured by the shiftless. These strong and sturdy vessels often found their way into private households just as plastic milk crates do today.

Two extraordinarily creative crimes hit the Kent Brewery. In April 1862, John Bryan placed an order at the brewery. He sent a group of children to deliver his request and fetch his beer. When payment failed to materialize, the owners, Hamilton & Morgan, investigated and discovered that Bryan was "a mere child" who, despite his tender years, had "a peculiar relish for a certain beverage." Bryan later faced a judge, but had the case against him dismissed since it was his first offence. Interestingly, the unlikely underworld mastermind was charged not because of his age, but because he had received goods under false pretences.

On the morning of March 14, 1893, Joseph Hamilton walked into a brewery office that had all of its windows blown out and its furniture knocked upside down. The chief clue to what had happened could be found amidst the mess and turmoil. The safe, in its twisted and mangled state, indicated that a team of old-fashioned safecrackers had visited the brewery the night before. Given that the sound of the explosion went undetected, the *London Free Press* surmised that "the tremendous rush and jar" of an early morning express train had drowned out the report of the explosive. This is logical and strongly suggests that the thieves had cleverly targeted the Kent Brewery owing to its proximity to the Canadian Pacific line. However, the safecrackers had more smarts than luck that night. They only got $35 for their trouble.

BEER LORE — Every common geometric shape has been incorporated into beer label artwork. The list includes the triangle, square, rectangle, trapezoid, diamond, pentagon, hexagon, heptagon, octagon, decagon, circle, oval, four-pointed star, five-pointed star, six-pointed star, seven-pointed star, eight-pointed star, crescent and half-moon.

The law was a last resort. To get satisfaction from delinquent debtors, Carling and Labatt had courts execute writs of attachment against hotel property and pressed for creditor auctions of insolvent hoteliers' goods and chattels. In extreme cases, the brewers just sued. Law suits were reserved for especially obstinate clients, who absolutely refused payment, fraudulently transferred property prior to creditor auctions or simply fled to that great home of the brave and the Victorian Canadian absconder, the United States. The case of George Lumby, a London hotelkeeper, is an interesting example of the latter. Considerably indebted to several parties, including Carling B. & M., he skipped to Detroit in 1887. Although knowing Lumby was beyond the reach of Canadian law, the brewer sued anyway. Since the former hotelman did not show to defend the suit, Carling received a favourable judgement. The court also issued a writ of capias (arrest order) against Lumby. Thinking that the coast was clear, the absconder returned to London to attend his father's estate sale in early November the next year. He was immediately "pounced upon by the bailiffs" and jailed until his wife paid his brewery debt.

TIED HOUSES

The subject of hotels and beer brings up the issue of tied houses. Tied houses were hotels which were figuratively tied to a given brewery through some sort of financial arrangement which gave the brewer the sway required to ensure that the hotels only carried his beer. Leverage usually came in the form of the brewer possessing the hotel's liquor license, holding a mortgage on hotel property or owning the hotel absolutely. In any case, tied houses were a capital intensive proposition and tended to be a phenomenon peculiar to the truly monstrous breweries in the United Kingdom and huge breweries in some American metropolises. As a general rule, the tied house was a rare bird in Victorian Ontario for two notable reasons. First of all, the provincially-controlled liquor licensing system effectively prohibited brewers from taking out hotel licenses (although not necessarily agency licenses). Moreover, breweries in Ontario, while including some of Canada's largest, simply did not have the awesome pools of extra capital needed to control large strings of hotels.

Of course, this is not to say that Carling and Labatt (and others, for that matter) did not try to influence hotelkeepers by spotting them loans of cash, furniture and equipment or, as the exception which proves the rule, by holding the occasional hotel mortgage. Still, questions of capital strength ultimately governed the issue as it related to local breweries and, to repeat an earlier point, Carling and Labatt could not really afford tied houses. It is unlikely that the county's other, much smaller brewers could do so either.

THE ENGLISH COME A-KNOCKING

In the late nineteenth century, England's largest brewers were amassing such mammoth fortunes that they literally could not spend their money as fast as they

G.E. TUCKEY'S WHEEL INN, GRANTON, ONTARIO, CIRCA 1906
Although dating from the very early twentieth century, this photo nonetheless reflects two notable themes of late Victorian beer selling — signage and the rarity of tied houses. If you look closely, you can spot a Carling beer sign above the gentleman to the far left and a Kent Brewery sign just barely pokes out from behind the head of the gentleman standing second from the left. The very fact that Tuckey carried brands from two London breweries strongly suggests that his hotel was not tied.
Courtesy, J.J. Talman Regional Collection

This Agreement made the

second day of March, A.D. 1897, between the several persons, firms and corporations, being Brewers, whose hands and seals or corporate seals are hereto affixed, of the first part; and E. R. C. Clarkson and Zebulun Aiton Lash of Toronto and I. F. Hellmuth of London, Ontario, Trustees, of the second part;

Witnesseth :

1. In this agreement " person " includes persons, firms and corporations; the singular number includes the plural, and the plural the singular, and the masculine includes the feminine. "Brewer" or "Brewers" means one or more of the parties of the first part. "Trustees" means the parties of the second part, and includes any new trustee or trustees appointed under this agreement.

"Purchaser agent" means a person not being a hotel or saloon keeper who purchases ale or porter from one brewer only in Ontario and who, though a purchaser, is usually spoken of among brewers as the agent of the brewer from whom he so purchases.

2. In consideration of the mutual covenants and agreements herein contained the Brewers severally, and not for each other, covenant and agree with the Trustees, and also severally and not for each other covenant and agree with the others of them and with each of the others, as follows:

3. This agreement shall not take effect unless and until it has been executed by or on behalf of The Dominion Brewery Company (Limited), The Ontario Breweries (Limited), The Davies Brewing and Malting Company (Limited), The Ontario Brewing and Malting Company (Limited), The Copeland Brewing and Malting Company, The O'Keefe Brewery Company (Limited), The Toronto Brewing and Malting Company (Limited), The Cosgrave Brewery Company (Limited), all of Toronto; The Walkerville Brewery Company (Limited), Walkerville; The Carling Brewing and Malting Company (Limited), London; John Labatt, London; George Sleeman, Guelph; Taylor & Bate, St. Catharines; The Grant-Lottridge Brewing Company, Limited, Hamilton; The Ambrose Winslow Brewing and Malting Company, Limited, Port Hope; Bowie & Company, Brockville; The J. McCarthy & Son Company, Limited, Prescott; The Prescott Brewing and Malting Company, Limited.

4. Upon this agreement being executed by or on behalf of the parties mentioned in paragraph number 3, it shall take effect and be binding and shall continue in force until the thirty-first day of December, 1897, and thereafter if agreed to be continued as provided by paragraph No. 25 hereof, and no Brewer shall be entitled to withdraw from this agreement while it continues in force. The execution by Robert Davies on behalf of The Dominion Brewery Company (Limited), and by William J. Thomas on behalf of The Ontario Breweries (Limited), shall be sufficient.

5. So soon as this agreement takes effect each Brewer having executed the same and each Brewer thereafter executing this agreement shall deposit with the Trustees the sum of Five Hundred Dollars, which shall be deposited at interest by the Trustees in a chartered Bank to a special account and shall be held and dealt with by the Trustees for the purposes and in the manner hereinafter mentioned.

INTRODUCTORY PAGE OF THE PRICE-FIXING AGREEMENT OF MARCH 2, 1897

Like every other business interest, Victorian brewers occasionally entered into "protective associations" to halt harmful price-cutting in their industry. Price-fixing was also a solution to the effects of the general economic depression that hit Canada during most of the 1890s.

could make it. Nearing the practical limits of their domestic and foreign markets, they began to buy up overseas breweries. At first, the Anglo beer barons cast their eyes upon the United States and scooped up a few of the biggest American breweries. By the late 1880s, the English were looking a little farther north.

In 1889, an unnamed English syndicate of brewers and other capitalists approached Carling and Labatt. Evidently, the Londoners were sufficiently tempted that John Labatt left for England that summer to negotiate the sale of both breweries. (Labatt had been authorized by Carling's directors to bargain on their behalf.) The *St. Thomas Journal* noted: "The plan adopted is to purchase [each] brewery at a fixed price, paying 60 per cent of the purchase money, the owner of the brewery at the time of the purchase to continue to manage it and to retain [a] 40 per cent interest in the concern." However, Labatt returned without a deal, as the English, despite their gobs of cash, had not offered enough. Nine years later, Labatt considered another English bid, this time to merge his business with Eugene O'Keefe's in Toronto. He declined to sell when he felt his brewery had again been undervalued. On the other hand, imagine if this deal had gone through. You might now be drinking Labatt-O'Keefe Blue — a brand name without the same ring to it!

PRICE WARS & PRICE-FIXING

Competition has long been both good and bad for business. As we have seen, the struggle for success stimulated some very creative impulses in brewers. However, heavy competition frequently triggered price wars. In an effort to improve market position in one place or another, a given brewer would lower his prices below those of his rivals. Anxious to fend off such a volley, competitors would respond in kind and thus a price war would flare up. In some cases, prices fell below the cost of production. Naturally, the consumer benefitted immeasurably, but, in the long run, price wars were certainly not in the brewers' best interests. Price-fixing was the solution to price wars (and, it should be noted, to the harmful effects of economic depressions, such as the one which hit Canada for most of the 1890s).

Every now and again, brewers joined together to set uniform prices. Of course, protective schemes depended upon universal adherence and, as one might guess, they rapidly collapsed once abrogated. During the late 1880s and early 1890s, several efforts fell apart owing to such breakdowns. Still, beer-makers pressed on. In 1897, for example, members of The Brewers' and Maltsters' Association of Ontario fixed the following wholesale prices for ale and porter: $1.40 per dozen quarts (bottle deposit of 50¢ included), 70¢ per dozen pints (bottle deposit of 10¢ included), 30¢ per barrelled imperial gallon for orders less than 1,500 gallons and 26¢ per barrelled imperial gallon for orders greater than 1,500 gallons. Discounts of five percent on bottled beer and ten percent on barrelled beer were allowed on accounts paid off within specified periods. To encourage compliance, fines for infractions were to be subtracted from the $500 that each brewer was required to post as a bond. Among the eighteen signatories to this agreement were Sleeman of Guelph, O'Keefe of Toronto, and Carling and Labatt of London. Harry Carling of Carling B. & M. and George Labatt of Prescott B. & M. sat on the cartel's management committee. It is not known if the parties renewed this agreement upon its expiry at year's end.

Now, lest you think that brewers were the only ones to act in collusion, be advised that every other business interest, including railways, steamship lines, grocers, dry goods merchants, druggists, shoemakers, flour millers, stove founders, oil refiners (even then — go figure!), physicians and lawyers, played the game. In Victorian Canada, price-fixing was an expected and accepted commercial reality. Furthermore, in certain organized forms, it was not then an illegal practice.

A NEW COURSE FOR THE KENT BREWERY

The very fact that London's small Kent Brewery survived at all is telling evidence that the awesome strength of industry giants and stiff agency competition were not enough to knock-out the proverbial little guy. However, this is not to say that the Kent Brewery stayed around because of sheer luck. On the contrary, the concern survived because its owners also drew upon such concepts as focused sales, branding and persistent advertising, albeit on a much more modest scale.

In the mid-1880s, John Hamilton took stock of the changing world around him and concluded that quietly going about things would do no longer. Recognizing that he did not have a snowball's chance in July to better Carling and Labatt on volume and area of distribution, he determined to outdo them (and others, for that matter) in the local niche market for English-style porter. Although not entirely abandoning his ale line, he nonetheless began to emphasize the porter side of his business in the ads which he now regularly placed in city newspapers. Unfortunately, Hamilton did not enjoy the fruits of his new plan for long. On October 9, 1887, at age sixty-three, the brewer passed away. Since he died intestate, the Kent Brewery immediately became the property of his widow, Agnes. In turn, Agnes sold it to their only son, Joseph.

JOSEPH HAMILTON TAKES THE REINS

In his mid-twenties, Joseph Hamilton lent a crucial flare to the business. He immediately branded his flagship beer as Hamilton's London Porter. The name did not solely derive from the Ontario city. If anything, it was an association with the widely

THE LABATT "SIGNATURE," 1900
John Labatt used this custom-stylized script as another means to distinguish the public face of his business. Although not the brewer's true signature, the personalized trademark appeared in Labatt advertising well into the twentieth century.

CARLING PRESIDENTS, 1882 TO 1900

John Beattie - 1882 to 1885
Daniel Macfie - 1885 to 1887
H. Becher - 1887 to 1888
Harry Carling - 1888 to 1894
Sir John Carling - 1894 to 1900

KENT BREWERY AD FROM THE *LONDON FREE PRESS* CHRISTMAS NUMBER FOR 1889
The enterprising Joseph Hamilton also used brand recognition techniques to promote his beers. Along with the bold headlines, the label facsimiles dominate this ad.

BEER LORE — According to a bartenders' guide book published in 1862, the recipe for "ale flip" called for the mixing together of a quart of boiled ale, four eggs, four tablespoons of sugar and half a nutmeg. What was "ale flip"? It was a cold remedy. Don't you wish you had a cold right now?

known catch-all, London Porter, that denoted any of the famous porters brewed in the great English metropolis since the mid-1700s. Hamilton's choice astutely equated his product with a century and a half of old-world tradition and quality. Britons had their London Porter and now thirsty Canucks in London-Middlesex had one too.

To promote his London Porter, Hamilton followed his father's advertising lead, but added a few twists. Firstly, he rescued the Kent Brewery ad space from the back pages of the *London Free Press* and put it next to the paper's masthead. Secondly, the brewer frequently changed the layout and content of his ads to give his prominent advertising corner a fresh look. Thirdly, in keeping with branding principles, he designed a mantra-like wording strategy to impress upon the beer-loving public exactly who brewed the best porter available. The following are but a handful of his promotional flourishes: "Hamilton's London Porter is Universally Acknowledged to the be the Peer of all Porters." "Hamilton's London Porter still maintains its high standard of excellence, never deviating except for the better." "Hamilton's London Porter is unsurpassed by any Canadian Stout. You can always rely on the quality of this article." "Hamilton's London Porter is equal to the best imported. Sells on its own merits. You cannot make a mistake if you ask for Hamilton's." "Hamilton's London Porter — The Most Recommended Beverage on the Market."

Hamilton's plan of attack quickly returned dividends. In October 1888, the *London Advertiser* observed that he had rapidly built up a large local trade. Over the next five years, the hardworking brewer nearly tripled his commercial worth. Indeed, a growing business allowed him to build a fine residence next to the brewery in 1893. (It still stands at 183 Ann Street.) Near the end of the century, booming porter sales prompted Hamilton to make "extensive alterations and additions" to the Kent Brewery. The remodelling doubled his capacity. Reporting on the expansion, a local scribe glowed that Hamilton's London Porter was "uniformly pleasant to the taste." Such praise seemingly confirmed the brewer's advertising claims. Ironically, Joseph Hamilton had pulled the whole thing off from 197 Ann Street, an address that literally put his brewery in the shadow of the goliath Carling plant some two blocks to the west. Ultimately, his success proved that even the humble could be mighty in their own modest way.

Shrinking Fortunes in Strathroy

In marked contrast to the Kent Brewery's upswing, Strathroy's brewery suffered a notable reversal in fortunes, but not until after the Bixel family sold

JOSEPH HAMILTON'S KENT BREWERY, 1905
This image shows the additions that a busy Joseph Hamilton made to the rear of his Kent Brewery in the 1890s. The main building still stands at 197 Ann Street. It is the largest surviving brewery artifact from Victorian London-Middlesex.

it in 1895. With glad hearts, the Bixels welcomed the fading of the Scott Act during the late 1880s. In this freer environment, things returned to normal and sales began to pick up. To accommodate a growing trade, both locally and at Brantford, Matthew and Cyrus formally admitted the two youngest Bixel boys, Oscar and Arthur, into partnership in early 1889. Styled as M. Bixel & Sons, the new firm was modelled on much the same lines as Carling & Co. had been fourteen years earlier. As such, M. Bixel & Sons operated the plants in Strathroy and Brantford, while Matthew and Cyrus retained ownership of the breweries' physical and real estate assets.

The Bixel Brewing & Malting Company

M. Bixel & Sons did not last long, however. On February 1, 1890, Matthew, at age sixty-one, died from lung trouble. He was buried with Masonic honours in his old home of Ingersoll. According to his testamentary wishes, his half-interest and Cyrus' half-interest in the breweries at Strathroy and Brantford were joined and

BIXEL B. & M. AD FROM THE *STRATHROY DISPATCH* OF MARCH 17, 1892 (ABOVE) AND AN AMBER STRATHROY B. & M. BOTTLE (OPPOSITE)
Although re-instituting ale production in the early 1890s, Bixel remained famous as a lager producer. Indeed, the success that Bixel B. & M. had with making lager at its Brantford branch prompted the company to sell off its Strathroy asset. The brewery eventually fell into the hands of a Strathroy investor group, whose members incorporated themselves as the Strathroy Brewing & Malting Company, Limited. (ad is computer enhanced) Courtesy, Jim Butler

then divided into three equal shares amongst Cyrus, Oscar and Arthur. Eleven days after their father's passing, the brothers, along with their wives, Emily, Dorah and Emma, applied for a federal charter to incorporate the Bixel Brewing & Malting Company, Limited to assume the assets and trade of M. Bixel & Sons. Letters patent were granted on May 6 and the new company's capitalization stood at $150,000 divided into 1,500 shares with a nominal value of $100 each. Like Carling B. & M., Bixel B. & M. was a private entity. Cyrus, Oscar and Arthur sat as the company's directors and were respectively president, vice-president and secretary-treasurer.

LUDWIG & BRENER
Bixel B. & M. operated both its breweries until 1895. On June 25 that year, thirty-nine-year-old Cyrus died from head injuries suffered during a freak carriage accident. He willed 150 shares in the family business to his wife, Emily, and the balance of his stock, amounting to 90 shares, to his son, Arthur Winlow. To Bixel B. & M., he left his portion of brewery real estate. Oscar and Arthur carried on, but preferred to operate the thriving, much newer and larger Brantford branch. In early November, they sold the Strathroy brewery to a pair of Londoners, Louis V. Ludwig and Otto E. Brener. Emily and Arthur Winlow retained their shares in Bixel B. & M.

We have already met Ludwig as Carling's lager brewer back in the early 1880s and as the vinegar- and cider-maker who had rented space in Slater's malthouse. Meanwhile, Otto E. Brener constituted one half of Brener Brothers. The Breners' Ridout Street cigar factory cranked out more than a million "Havana Cat" stogies per year. It seems that Brener saw brewery ownership chiefly as an investment opportunity, although his experience with distributing cigars to hotels made the move into brewing a natural one. In any event, a hopeful *Strathroy Dispatch* predicted: "In the hands of such capable men as the [new] proprietors, success is almost assured." Unfortunately, the operative word in this quotation turned out to be *almost*.

A house divided always falls and so was the case with Ludwig & Brener. Essentially, the partners could not get along, although over what issues remains unknown. Within a year, Ludwig wanted out and he launched a law suit against Brener on October 6, 1896. In particular, Ludwig petitioned the court "to have the affairs of the partnership wound up." Eleven days later (justice was much swifter then), Judge Edward Elliott of the High Court of Middlesex ordered an accounting of the firm's assets, the placement of the business into receivership and the dissolution of the partnership contingent upon the sale of the brewery as a going concern. Frank Brookes, a Strathroy accountant, was appointed as receiver and thenceforth supervised the brewery's operation. Meanwhile, Ludwig returned full-time to vinegar- and cider-making and Brener returned full-time to cigar-making.

The whole affair was messy and in its wake was left a greatly diminished brewing enterprise. When Ludwig & Brener took over the Bixel brewery, the credit-reporting house of R.G. Dun & Company estimated the value of the business to be in the robust $35,000 to $50,000 bracket. When the brewery was sold out of receivership, Dun had dramatically lowered its rating to the $5,000 to $10,000 range. At the end of 1896, the once great brewery was but a shadow of its former self.

THE STRATHROY BREWING & MALTING COMPANY

However, a brave group of locals made a go of things anyway. On February 24, 1897, Ontario letters patent were granted to Patrick O'Dwyer, William O'Dwyer (both grocers and liquor dealers), Frank Brookes (the accountant), George Wilson, Richard Dumbrill (both gentlemen), Alexander Stevenson (a harness-maker) and Adolph Freund (a brewer formerly with Bixel) to incorporate the Strathroy Brewing & Malting Company, Limited (Strathroy B. & M.). A private joint-stock company, it was capitalized at $11,000 divided into 220 shares each with a nominal value of $50. Freund, Stevenson, Dumbrill and Patrick O'Dwyer formed the company's first board of directors. Freund also served as brewmaster. Interestingly, the involvement of two liquor dealers suggests that Strathroy B. & M. was more than just an investment for some. Under the Strathroy B. & M. banner, the brewery found some much needed stability and it gradually healed from damage inflicted under the bickering Ludwig and Brener. While never recapturing the Bixel glory of old, the concern lived out the rest of the century as a steady regional player nonetheless.

MORE FIRES

Besides minor physical additions, including the installation of an artificial ice-making plant at Carling's and the adoption of such technologies as the telephone, fires were the other notable miscellaneous occurrences at area breweries during the period 1885 to 1900. On June 25, 1886, an arsonist used rags and coal oil to set fire to the stables at Labatt's brewery. Thankfully, a properly equipped fire department (at last, the city council had rectified a once sad state of affairs!) extinguished the flames before they caused serious harm. A fire which broke out in Carling's chimney several years later was also put out before causing significant damage. The Bixels were not as fortunate, however. In 1893, they lost one of their ice houses to the "devouring element." Near the end of the century, John Labatt was even unluckier.

At 5 p.m. on Tuesday, July 4, 1899 — a day baked to 100° Fahrenheit — some employees at Hunt's flour mill noticed thick black smoke billowing from the cupola

THE LABATT BREWERY FIRE, JULY 4, 1899
Taken from the banks of the Thames River near Ridout and Carfrae Streets, this rare amateur snapshot shows the Labatt fire of 1899 not long after it started. Can you possibly imagine what John Labatt was feeling the moment this photo was snapped? After all, he had already lost one brewery back in 1874. Courtesy, London Public Library

over the drying room at Labatt's brewery. Three companies of the fire department responded to the alarm and within minutes had eight or ten streams of water aimed at the burning brewery. It took some four hours to conquer the fierce blaze, which consumed two malt kilns and the drying room. All told, the brewer suffered an estimated loss of $30,000 to $35,000 in barley, malt and physical plant. Still, the firefighters' heroic actions, along with the aid of brewery workers and private citizens, ultimately saved Labatt's enterprise from absolute ruin. Acting together, they had kept the flames from a third malt kiln and the brewery building itself. Moreover, insurance covered all damages. Incidentally, the honest Labatt returned that part of the insurance settlement he did not need to finance rebuilding.

THE CURTAIN CLOSES ON THE VICTORIAN ERA

On December 31, 1900, the end of the Victorian century, four brewers called Middlesex home — the Kent Brewery, Strathroy Brewing & Malting, Carling Brewing & Malting and John Labatt. As one might expect, the size of the latter two distinguished the county as one of Canada's major brewing centres. Indeed, the combined output of Carling and Labatt accounted for over 1,000,000 of the 14,000,000 gallons of malt liquor produced in the country during the tax-revenue year ending June 30, 1901. Impressively, the two London giants were among the top ten producers in a domestic industry that consisted of 131 breweries at the time. In pure financial terms, they were also among the top ten nationally. In September 1900, the R.G. Dun credit-rating bureau estimated the strength of each brewer's business to hover around the $200,000 level, with Labatt just a nose ahead of Carling. While Labatt's tremendous advertising campaign had given him the edge to best his crosstown rival, a most successful Carling B. & M. declared dividends in the healthy four to eight percent range over the last two Victorian decades.

Numbers, however, only tell part of the story. In 1897, the *Toronto Globe* glowingly remarked upon Carling B. & M.'s prominence: "What Guinness and Bass are to Great Britain, or Pabst to the United States, so Carling is to Canada." Three years later, the *London Free Press* applauded John Labatt's brewery management: "His name is inseparably linked with its [the brewery's] rise and progress."

CONCLUSIONS

Nineteenth-century brewers functioned within a wider drink culture brought to Canada by waves of immigrants. If it were not for settlers' demands for beer and tavern life, the domestic brewing industry would have never taken root. In this sense, beer and brewing are fundamental components of Canada's economic and social history. Indeed, among other standards, we define who we are as a nation by the very beer we drink. If you find this a stretch, then why do we pride ourselves on having better beer than our neighbours to the south?

Brewing developments in Victorian London-Middlesex are among the most important in our country's brewing past, as two of the three most prominent beer names in modern Canada — Carling and Labatt — originated in London. In fact, of all Canadian municipalities, only London can rightfully claim such an honour. Neither Montreal, nor Vancouver, nor even Toronto are so distinguished.

London's special place in Canadian brewing history boils down to three inter-related issues: the transportability of malt liquor, prudent entrepreneurship and good beer. Despite the claims of some historians to the contrary, beer in nineteenth-century Canada was a highly transportable commodity. Brewers in London-Middlesex not only recognized this, but also understood that beer could be shipped to distant places at a profit. However, knowing that beer could be sent far and wide was merely a prelude to battle. Competing beyond the local level demanded keen entrepreneurial skills, significant capital strength and product quality that met consumer expectations. The Carlings and the Labatts enjoyed these things and they used the railway, sales agencies, promotional innovations and timely investments in physical plant and technology to build their national brewing empires.

Of course, the local market remained important. Indeed, London's vibrant beer

GOOD CARDS, GOOD STOGIES AND GOOD BEER FROM A QUART BOTTLE OF LABATT'S INDIA PALE ALE, CIRCA 1900
Enough said! Courtesy, Don Cosens

scene, with its favourable demographics, thriving barroom culture and garrisoned regiments of beer-thirsty soldiers, gave the city's early brewers a significant edge over brewers in most other places. In particular, brisk local sales afforded Carling and Labatt the crucial pools of capital from which they financed their initial agency networks. This itself was the first step in the march towards national prominence. Moreover, persistent local players, such as Thomas Snell, the Tupholmes, the Hamiltons and John Allaster, further illustrate the significance of the local market. Even the regionally oriented Bixels relied upon local sales to a large degree.

Ultimately, however, it was the struggle to survive on the wider stage which crowned London as a major brewing centre in Victorian Canada. Competing in an increasingly integrated domestic marketplace literally toughened Carling and Labatt into industry leaders. In a nutshell, their triumphs were the engines that drove the county's brewing economy. Most interestingly, perhaps, is that the promotional techniques which they adopted and refined during the last quarter of the nineteenth-century — namely, branding, brand-driven marketing, national ad campaigns, image advertising and crafting corporate identities — continue as the pillars of modern beer marketing. Today's brewers owe a great deal to their Victorian predecessors.

EPILOGUE

The twentieth century brought even more change to the local brewing landscape. In 1910, ever-expanding forces of market integration spelled the end of brewing in Strathroy. On November 6 the next year, eighty-three-year-old Sir John Carling passed away. On April 27, 1915, that other grand old man of brewing, John Labatt, died at age seventy-six. A year and a half later, the passage of the Ontario Temperance Act saw the Kent Brewery close, and it was only by hook and crook that Carling and John Labatt Limited (incorporated in 1911) survived prohibition in its various provincial and federal forms over the period from 1916 to 1927.

The Great Depression worsened matters for Carling in particular. Severely weakened by family disinterest and an ill-prepared new ownership, the London concern became easy prey for E.P. Taylor's frenzied program of brewery consolidation. In 1930, Taylor absorbed the Carling plant into his Canadian Breweries conglomerate. Six years later, he closed the facility and transferred its production to the Kuntz brewery in Waterloo. (Ironically, John Labatt Limited bought this brewery in 1977.) As events turned out, only Labatt proved strong enough to survive the combined effects of prohibition, the Great Depression and "Taylorization." Today, Labatt's London plant proudly stands as one of North America's oldest operating breweries. The labels might say "since 1847," but brewing has taken place at the site ever since John Balkwill first fired his kettle back in 1828.

BEER QUOTE —
He that drinks strong beer,
And goes to bed mellow,
Lives as he ought to live,
And dies a hearty fellow.
          Eighteenth-Century English Pub Rhyme

SELECT BIBLIOGRAPHY

MANUSCRIPTS

Archives of Ontario. John Denison Papers.

J.J. Talman Regional Collection, D.B. Weldon Library, University of Western Ontario. Richard Airey Papers.

_____. London Assessment Rolls, 1844 to 1870.

_____. Middlesex County Court Records.

_____. Rance Papers.

Labatt Archives. Various collections.

National Archives of Canada. R.G. Dun Collection.

National Archives of Ireland. Various collections.

National Library of Ireland. Various collections.

EARLY MONOGRAPHS

Carling, Louisa. *Sketch of Sir John Carling*. London, Ontario.

History of the County of Middlesex. Toronto: W.A. and C.L. Goodspeed, 1889.

Montreal Illustrated, 1894. Montreal: Consolidated Illustrating Company, 1894.

Murray, Hugh. *An Historical and Descriptive Account of British America* (two volumes). Edinburgh: Oliver and Boyd, 1839.

Smith, W.H. *Smith's Canadian Gazetteer*. Toronto: H. and W. Roswell, 1846.

Tizard, W.L. *The Theory and Practice of Brewing*. London: self-published, 1857.

Traill, Catharine Parr. *The Canadian Settlers' Guide*. Reprint of 1855 edition. Toronto: McClelland and Stewart, 1969.

DIRECTORIES

The Canada Directory. Montreal: John Lovell, 1851 and 1857.

County of Oxford Gazetteer and General Business Directory for 1862-63. Ingersoll, Canada West: James Smith, 1862.

Directories for the City of Cleveland. Various titles and various publishers, 1882 to 1893.

Directories for the City of London and the County of Middlesex. Various titles and various publishers, 1856 to 1901.

Directories for the City of Ottawa. Various titles and various publishers, 1876 to 1901.

Directories for the City of Quebec. Various titles and various publishers, 1881 to 1901.

Directories for the City of Saint John. Various titles and various publishers, 1890 to 1901.

Directories for the City of Toronto. Various titles and various publishers, 1875 to 1901.

Great Western Railway Gazetteer, Commercial Advertiser and Business Directory, 1861-62. Toronto: J.L. Mitchell and Company, 1861.

Lovell's Montreal Directory. Montreal: John Lovell and Son, 1880 to 1905.

The Mercantile Agency Reference Book for the Dominion of Canada. Montreal: Dun, Wiman and Company (later R.G. Dun and Company), 1864 to 1901

GOVERNMENT DOCUMENTS AND PUBLICATIONS

Canada. *Census of Canada*, 1871, 1881 and 1891.

_____. *Report, Returns and Statistics of the Inland Revenue of the Dominion of Canada*, 1871 to 1901.

_____. *Royal Commission on the Liquor Traffic, Minutes of Evidence*, 1894.

_____. *Statistical Year-book of Canada for 1901*.

_____. Various statutes.

Ontario. *Report on the Working of the Tavern and Shop Licenses Acts*, 1881 to 1901.

_____. Various statutes.

Province of Canada. *Census of the Province of Canada*, 1842, 1851 and 1861.

_____. *Tables of Trade and Navigation of the Province of Canada*, 1859 to 1865.

_____. Various statutes.

Province of Upper Canada. Various statutes.

NEWSPAPERS AND SERIALS

(Ancaster) *Gore Gazette*.

Brantford Expositor.

Chatham Planet.

Clinton New Era.

Collingwood Enterprise.

Dominion Mechanical and Milling News.

Galt Reformer.

Glencoe Transcript.

(Goderich) *Huron Signal*.

Goderich Star.

(Gore Bay) *Algoma Conservator*.

Guelph Mercury.

(Hamilton) *Canadian Illustrated News*.

Hamilton Spectator.

Ingersoll Chronicle.

Kingston Chronicle.

London Advertiser.

London Daily News.

(London) *Farmer's Advocate.*

London Free Press.

London Gazette.

London Herald.

London Inquirer.

London Prototype.

London Sun.

London Times.

(Montreal) *Canada Temperance Advocate.*

Ottawa Citizen.

Peterborough Review.

St. Thomas Dispatch.

St. Thomas Journal.

Sarnia Observer.

Stratford Beacon.

Strathroy Age.

Strathroy Dispatch.

(Toronto) *The Advocate.*

(Toronto) *Christian Guardian.*

Toronto Empire.

Toronto Globe.

(Toronto) *Industrial Canada.*

(Toronto) *Irish Canadian.*

(Toronto) *The Labor Advocate.*

(Toronto) *Saturday Night.*

(Toronto) *The Sentinel and Orange and Protestant Advocate.*

(Toronto) *The Week.*

(Walkerton) *Bruce Herald.*

Watford Guide.

Winnipeg Daily Tribune.

Woodstock Sentinel-Review.

SECONDARY WORKS

Armstrong, Frederick H. *The Forest City: An Illustrated History of London, Canada.* Burlington, Ontario: Windsor Publications, 1986.

_____. "John Kinder Labatt." In *Dictionary of Canadian Biography, Volume IX: 1861 to 1870.* Toronto: University of Toronto Press, 1976.

Bloomfield, Elizabeth et al. *Industry in Ontario Urban Centres, 1870: Accessing the Manuscript Census.* Guelph, Ontario: Department of Geography, University of Guelph, 1986.

Bowering, Ian. *The Art and Mystery of Brewing in Ontario.* Burnstown, Ontario: General Store Publishing, 1988.

Burant, Jim and Judith Saunders. *The Garrison Years, London, Canada West.* London, Ontario: London Regional Art Gallery, 1983.

Campbell, Clarence T. *Pioneer Days in London.* London, Ontario: Advertiser Job Printing Company, 1921.

Clemens, James M. "Taste Not; Touch Not; Handle Not: A Study of the Social Assumptions of Temperance Literature and Temperance Supporters in Canada West." *Ontario History* 64 (1972): 142-160.

DeKay, George P. *Carling, Beverley, Gray, Hildred, West, Mason, and Their Descendants: Pioneer Families of London Township, Middlesex County, Ontario.* Hyde Park, Ontario: self-published, 1976.

Denison, Merrill. *The Barley and the Stream: The Molson Story.* Toronto: McClelland and Stewart, 1955.

Garland, M.A. and J.J. Talman. "Pioneer Drinking Habits and the Rise of Temperance Agitation in Upper Canada Prior to 1840. *Ontario Historical Society Papers and Records* 27 (1931): 341-360.

Gilmour, James M. *Spatial Evolution of Manufacturing: Southern Ontario, 1851-1891.* Toronto: University of Toronto Press, 1972.

Gourvish, T.R. and R.G. Wilson. *The British Brewing Industry, 1830-1980.* Cambridge: Cambridge University Press, 1994.

Herr, J.A. *Breweries and Soda Works of St. Thomas, Ontario, 1833-1933.* St. Thomas, Ontario: self-published, 1974.

Mathias, Peter. *The Brewing Industry in England, 1700-1830.* Cambridge: Cambridge University Press, 1959.

McBurney, Margaret and Mary Byers. *Tavern in the Town: Early Inns and Taverns of Ontario.* Toronto: University of Toronto Press, 1987.

Miller, Orlo. *London 200: An Illustrated History.* London, Ontario: London Chamber of Commerce, 1992.

Noel, Jan. *Canada Dry: Temperance Crusades before Confederation.* Toronto: University of Toronto Press, 1995.

Phillips, Glen C. *The Ontario Soda Water Manufacturers and Brewers Gazetteer and Business Directory.* Sarnia, Ontario: Clearwater Publishing, 1987.

Smart, Reginald and Alan C. Ogborne. *Northern Spirits: Drinking in Canada Then and Now.* Toronto: Addiction Research Foundation, 1986.

Spence, Ruth E. *Prohibition in Canada.* Toronto: Ontario Branch of the Dominion Alliance for the Total Suppression of the Liquor Traffic, 1919.

Sweet, Richard L. *Directory of Canadian Breweries.* Saskatoon: self-published, 1990.

Van Wieren, Dale P. *American Breweries II.* West Point, Pennsylvania: Eastern Coast Breweriana Association, 1995.

INDEX